PINHEAD is more than just a love story. It's a timeless tale of what it means to be young. If you were a college student in the middle of the last century, you'll relate. If you're a college student now ... well, perhaps things haven't changed all that much, at least when it comes to looking for love and struggling to find your place in an increasingly complex and often contradictory adult world. It still is, after all, a kind of a crap shoot.

Here are a few early reactions to *PINHEAD*.

"Bazzett's unique style combines anecdotes, digressions, and uncensored musings on his lustful search for love in this memoir which captures, I think, what it was like to be a veteran returning to small-town college life in the early 60s."
Helen Popovich, former President of Ferris State University

"Tim Bazzett has done it again – he's told the story of a small town with bravado and unfailing honesty. The guy's a hoot! Part American Graffiti, part coming-home tale, Pinhead is a barrelling road-trip into a long-ago America – not a simpler time, just funnier. Poignant. Vote for Pinhead!"
Doug Stanton, author of the *NY Times* bestseller, *In Harm's Way*

"A delightfully nostalgic work, this was an enjoyable stroll down memory lane for me. Pinhead is straightforward, frank, and honest, yet delicate and sensitive. The narration is in a pleasant and conversational tone, like listening in person to a friend telling an absorbing story ... I enjoyed it greatly."
Herbert L. Carson, Ph.D., Professor of English at Ferris State University, 1960-1994

"I was caught by Reed City Boy, and held by Soldier Boy – an all-American story, I thought. Pinhead is as good as the other two. I don't see why Tim Bazzett should ever stop writing Reed City into the history of small-town America."
Samuel Hynes, Professor Emeritus of Literature at Princeton University and author of *The Growing Seasons*

Pinhead

Pinhead
A LOVE STORY

Timothy James Bazzett

RATHOLE BOOKS

PINHEAD

The photo of the W.N. Ferris statue on back cover was used by permission of Ferris State University.

Published by Rathole Books
Reed City, Michigan
www.rathole.com/Pinhead

Publisher's Cataloging-in-Publication Data

    Bazzett, Timothy James.

    Pinhead : a love story / Timothy James Bazzett. – 1st ed. –
ReedCity, Mich. : Rathole Books, 2006.

        p. ; cm.
        ISBN-13: 978-09771119-2-3
        ISBN-10: 0-9771119-2-X

        1. Bazzett, Timothy James. 2. Man-woman relationships–
United States. 3. College students–United States. 4. Veterans–
United States–Social life and customs. 5. United States. Army–
Military life–Anecdotes. 6. Ferris State College. I. Title.

U766 .B394 2006
355.1/00973–dc22

2006930901
0609

Printed in the United States of America
10 9 8 7 6 5 4 3 2 1

Cover and interior design by Scott Bazzett
First Edition: October 2006
First Paperback Edition: October 2006

To order additional copies send check or money order made payable to TJ Bazzett to:

330 West Todd Avenue
Reed City, MI 49677

For more information, visit us online at:
www.rathole.com/Pinhead

For Treve,
my brown-eyed girl

"Them damn Ferris pinheads think they know everythin'. Hell, most of 'em ain't got enough sense to pound sand in a rat hole!"
   - Milt Steinhaus, circa 1961

Pinhead – 5. A brainless or stupid person; a fool.
   - Webster's Dictionary

Pinhead – A student, usually male, who attends Ferris, variously known historically as Ferris Institute, Ferris State College and Ferris State University, in Big Rapids.
   - West Michigan vernacular

"In all my schoolroom work I have never called any human being a 'stick', a 'blockhead', or a bonehead."
   - Woodbridge Nathan Ferris

"A NOTE
FROM THE AUTHOR'S WIFE"

I went to Ferris from September of 1965 through August of 1967 and I do not recall ever hearing the term "pinhead." However, I am here to say that this book is indeed "a love story" – our love story, told by one half of this couple, i.e. the half who always wanted to be a writer.

I, on the other hand, before leaving for college, said to my mother in all sincerity, "Mom, I'm going to find the biggest guy I can and bring him home."

Now, mind you, Tim was not the first or only love of my life, but he was indeed the tallest at six foot five. So when I met Tim, I said to my suitemate, Marilyn, "That's the one." I knew I had found the last love of my life!

So now, after more than thirty-eight years together, Tim has written this, his third book, telling his own unique version of our sixties love story as he remembers it. Hopefully it won't embarrass our children too much (sorry, kids) – or anyone else. I hope you enjoy it as much as I did.

Terri Bazzett
August 3, 2005

TABLE OF CONTENTS

PART I

Lookin' for Love
(The Pinhead Part)

1

COMING HOME, CARS,
AND BROTHERS BIG AND LITTLE

The intent of this book, my third in the continuing saga of a
Reed City boy's version of *Remembrance of Things Past* (although
I ain't no Proust), is to cover a portion of my college years,
specifically the two years I spent at Ferris State College in the mid-
sixties. I've been struggling literally for *weeks* now trying to figure
out how to just *start* this thing, and it suddenly struck me that, in
spite of all the importance we place on getting a college education
in our society, as I was jotting down everything I could remember
about those years, almost *nothing* seemed to surface from the
classroom itself. I mean, for cripes sake, the reason we go to
college is to learn all this supposedly really important stuff, right?
And all this vital information and knowledge that we spent
hundreds or perhaps even *thousands* of hours absorbing, writing
down, memorizing and dutifully regurgitating back out into
bluebooks and onto exam papers in multiple choice, true or false,
or essay form is absolutely essential to making us better educated,
more rounded individuals and contributing members of society,
right? And I know that I *did* study hard (well, *pretty* hard) and
wrote all those term papers and took all those notes and exams and
sweated bullets and worried plenty about all that stuff at the time.
So how come I have no memories of all those classroom hours?
Weren't they supposed to be the very reason I was *there*? Aaah,
what the hell. It's a mystery, I guess, but maybe it will sort itself out

as I sift through the things I *do* remember. Because somehow I did manage to become a productive and contributing member of society. At least I *think* I did. I mean I'm retired now, and that same society is now paying me, so I must have done *some*thing worthwhile in the past forty years, right? … Ominous silence … No answer. I think I know now what those Pink Floyd guys meant when they sang, "Is there anybody out there?"

So why don't I just start anyway, okay?

I came back home from the army in late August of 1965. I was only twenty-one years old, but by local standards I was an extremely well traveled individual. In the past three years I had spent time in Missouri, Massachusetts and Maryland. I had roamed the crowded streets and seen the historical and scenic sights of Boston, Baltimore and Washington, D.C. I had lived a year in Turkey and a year in Germany, and en route to and from these duty stations I had even gotten brief glimpses of the major world cities of Ankara, Dublin, Frankfurt, Paris and Rome. Looking back now, I am astounded. *Wow*! I saw and did all that stuff by the time I was twenty-one? *Far out*! as John Denver used to say.

You'd think that the people around Reed City would have been pretty impressed when I finally got back home, and would have wanted to hear all about my world travels and adventures, wouldn't you? Nope. No such luck. In fact, the response that was most common those first few days back, when I would casually mention how it sure was good to be home again, was, *Whaddayamean? Were you gone somewhere or somethin'?* At first I got rather ruffled and indignant, informing these oblivious dolts that, Hell, *yes*, I'd been gone. I was in the *army*! I'd been gone for nearly three *years*, and had been *overseas*! Probably one of the more profound responses to my outraged pronouncements went something like, *Well, I'll be durned. Welcome home then, I guess*. And that was it. It didn't take me too long to figure out that folks were generally pretty pre-occupied with their own lives and problems, and didn't really much care what I'd been doing or where I'd been for the past few years. While I had been drinking and carousing on distant shores and "trying to *find* myself," they had been busy getting on with things here at home, and still were.

So I got over myself, and began the business of getting on with my own life.

I quickly realized that one of the first things I had to do was get mobile. I would be starting school at Ferris in just a few weeks, and it was nearly fifteen miles from Reed City to the Big Rapids campus, so wheels were essential. It was time to buy my first car.

Let's talk a little about cars, okay? I had, of course, wanted a car of my own ever since I'd gotten my driver's license way back in 1960, but a vehicle had always been something that seemed to be just out of my financial reach. High school kids did often own their own cars at that time, but those cases were usually either because Mom and Dad bought them the car, or else they had part-time jobs and had scrimped and saved to buy the car. And then, as was often the case, the cars owned *them*, rather than the reverse, because there were always all those pesky insurance, repairs, gas and maintenance bills to pay. It helped considerably if a kid was mechanically inclined and could do his own oil changes and minor repairs, but I'm not really sure exactly how many grease monkey wizards there were in our high school ranks.

There were, however, a few slightly older kids at Reed City High whose reputations were exponentially enhanced by the cool cars they drove. Ken Roggow and Boyd Buerge were always busy modifying, painting, customizing and perfecting some vintage car in Roggow's garage up in Holdenville. Their senior year, in 1960, there was a gleaming, sculpted '52 Oldsmobile that Ken tooled about town in. It was called "The Radiant Rocket" and was a deep rich maroon color. All the chrome and trim had been meticulously removed, even down to the door handles. Buerge had a '54 gold Ford that was nearly as impressive. Roy Tubbs, in the same class, drove one of those perfectly chopped and channeled '49 Mercs that were all the rage in the custom car magazines of the day. And Milt Stanton had an old Chevy he had transformed into an equally enviable machine.

Paul Eichenberg had a sleek black '54 Ford coupe that he sold to his brother Keith, probably somewhat reluctantly, when he left home to join the navy. Keith and I spent many carefree hours prowling the streets of town and the country back roads our last couple years of high school. Well, carefree for *me*, I should probably say. Keith always seemed to be listening carefully, head

3

Ken Roggow and original '52 Olds, the "Radiant Rocket"

cocked, for strange and mysterious rattles and clunking sounds from under the hood or the rear end, wondering fretfully if the universal joint was about to go out again, and were those just normal tappet noises, or was he about to throw a rod? Cars only seemed like carefree magical machines to me because I didn't own one.

And my oldest brother, Rich, owned one of the most perfect automobiles ever designed, one that is still considered a classic in the car world nearly fifty years later – a 1957 Chevy. Some of my finest moments my senior year in high school were spent behind the wheel of that perfect gleaming chariot. And it always *was* perfect and gleaming whenever I drove it, because one of the many "conditions" that went with the privilege of driving the car was that I wash it and carefully rub it down afterward, as if it were a prize Thoroughbred. I don't think Rich would have trusted me to wax the car. He did that job himself, and did it often, carefully applying the paste wax to only a small area at a time, allowing it a few minutes to dry to a haze, and then vigorously rubbing it out to a shimmering metallic sheen in which he would often pause to admire his own reflection. It was a red and white Bel Air two-door hardtop convertible with a V-8, twin glass packs, and a Continental spare kit on the back, and I never felt more important or special than when

Rich would allow me to drive it slowly around town by myself (some other conditions: don't go over 25 mph, no passengers, and don't go beyond the city limits). I would cruise slowly down Church, turn north up Chestnut, roll slowly past the line of little kids waiting for their cones at the Dairy Queen, and then on past Dobben's Chevrolet and Crane's Ford dealerships. Sometimes I would pull into Sonny's service station and request fifty cents worth of regular. All gas stations were full service then, so I didn't even have to get out of the car. I always told Sonny not to bother checking the oil or cleaning the windshield though. After all, I had just finished cleaning the whole car, and I was terrified that a single drop of oil might fall on its sparkling pristine finish. Pulling away from Sonny's, I would sit rumbling majestically at the main traffic light in the center of town, then head on north, past the A&P, Remenap's Hardware and the Kent Elevator, bumping gently over the railroad tracks, and then on up the road past the state liquor store, the Sinclair station and over the bridge spanning the Hersey river. My usual destination was the A&W, a drive-in restaurant on the north end of town, one of the popular watering holes for Reed City's youth.

The A&W had a circular gravel drive that went all the way around the restaurant, and it was customary to circle the whole establishment at least once before pulling into a parking place where a girl carhop would come and take your order. It was a powerful exhilarating feeling for me to crunch slowly around over the gravel, my arm draped casually out over the car door. Clutch pushed all the way in, I would gently pump the gas pedal. The powerful V-8 would rumble and thrum loudly, and then, when I let up on the accelerator, the glass packs would rap off and do their stuff, the whole sequence resulting in a most impressive *VROOM-VROOM, BUP-Bup-bup-bup-bup* kind of holy litany. This never failed to turn the heads of everyone at the place, even the accomplished car buffs like Roggow, Buerge and Tubbs.

After enjoying an ice-cold root beer served up in a frosted mug and placed on a metal tray hung carefully over my half-raised window, I would toot the horn discreetly to have this paraphernalia removed and restart the engine with a reverberating roar. Then I would slowly make the circuit one more time, rumbling and rapping and crunching over the gravel, and finally turning back south toward town. If I were feeling especially brave and cocky, I would disregard Rich's rule about leaving town, and head west on 10, pushing the car up to 60 or more in seconds flat and feeling its power. I never went any further than the Catholic cemetery though, where I would pull off, look up and down the highway, and execute a careful U-turn to return home.

I know this has been a rather lengthy digression, but my brother Rich died of cancer in 2001, and I still miss him, so I'm writing this down for him too. Rich, those few times you trusted me to borrow your car were without question some of the best times of my adolescent life, a real ego-booster. Thank you, Big Brother.

My first car was a Chevy too, but nothing like Rich's. It was a Biscayne, which everyone knows was the lowest, bottom-of-the-food-chain model of Chevrolet, the one a conservative farmer or a family man buys. I apologize deeply, but it was the best I could do at the time, that September of 1965. It was a 1960 model, so at least it had a respectable set of "fins" on the back. Remember when cars had fins? The car was black and a four-door model to boot, the kind a frugal farmer with four or five kids might buy.

I have to admit that I had an ulterior motive for buying that particular car though. I had spent the previous year in Germany, riding in and surrounded by small runty European cars like Volkswagens and Opels, so that '60 Chevy looked enormous to me. Hell, it *was* enormous. American cars were still big and heavy in the sixties. And there was a tremendous amount of room inside them. That '60 Biscayne looked pretty damned good. The body and paint were in excellent condition with no visible rust. But what really attracted me was that enormous back seat. I had had one of my earliest sexual encounters in the back seat of a Volkswagen Beetle. Picture the back seat of a Bug, and keep in mind that I was six foot five, and that there was another whole *person* back there with me, and if she hadn't been extremely cooperative and friendly (and more than a little inebriated, as was I) probably nothing much would have happened. Somehow we managed, but the contortions required on my part bordered on being outright painful. The old expression "it hurts so *good*" was finally made clear to me in the back seat of that VW. So, yeah, I'll admit it. I had high hopes for the back seat of that Chevy, and in my mind had already added a blanket, and perhaps a pillow or two.

Chris and me and "Black Betty," my '60 Chevy

I found the Chevy on the used car lot at Henry Dobben's Chevrolet dealership. I had already looked over the offerings at Bud Crane's Ford just up the street and found nothing I could afford. My bankroll wasn't all that big to begin with. I had sent money home from the army on a fairly regular basis, but the total sum I'd managed to save was something less than a thousand dollars. Dobben's was having a Dutch auction that week, which, simply stated, meant that several cars on the lot were featured as sale vehicles, and each day they remained unsold their prices would be reduced by twenty or thirty dollars. Once I'd picked out this black behemoth and fixated on her wide inviting back seat, I was only able to hold out for a couple of days before I made an offer, so sure was I that someone else would see her fleshy potential and snap her up.

Since it was my first time purchasing a car, I took my dad with me to look it over. I figured just his presence might give me a bit more credibility as a buyer, and it made me feel a little less nervous too. Of course, Dad was nearly as mechanically clueless as I was when it came to cars and engines and such. But we walked frowning around the car, opening and slamming the doors and kicking the tires, and even actually looked under the hood. *Yup, there's the motor-thing, sure enough, yup, yup.*

7

Here I have to tell you about that engine. It's true I don't know squat about engines, but what I noticed and still remember about the engine compartment in that Chevy was how *roomy*, or, perhaps more accurately stated, how *empty* it seemed. Remember that a '60 Chevy was a big wide car, like most domestic autos were back then. But the Biscayne was the most basic, stripped-down model available. Air conditioning was very rare in cars (at least in Michigan) those days, so there was no compressor or extra belts. There were no power accessories and certainly no automatic transmission (a "three-on-the-tree" stick shift was standard in most cars). The engine was what I think was called a "straight six" which ran right up the center of that huge gaping compartment under the hood. So, unlike the densely packed and cluttered space under the hoods of today's cars, there was all this empty space on both sides of the engine block. I think it was probably empty and spacious enough so that a mechanic, if he had wanted to, could have climbed in over the fender and stood inside the engine compartment on either side of the block to work on it. I guess what I'm trying to tell you is that there was more empty air and space under the hood than anything else. Small wonder then that the car wasn't exactly a hot rod going down the road when we took it for a short test drive. It would have probably done zero to sixty in about sixty seconds flat – *maybe*, with a good tail wind, I mean.

In any case, Dad and I made our final cursory inspection of the car. The last thing we did was look inside the trunk, and it's probably a good thing Dad was there, because he was the one who noticed, after rummaging around a bit, that there was no jack to go with the nearly bald spare tire we found. The salesman promised to find a jack for us, whereupon Dad reluctantly allowed that he guessed the car would probably do for my purposes as transportation to school and work. Of course, I was already mentally making up that back seat bed, and imagining future romantic rendezvous, but I kept my mouth shut about that, and counted out my money, at six hundred bucks a real bargain, or so it seemed at the time.

That "bargain" would come back to bite me in the ass, er, pocketbook, more than once over the next six months or so, which was as long as I owned the car, which I christened "Black Betty." Betty was an oil burner from the word go. I think she got about a hundred miles to the quart, if that, so it wasn't long before I opted for radical surgery. I took her in to Tucker's garage, just east of Godbold's house, for a ring job. Or was it a valve job? Whatever the hell it was, it was damned expensive, but it did alleviate Betty's terrible 10-W-30 thirst, at least for a little while.

But Baby also needed new shoes. I discovered this in a most inconvenient manner. I had decided to take Betty on her first long-ish road trip, down to Chicago to visit Bob and Maureen, and to meet my first niece, Laura. I took along my little brother, Chris, who was just twelve at the time. We had only gotten as far south as Sand Lake when I was startled by a muffled *whump* and then a flapping sound and the car began pulling hard to the right. It was my first blowout. I had never changed a tire before. After wrestling the car over onto the shoulder of the highway, we got out and stood looking at the offending right rear tire, which was half shredded on the rim. Feeling extremely frustrated, and muttering angrily to myself, I think I may have taught my little brother a few brand-new words. But we opened up the trunk and wrestled that aforementioned "nearly bald" spare out and rolled it around to the flat tire. Then Chris proceeded to surprise me with his precocious mechanical insight. While I was still mumbling to myself and scratching my head, he got out the jack stand and lug wrench, neatly popped off the hubcap, loosened the lug nuts, and then got down and looked under the car, located the slot where the jack fits, and efficiently ratcheted the rear end of the car up off the ground.

He had already pulled the mangled tire off and fitted the spare into place when I asked him, amazed, "Chris, where'd you learn to do that?"

"Oh, I dunno," he replied. "Just watching other people, I guess. And I looked at your jack and stuff when you first brought the car home."

So I got my first lesson on how to change a tire from my twelve year-old brother, who always was – and still is – interested in all things mechanical and automotive. (I won't count the time in Germany when I was one of four farting GI drunks holding up the front end of Bill Wilkes's VW while he changed the tire.)

At any rate, Chris and I continued somewhat gingerly on our way, and made it down to Roselle, the Chicago suburb where Bob's family lived, and, after a pleasant weekend visit, we headed back home, all the while very conscious of the fact that we were driving

Chris and me

without a spare, and the other three tires suddenly weren't looking that good either. So my first order of business upon arriving back home was buying a whole new set of tires, which I got on sale at OK Tires on North State Street in Big Rapids. See what I mean? This car was still costing me money weeks after I bought it! *Hey, welcome to the wonderful world of auto ownership, Numbnuts!* It was only the beginning of what was to become a lifetime of frustration for me with cars.

* * * * *

2

GRANDPA BAZZETT

I had been home from the army less than two weeks when my Grandpa Bazzett died rather suddenly after apparently developing a kidney infection, which, characteristically, he kept to himself and endured stoically until it was too late. It was quite a shock to everyone, because Grandpa was one of the people who almost never complained and was rarely sick.

Grandma and Grandpa Bazzett in happier times, Wayland circa 1951

He and Grandma had been an integral part of our lives since 1953, when I was nine years old and they had moved from Wayland up to Reed City and taken up residence in the farmhouse just across the field from our place on West Church. Grandma had been overjoyed to be suddenly living nearly next door to six of her grandkids. (Chris was just a baby when they moved in, and my sister Mary was only two.)

The only time I could ever remember Grandpa being sick was when he'd been briefly hospitalized for a hernia

11

operation, and that had been after years of pain and wearing a truss, and he had only agreed to the surgery after my dad insisted. It seemed like Grandpa had just always been there, either working in the fields or around the barn, or sitting at his usual spot in the corner of the kitchen, reading the *Osceola Herald*, *Farm Journal*, or *Michigan Farmer*, his reading glasses perched on the end of his nose. Practically all of my scant knowledge of farming or gardening had come from this stooped and stern old man. He had taught my brothers and me the most efficient way to use a pitchfork, whether it was forking hay down a chute from the haymow to the cows, or turning over the windrowed hay in the field to dry and then cocking it in preparation for loading it onto the hay wagon. He showed me how to swing a hand scythe to clear weeds in the stunted, overgrown apple orchard between our place and the Hendersons. I had spent countless fall days with Grandpa sitting on overturned crates near our old tarpaper-covered corncrib, husking field corn to grind into winter feed for the cows. He had these leather-strapped contraptions that fit around your hand with a metal claw on the palm that easily grabbed the dried husks and stripped them away from the bright-colored kernels – husking pegs, I think they were called. I remember the first time I used one, I was probably nine or ten, and I couldn't seem to make it work, so Grandpa showed me how to seat it and fasten it correctly onto my smaller hand, and then demonstrated the proper one-two-three method for stripping the cob. He showed me all this in his usual matter-of-fact manner, saying little, but making sure I understood.

I loved digging potatoes with my grandpa in the fall. It had always seemed almost like a kind of magic to me, the way this small simple-looking green-leafed plant could yield a dozen or more of these perfect, firm red or white potatoes from under the dirt. All it took was a turn of the fork in the black earth. And I knew that many of the smaller ones would soon turn up on the supper table mixed with new green peas and covered in Mom's special buttered and salted white sauce.

Grandpa also taught us how to peel cedar posts with a simple two-handled planning tool called a draw-shave which he drew from his ancient wooden tool chest in the barn. One summer Bob and I probably stripped the bark from nearly a hundred posts, and stacked them in neat criss-crossing rows in a pile by the garage.

Grandpa B. in Reed City circa 1960 – always working

Later that summer and into the fall we would from time to time load some of those posts into the wagon hitched behind Grandpa's John Deere, and then we would drive slowly along the fence lines in the fields back behind the house and barn, looking for rotted or loose posts and replacing them with the new ones. It was hard sweaty work, but somehow, working with Grandpa always made me feel just a little more important and grown up. He never criticized, although sometimes he would "suggest" what might be a better way to do something. In this way I learned how to handle a pair of posthole diggers and a little about how a wire stretcher works, as we re-fastened the strands of barbed wire to the new posts, securing them firmly in place with fence staples. It was a new and powerfully masculine feeling for me, at the age of twelve, wielding a hammer and watching the staples bite deeper into the yellow wood with each blow.

Yeah, Grandpa was always teaching us things without our even being aware we were learning. It was hard work, yes, but it was also interesting and gave us a renewed sense of self-worth. And sometimes it wasn't until months, or even years later, that we realized just how much our grandpa had taught us, and not just about farming or fixing fences, but about how to take pride in a job done well, no matter how humble the task.

Grandpa had a few rituals that all my brothers and I remember. Whenever one of us had a birthday, He would solemnly present that child with a silver dollar, and admonish him to save it. Even back in the fifties silver dollars had already become something of a rarity, and weren't much circulated anymore, so we knew that Grandpa had walked into town to the bank and exchanged a paper dollar for the silver one, which in his eyes was obviously worth more. We treasured those silver dollars, and I did save mine for many years.

One of Grandpa's other annual rituals was buying an Easter ham, which would also necessitate a walk into town (Grandpa didn't own a car) to either the Kroger store or the A&P, where he would carefully select what seemed to him to be the best ham available, often making small talk with Bob Pontz behind the Kroger meat counter, or Brandy Mellberg at the A&P in one of his rare social encounters. Then, tucking the wrapped and bagged ham under one arm, he would trek the six blocks back to West Church and solemnly present the ham to Mom at the kitchen door. Of course, Grandpa and Grandma Bazzett always came to our house for Easter dinner, for which Mom would prepare the ham and all the other "fixings", as Grandpa called the side dishes. Grandpa would beam proudly each year when Mom would proclaim the ham to be the very best and the sweetest she had ever tasted, and wonder how he always managed to find one so good.

Grandpa didn't go into town very often, being very parsimonious by nature, and pretty tight with a dollar, as were most men of his generation who had endured the worst years of the Great Depression. My mom still likes to tell the tale of "Grandpa Bazzett and the Hot Salted Nuts." Grandpa had a weakness for cashews and fancy mixed nuts, the kind they used to sell hot from a heated display case in two of Reed City's downtown drugstores, Bonsall's and Dykstra's. On one of his rare forays into town one cold winter day, Grandpa had gone into Dykstra's, probably just in order to warm up a bit before starting back home. He was standing in front of the hot nuts display and gazing longingly at the slowly rotating trays of peanuts, cashews and mixed nuts inside the case.

Carl Dykstra, the store's owner, saw Grandpa standing there and came over to see if he could help.

"Good morning, Mr. Bazzett," he said. "What can I do for you today?"

Coming slowly out of his nut-induced reverie, Grandpa looked at Carl and said, "I was just thinkin' about buyin' some of them nuts."

"Why certainly," replied Carl. "Which kind of nuts were you considering?"

"Them there cashews, most likely, but I ain't really decided just yet."

"Would you like to sample some first, Mr. Bazzett?" asked Carl.

"I reckon I would," allowed Grandpa.

Opening the back of the display case, Carl scooped several large steaming-hot cashews onto a paper napkin and handed them to Grandpa, who took them gingerly in his left hand. Then he slowly ate the cashews, one at a time, obviously savoring them, chewing slowly and thoroughly, appreciative *mmmm*'s escaping his lips between bites. Finishing the last nut, he carefully licked the salt from his fingers and declared, "Them are mighty good nuts. I'll take a nickel's worth."

A bemused expression on his face, Carl Dykstra responded, "Mr. Bazzett, you just *ate* a nickel's worth."

Without missing a beat, Grandpa replied, "Well, never mind then. I guess I won't buy any today. Much obliged for the taste though." And tipping his barn cap, he opened the door and went back out into the frigid cold weather, his belly warmed by one of his favorite treats for the walk home.

Mom got this story third-hand from Dad, who had gotten it from Carl Dykstra later that week. It has become a traditional favorite story in our family and is still often told whenever we gather together.

The night before Grandpa's funeral, after the visitation hours at McDowell's Funeral Home, my brother Bill and I went with Keith and Dianne Eichenberg back to their apartment upstairs over Dr. Gogolin's dental offices and sat and drank beer and reminisced about Grandpa Bazzett and all the things he had taught us, and toasted him for bringing us all together one more time, and got rather drunk in the process. The Eichenbergs and the Bazzetts had always been close. Keith and I had been friends nearly all our lives. It couldn't have been easy for Keith to have us there that night before the funeral, since his own father, George, had died suddenly of a heart attack scarcely three months earlier. George hadn't even been fifty years old when he died. I had still been in Germany when George died, so I hadn't been there to offer Keith my support, but he was there for me when my Grandpa died, and he was there again for me years later, in 1989, when my dad died and I bawled like a baby at the cemetery. People around here, particularly the Germanic farmer types like the Eichenbergs, are not naturally demonstrative, and are not given to public displays of emotion or affection, but Keith never said a word about my unseemly, womanish outpouring of grief. He just walked around the open grave and folded me into his arms and let me weep, perhaps remembering his own dad's untimely death so many years before. I don't think I ever thanked Keith for that, so I am now. He is, and has always been, a true friend. He only recently told me the story about how, when his dad died, they were in the middle of the potato harvest at their farm, and Dad left his business at the elevator and came over and spent most of the day helping Keith and his brothers dig potatoes, not saying much, just working beside them and being there with them.

My grandpa. My dad. My friend.

* * * * *

In Memory Of
JULIUS (JUDA) BAZZETT
March 9, 1883   September 5, 1965

Services Held At
McDowell Funeral Home
1:30 p.m.   September 7, 1965

Officiating
Rev. Brian Spencer

Music
Mrs. Lamont Ford

Interment
Woodland Cemetery

Casket Bearers
Grandsons
Christopher Bazzett   Ronald Bazzett
Donald Bazzett   Timothy Bazzett
Duane Bazzett   William Bazzett

3

DRUGSTORE STORIES

A lot of things happened those first few months after I got back from the army. It wasn't just that I was trying to cram a lot of "catching-up" kind of stuff into those first weeks and months, although in retrospect I suppose I probably was doing that too. The fact of the matter was I *did* have a lot of things I needed to do right away, not the least of which was finding a job.

I never once thought of applying for a loan or financial aid of any kind while I was registering for classes that first term, although the opportunities and all the literature and pamphlets were there. I think it was a result of the way Dad brought us all up, because the thought of going to school and then being in debt for it afterwards scared the hell out of me. There was never any doubt in my mind that if I wanted to go to college I'd have to pay for it myself, and right up front too, not years down the road sometime. Well, after buying that Chevy, my savings account was nearly depleted, and that damn car continued to suck away my funds almost as fast as I could earn them for most of the time I owned it.

My first job was at Bonsall's Drugs in Reed City. There was probably a bit of shirt-tail nepotism at work in my getting on the Bonsall's payroll, since my brother Bob had worked at the drugstore for nearly five years, or for the whole time he attended Ferris as a pharmacy student. It was a great deal for him. Joe Bonsall let him practically set his own hours, Bob was able to complete his pharmacy internship there too during his fifth and final year of school. So it was a natural fit for Bob.

Not so for me. My tenure at Bonsall's was to be fairly short, probably only six or eight weeks, I can't remember for sure. To be honest, Mr. Bonsall – Joe – made me uncomfortable. It seemed like he was always hovering nearby, looking over my shoulder, wherever I was working in the store, whether I was stocking shelves or waiting on a customer. Of course it wasn't a very big store, so maybe it was just my imagination, but it seemed like Joe hardly ever took a day off, and he was always right there, lurking just a few feet away, or in the next aisle, watching me, judging me.

But maybe this was just paranoia on my part, or perhaps even some residual feeling of guilt, because once, when I was about thirteen or fourteen, I swiped a book from Bonsall's, just took it off the paperback rack, stuffed in my coat pocket, and was out the door. And what was even worse was that I got away with it. But maybe you never really get away with that kind of stuff, because I was so consumed with guilt at my theft that I found it impossible to live with myself. So the following week I went back into the store and paid for it. It was extremely awkward. Joe was at the front cash register behind the cigar counter, right next to the comics and bookracks, the scene of my crime. I put a dollar on the counter. (This was a time when even the most expensive paperback rarely cost more than ninety-five cents.)

Joe looked at the dollar and then looked at me and asked, "What's this for?"

Unable to meet his gaze, I mumbled something about having "forgotten" to pay for a book I got last week, and told him it was ninety-five cents.

Joe gave me a long, thoughtful, rather fish-eyed look, then rang up the sale and gave me back a penny change.

I muttered, "Sorry," and scuttled, or slithered, out the door, like the vile, thieving snake I was, and back under the rock where I felt I belonged.

There's a little more to this story, actually. The pilfered book was Vladimir Nabokov's *Lolita*, an extremely controversial work at that time. (It still is today in certain right-wing conservative circles.) A rather precocious reader, I had read all about the book when it was first published in hardcover. Its release was covered in many of the major newspapers and magazines. I think I read about it in *Life*. Anyway, from all I had read about the book, it sounded like a pretty hot number, very racy stuff. So when I saw the paperback edition a year or two later in Bonsall's, I knew I just had to have it. But I knew too that I couldn't openly buy it. I'd have to sneak it into the house. It was, after all, a notoriously "dirty book." So I filched the book, smuggled it into my room, read it (or *tried* to) secretly in my room while Bob wasn't around, and kept it "hidden" under my bed. *Bad idea, Bazzett!* What a perfectly *stoopid* place to hide anything illicit or important. Anyway, Mom found it, and, recognizing it as questionable material for a good Catholic boy to be reading, confronted me with it, and confiscated it. (I'm not sure if she actually burned it like she said she was going to do, or read it herself. I suspect the latter, since, like me, Mom could never bear to destroy a book – any book.) Suffice it to say, it was, overall, an embarrassing and shameful blot on my adolescence, and, to top it all off, I couldn't make much sense of *Lolita* either. It was a notch or two too sophisticated for me at that age, and I ended up wondering what all the fuss had been over this book which didn't really seem very "dirty" at all to me, darn it!

So perhaps Joe Bonsall still remembered that suspicious episode and thought he'd better keep an eye on me. Or maybe it was just my still-guilty conscience, even several years later, working overtime. (That darned Catholic-school education again!)

But it wasn't just the perhaps unfounded feeling of being watched constantly that soured that job for me. No, I was just never very comfortable "clerking", or waiting on people. The whole "may I help you" milieu gave me the creeps, to be honest. I guess I just wasn't cut out for the customer service game.

Perhaps my daughter, Susan, best expressed the crux of this problem not long ago. She has worked as a telemarketer and in other menial clerking jobs, but never liked them much, and once said to me, "I *like* customer service; it's just that I much prefer being the *customer*, and *not* the one providing the service."

At least she was honest, and I think I felt much the same way when I was twenty-one and trying to follow in my brother's footsteps at Bonsall's. But it just wasn't working for me.

There was one job I was tasked with at the store that was kind of the proverbial straw that broke the camel's back. It was books, once again, that ultimately drove me away from the job. I had to *burn* books in the basement furnace.

Yes, burn books! I *love* books – always have – and to *burn* a book seemed to me like the most egregious of mortal sins. However, back then – and perhaps this is still true – book publishers and distributors didn't want unsold books returned. If retailers wanted a partial refund for unsold books, they only needed to return the front covers. The leftover "beheaded" books were then supposed to be destroyed. So this was one of my assigned jobs – book burner. No fucking way, man! I tried to do it once, but nope, I just couldn't do it. I quit. My explanation to Mr. Bonsall for leaving was that my new job, working as a part-time custodian at Ferris, was more convenient to my class schedule. And this was mostly true, actually. But the real reasons I preferred my new job were: no customer service involved – and no book burning.

I will talk more later about my new role of "JANITORMAN", but first, in an at least half-assed attempt at keeping my story somewhat chronologically correct, I want to talk about one of the first friends I made at Ferris.

* * * * *

4

NEW FRIENDS –
DON AND MARY ELLEN DOBSON

Don Dobson and I met on the first day of school at Ferris that September of 1965. Maybe I shouldn't say "on the first day of school." It sounds too much like we were five years old and our moms had just left us behind at kindergarten and on our own for the very first time. Well, in a sense it actually did feel kind of that way, and for a couple of reasons. For one, Don and I clicked so immediately as friends – as kindred spirits – that it wasn't long before we *felt* like we'd known each other forever. But perhaps the *real* reason our friendship was so easy, so *com*fortable, was that we really *did* feel, at this time in our lives, like we were indeed finally on our own and starting over. We were "clean slates", and it was, at least to me, more than a little frightening.

For eighteen years we'd had our parents and families to lean on, to depend on. Then we'd had our benevolent Uncle Sam looking after us for three or four years – in the army, and, in Don's case, the navy. Now suddenly we'd cut ourselves loose from all that, and it was up to us to get an education, to find jobs and to make a living. Even at the "advanced" age of twenty-one this can be a pretty daunting prospect. At least I was still living at home. My folks were there for me, so I did, technically, have something and someone to fall back on if necessary.

For Don it was different. He was a long way from home and family. Well, from home anyway, because Donnie had brought his "family" with him. I'd better explain. Don was discharged from the navy on September 9. On September 11 he got married. On September 15 he had to be at Ferris to start school. That's an awful lot of life-changing stuff to be packed into a single week, and I didn't even mention the 1500-mile trip that Don and his new bride had to make from their hometown in northern Maine to the middle of the Michigan mitten. And then, when they got to Ferris, where they didn't know a soul, they still had to find a place to live. *Whew!*

There's undoubtedly a lot that I *don't* know about Donnie and Mary Ellen's story, but I'll try to tell you what I *do* know.

They had known each other since they were teenagers going to high school in Presque Isle, a town of about 9,000 located near the border of the Canadian province of New Brunswick. As Don remembers it, it was a classic case of "lust at first sight". Mary is gonna hate me for this, but when I asked Don recently what he remembers most about Mary Ellen and those early days of their adolescent courtship, he replied with absolutely no hesitation, "It was her rack." Laughing, he continued, "Even at fifteen, Mary had a rack on 'er that a guy couldn't help but notice, and I just knew I had to get to know this girl."

Well, Don must have had all the right moves. He remembers their first date – this would have been in the late fifties, understand – and how he got himself all cleaned up and even into a coat and tie to go pick Mary Ellen up at her house. He didn't want her folks, particularly her dad, to find anything to disapprove of or object to. He must have passed the parent muster, because they continued to date through high school, until Don graduated and went into the navy. Mary, I think, went to Beauty School after high school and worked as a hair dresser for at least part of the time Don was away in the service. Somehow they managed to stay connected during that period of nearly four years, and even got engaged, I assume, somewhere in there, while Don bounced around between assignments in Illinois, Washington, D.C., and Virginia.

I don't remember for sure why Don picked Ferris as a college and ended up in Michigan after the navy, but I'm glad he did. Like I said, we met on the first day of freshman orientation week at Ferris. I've been trying to figure out just how to best explain the "setting" in which we met. I need to get it right and describe it in such a way that my readers won't suspect there was any kind of "special friendship" between us (the kind the clerical faculty at St. Joe's Seminary actively discouraged among the all male student body). Oh, what the hell. We met in the john, okay?

We had spent the whole morning sitting in long rows of student desks set up on the basketball court of the field house, taking placement tests. It had been a long grueling forenoon, with all those multiple choice exams, hours spent filling in those little bubbles with dull-pointed number two pencils. We'd just finished with the math section of the test, which didn't leave me feeling any too good about myself. I marked "C" a lot – whenever I had no idea what the correct answer was. Anyway, we finally broke for lunch, and a few of us headed off to the bathroom to empty our clamoring bladders. There were enough guys that we actually had to stand in line to get to a urinal. Don and I got to talking. I can't remember what we talked about, maybe all those "C" guesses at unfathomable math problems. Turned out Don didn't have very many mathematical smarts either.

Finally I got myself up to a vacant urinal for that sweet relief that only comes with the release of too long pent-up piss. I had barely unzipped and let loose when the urinal right next to me was vacated. Don could have stepped up and used it, but instead he waited until the next urinal over was free, and then stepped up to that one. At that moment I knew that Don and I would be friends. Here was a guy with guy manners, a guy who knew something about latrine etiquette. Any ex-GI knows that you always try to leave a vacant urinal between you and the next guy. It's just common courtesy. Women probably won't understand this, but trust me; it's an important guy-thing, a kind of homophobe comfort zone, if you will. Don had passed the test.

Let me tell you a little about Don, to try to give you a kind of mental picture of him. First of all, he's short. I don't know why so many of my friends are nearly a foot shorter than me, but they are, and that's been the case for most of my life, so I'm kind of used to it by now. Don is perhaps five foot six, if that. He's a solid, blocky sort of guy, with thick, dark, wavy hair usually kept cut pretty close. Wait, should I do this in the present tense or past? Because I doubt if his hair is dark any more, or thick either. I say this from personal experience. My own formerly thick dark hair is now thinning fast and going mostly grey, and my forehead keeps moving farther north every year. But no one wants to hear about creeping geezer-dom, so I'd better keep this narrative in the past, mostly anyway. This is, after all, a *memoir*. Don was also kind of square-jawed, nearly lantern-jawed, actually. If Jay Leno had been around back then, I would have likened Don's square-jawed countenance to Jay's. As it was, I had to tell him that he reminded me a bit of Dudley Do-Right, the well-

Don Dobson

meaning but buffoon-ish cartoon Royal Canadian Mountie. (Dudley, by the way, was, I think, the inspiration for that old joke: "Dja hear about the mixed up Mountie that jumped on his whistle and blew his horse?") If that image (or the joke) makes you smile, good. Don was – *is* – a very funny guy, and we laughed a *lot* in the years we knew each other, all through college.

I think Don and I had lunch together that first day. We were probably brown-bagging, since we were both painfully aware of how poor we were. The new GI Bill hadn't started yet in the fall of 1965, so financing our education was a matter uppermost in our minds, and we probably talked some about jobs that day too. Of course, the fact that we were both just fresh out of the service gave us plenty to talk about, and we undoubtedly compared our military experiences too and discovered we had much in common as we heaped scorn on the "fuckin' army" and the "goddamn navy".

I don't really know how important our friendship was to Don at the time, but it was a lifesaver to me. This might seem odd, since I was back living in the town where I grew up and was in fact surrounded by family and old friends from school, many of whom I'd know all my life. But the fact of the matter was, ever since I'd returned home from Germany I'd felt something of an outsider. It was true that I'd only been gone a few years, but during that short time it seemed like all my friends – and family too – had moved on somehow with their lives. My best friend, Keith Eichenberg, was already married and had been working at the local tool and die plant for over three years. My other high school buddies were scattered here and there. Jerry Whitman was at General Motors Institute over in Flint and engaged to his high school girlfriend, Fran Perdew. Rex Dolley and Art Gerhardt were both attending Ferris, but were seniors already and busy with their own upperclassmen schedules and planning for their futures. My oldest brother, Rich, was out of the army, but still working overseas. Bill and Bob were finished with college and had moved away to Minnesota and Illinois, respectively. That left only my sister Mary, seven years younger than me, and my little brother Chris, nine years my junior, still at home with my folks, who seemed to be having a kind of second honeymoon ever since they'd returned from their European trip. My grandma Bazzett was living with us too. She had moved in with us after Grandpa died, not wanting to live all alone in the big farmhouse next door, but she seemed to become a little more confused and vague with each passing day, living more in the past than in the present.

So I *needed* a friend badly, and Don fit the bill and filled that void. I suppose he was grateful too to find a friend so far from home, but Don had something, or rather some*one* I didn't have. He had a wife, and a brand new one at that. He and Mary had only been married a week when I first met Don, so marriage and "having a wife" was still a real novelty to him, and, as I remember it, he couldn't wait to get his horny ass back home to Mary Ellen each day when school was out.

"Home" to Don and Mary Ellen that first year at Ferris was, I was pleased to learn, in Reed City. As a first-year student, Don hadn't managed to get them into an on-campus apartment. Instead he had answered an apartment-for-rent ad posted on the bulletin board at the college housing office. They were renting a furnished upstairs apartment in the home of Mr. and Mrs. Marold Kienitz on the northwest corner of Park and Franklin. Perhaps the key word here was "furnished," because both Don and Mary would be quick to tell you that they didn't even have the proverbial "pot to piss in" at this very early stage of their life together. But they seemed – at least to *me*, on the outside looking in – to be quite blissfully happy, and I envied them.

But I do have to tell you the story of the first time I met Don's bride. I think it may have been only a week or so after we'd met when Don invited me for Sunday dinner at their apartment, which means their marriage was only a couple weeks old, so maybe this sort of invitation was just a wee bit premature on Don's part. But as far as newlywed etiquette went, Don was probably at least as dumb as I was. I mean, who *knew* what a traumatic thing it is for a new bride to hostess her first dinner guest?

So, that Sunday afternoon completely clueless Tim Kadiddlehopper came clomping up the outside stairs that led up to the tiny upstairs residence, humming tunelessly to himself and probably already beginning to salivate at the thought of a sumptuous and flavorful meal in the company of his new friend and his friend's bride. I had gotten about halfway up the steps when I heard a muffled clatter inside the apartment, followed immediately by a wailing, distinctly female cry of dismay. I stopped in mid-step on the stairs and listened, as the wailing continued, mixed with a muffled male voice, Don's, then some high-pitched nervous laughter, also unmistakably Don's. (*Big* mistake, Don, that laughing.)

Not knowing the proper protocol regarding first-time dinner guests, and eavesdropping, I stood stock-still and continued to listen, as Mary's initial horrified wail subsided into a more subdued sobbing, accompanied by Don's muffled muttering, which I sincerely hoped was meant to be reassuring or comforting, whatever the crisis was. Finally, satisfied that the worst was over, I tiptoed softly back down to the bottom of the staircase, then started back up again, this time clomping and creaking loudly, coughing and clearing my throat, making sure the people inside could hear me coming. Don threw open the door just as I arrived on the landing, and, smiling broadly, invited me in, and announced, "Mary, Tim's here. Come on out and meet him."

Mary emerged from the next room, which must have been the bedroom, clutching and twisting a kitchen towel. Looking a bit flustered and flushed, she smiled bravely and came over and greeted me warmly as I stood in their tiny kitchen, nervously shuffling my feet, which suddenly seemed obscenely large in the presence of this petite, attractive blonde girl. Because – wife or not – she *was* still just a girl.

I've already mentioned that Don was barely five and a half feet tall, and Mary Ellen was probably an inch or two shorter than him as they stood side by side, welcoming me into their first home. I could see immediately why Don was always in such a hurry to get back home after school or work. Mary was a "looker," and even though she was quite tiny, the aforementioned famous "rack" was an immediate attention getter, so now it was my turn to flush deeply as I tried valiantly not to notice.

You have to understand that both Don and I were only about twenty-one, and like most American males of that age group, we were afflicted with the usual breast fixation thing that had only been intensified by a steady diet of glossy skin magazines over the past few years of our military service. It would be a few years yet before we developed a deeper appreciation of women and matured enough to appreciate their finer points – like the upside-down heart of a shapely ass, say.

In any case, I was quite smitten with Don's new bride, perhaps even a bit envious of him, because he had someone like Mary to come home to, while I was still searching. (And there will be more on that later, I promise.)

Ever the gracious host, Don told me to sit down and make myself at home, and thrust a cold sweating bottle of Blue Ribbon at me. Then, chuckling, he explained, none too tactfully, considering Mary was right there in the room with us, that he wasn't sure what we were going to eat now, since Mary had just accidentally dumped the meatloaf on the *floor* while taking it out of the oven. Mary, red-faced, stammered that it would still be okay to eat, but Don just laughed and said, "*Oh* no, not *me*! There's no *way* I'm gonna eat something that went on the *floor*!"

Poor Mary looked, unbelieving, at her callow husband's laughing face, and, bursting into tears, she ran out of the apartment door and went clattering down the stairs. After a moment, we heard her knocking on the Kienitzes' back door, then more muffled sobbing, and a door closed. After a few moments of embarrassed, uncomfortable silence, Don shrugged it off, or tried to, and we chatted briefly about school and other unimportant things. (Isn't it ironic that I would include "school" with "unimportant" things, especially since this is a book about my college years? But it's true that we felt that way. The whole college thing was, for the most part, a pesky nuisance that we were just trying to get through so we could get on with our *real* lives, and stuff that really *mattered*.)

After a short time, we heard footsteps coming back up the outside stairs, and Mary Ellen came back in, still visibly red-faced and upset, followed by Mrs. Kienitz, the landlady, a sweet, warm-hearted woman whom Mary had befriended in the past few days. Pointedly ignoring us insensitive clods, the women went to the kitchen counter where Mrs. Kienitz carefully examined Mary's "floor-pie" meatloaf which had been cleaned off and put back into its pan. Taking a knife and fork, Mrs. Kienitz cut off a small piece, bravely took a bite, and declared it "delicious." Donnie cackled nervously, and, looking perhaps just a bit ashamed but still defiant, he reiterated his position against eating anything that had been flipped onto the floor.

Finally asserting herself and showing just a bit of fire in her eye, Mary snapped back, "*Fine!* You can just drink your damn *beer*, and Mrs. Kienitz and I will have *dinner*!"

And so they did. And we drank our damn beer.

I'll admit I felt torn. Don was my new friend, so of course I wanted to show solidarity, but I also sympathized with Mary, and that meatloaf *did* smell good! Thinking back now, nearly forty years later, on that first meeting, I am vaguely ashamed that I was such an ungracious and boorish guest. I *am* sorry, Mary. We really *were* jerks. (*Weren't* we, Don?)

But Don and Mary Ellen somehow survived this early bump in their road of life together, and probably numerous others too. They will celebrate their fortieth anniversary this year, so Don must have done *some*thing right in all those years. We should never underestimate the power of love, lust and a fine set of headlamps.

Now you've met my good friends, Don and Mary Ellen, and they will play a recurring role in my continuing chronicle of the college years.

* * * * *

5

EARNING MY WAY, OR
"JANITORMAN"

I was a "townie" during my two years at Ferris, which means simply that I was a local, and commuted to school every day. There were probably hundreds of kids from all around west central Michigan who drove themselves or car-pooled in to Ferris daily, or, if they were lucky enough to get a more cost-efficient schedule, maybe only three or four days a week. For me it was a two-way daily commute of approximately thirty miles. There was no expressway between Reed City and Big Rapids in the mid-sixties, so I would head south down 131 each morning, pushing Black Betty to her limit, belching oil fumes as we barreled past Tiel Oil on the south end of town, where my dad, semi-retired, worked part-time as a book-keeper. Rounding the pond and cresting the hill, I'd really open her up as we flew low across Crapo flats, the only level straightaway between Reed City and Big Rapids. Barely slowing as I cruised past the fish hatchery and through Paris, I would continue up hills and down until I reached the long curve on the northern edge of Big Rapids, where I would slow down as I passed Roben-Hood airport and followed the Muskegon River along State Street, passing OK Tires on the right, and then Hanchett Manufacturing, Grunst Bros. party store, Bowers Restaurant, the A&W, the Dairy Queen and the Pontiac dealership along the left side of the road. The final stretch of State, after crossing Maple, was flanked with rooming houses and old homes chopped up into apartments mostly occupied by Ferris students.

Ferris was considerably smaller in 1965 than it is now, although it had already begun its sprawl to the west side of State Street (Business 131) by then. I would pass Southland Pharmacy and its small shopping strip on the right and turn left at the traffic light into the college's main entrance, and then swing into the large parking lot on the west side of the Student Center. Parking wasn't such a problem in those years, or at least I don't remember it as a problem. Maybe that's because I always had early classes, at eight or nine o'clock, and once I'd parked my car I often wouldn't move it again until after nine that night when I would finish work and finally head home again.

Like most townies, I was working my way through college. For us less financially fortunate students, college was strictly a "pay as you go" proposition. I was more fortunate than some, in that I didn't have to worry about paying rent. I was living at home, and the "room and board" expenses were Mom and Dad's contribution to my college costs. I probably didn't appreciate that enough at the time, but, looking back, I certainly do now. I did know a few guys at Ferris whose budgets were so tight that they often had to drop out for a semester and work full-time until they'd gotten together enough money to start classes again and still pay their rent too.

Let's talk about my job. After several unhappy weeks working at Bonsall's Drugs, I finally quit and got a job working on the custodial crew at Ferris. I can't remember any more if this job was part of a formal work-study financial aid arrangement, or if students like me were just a convenient source of cheap labor to help keep the campus clean and tidy, but whatever it was, it worked well for me.

My pal, Don Dobson, had a job on a grounds crew, meaning he was one of those guys with a trash bag and a long stick with a nail on the end of it for picking up paper and trash. (Another slightly older friend of mine, Doug Call, who was later to be honored as a distinguished alumnus, had worked his way through Ferris as part of the grounds crew too, moving tons of snow and mowing acres of grass during his four years there.) I was part of the inside maintenance crew, and my duties varied between week nights and

Saturdays. On weekdays I was assigned to the Science Building. Monday through Friday I punched in at 5 PM and punched out at 9. There were a couple of regular full-time custodians who worked with me, and were, at least nominally, I suppose, my bosses, but they never acted like bosses. They were more like a pair of friendly, sometimes mischievous uncles.

Ed Howe was, I think, from Big Rapids and was probably somewhere in his forties, or perhaps fifty, I don't know for sure. He was a pretty laid-back sort of guy with thinning, sandy-colored hair combed straight back from a high forehead and steel-rimmed glasses that were forever sliding down his nose, and over which he would peer at me when he would inquire occasionally about how was my love life doing. (My standard reply was, "*What* love life?") I learned a lot from Ed – things like how to look cool and casual while leaning on a push broom, or don't ever lean over a mop bucket while you're pouring ammonia into hot water. Although I think he may have offered this latter morsel of advice only *after* I'd already done it and then staggered away gagging and coughing.

Woo-EEE! Burn yo' lungs, boy!

My other "boss" was Harold "Red" McClain, who lived, if I remember correctly, in an old stone farmhouse on the north end of Paris. Red was actually the janitor over in the Starr Building, next door to the Science Building, but he was always wandering over to shoot the shit with Ed, so I got to know him pretty well too. Red had a ruddy complexion and was pretty much completely bald. I think the nickname came from his younger days when he was still a red-haired kid, although his bald pate was often a rather rosy hue, so I could be wrong. Red played the kindly old uncle role, and was probably a bit older than Ed. Good ol' Ed 'n' Red.

My duties during my 5 to 9 shift each night were fairly simple. First I'd pull a large canvas trash container on casters along the hall on the office side of the building and, using my set of pass keys, I would open up each office and empty the waste baskets and put fresh plastic bags in them, pick up any stray trash that might have missed the basket, then re-lock the office door. Once a week I would also vacuum the office carpets. Once the faculty offices were taken care of, I would go into the classrooms on the opposite side of the hall and stack the chairs on the tables and sweep the floors, sometimes using a little sweeping compound. Then I would put the

The Science Building

chairs back down. When all the classrooms were done, I would sweep the floor of the main hallway, and if there were any spills or splotches of coffee or soft drinks, I would get a mop and bucket and clean those up. A couple times a week I would get out a buffer and polish all the floors in both the classrooms and the hallway. There were two levels in the Science Building and I cleaned both floors, so I usually kept pretty busy for at least two or three hours. But once I'd gotten used to the nightly routine, I gradually perfected it until I could get everything done by around 7 PM, leaving me two hours of free time. Neither Ed nor Red had any objection to my sitting at the counter in the custodians' room when I was done with my work, where, papers and books spread out in front of me, I would study and do my homework for the next day. Then at 9 o'clock I would punch out, haul my books back to my car, and head back home. This was largely my schedule for two years. I would leave home around 7:30 AM and get back about fourteen hours later. I get tired just thinking about it now, but I was a lot younger then and just figured that was the way you got a college education. I guess this is my version of everyone's grandpa telling about how he used to walk five miles uphill through three feet of snow to school every day. Everyone has his own tale of hardship and woe to tell to his grandkids. Comparatively speaking, I guess I didn't have it so tough, but this is my story and the only one I've got – and I'm stickin' to it.

My weeknight job undoubtedly sounds pretty tedious and boring, but it was my bread-and-butter job, twenty hours of my twenty-eight-hour work week. Because on Saturdays I worked a full day, usually in some other campus building, as part of a scrub crew.

One of the things I remember about those Saturdays is how hard it was to get out of bed again at 7 AM after a whole week of classes, study and working every night. It seemed so horribly unfair. Maybe that's when I really learned for myself the truth of the old axiom I often used to recite to my own kids years later when they would whine about something being *not FAIR!* I would smile and say, "Kids, life isn't fair."

But those Saturdays are what I actually remember most about my custodial job at Ferris, because those were the days you got to meet and talk with – and work with – all these other guys, the hapless souls who were doing the same thing you were, slogging their way through a higher education, one painstaking day at a time, and working their asses off to pay for it, earning the princely sum of about $1.15 an hour. Yup, that's right. If we were lucky, we made about twenty bucks a week, after taxes.

The Alumni Building

The East Building

Every Saturday morning all of the part-timer student workers who kept the classroom buildings clean around campus would assemble in the of office of the head custodian in the East Building, which adjoined the Alumni Building on the northeast corner of campus. Lloyd Dysard was the head poobah of the custodians and all the scrub crews. I think Lloyd especially enjoyed those Saturday morning gatherings when a couple dozen of us would crowd into his small smoke-filled domain, still rubbing the sleep from our eyes, sipping coffee and moaning and grumbling about how little sleep we'd gotten the night before. Lloyd would sit grinning behind his battered old wooden desk, his weathered wrinkled face wreathed in smoke from an ever-present cigarette, and dispense such pearls of wisdom as, "Hell, if you wadn't out chasin' pussy 'til all hours of the mornin', you wouldn't be so damn tahrd!"

Well, I don't think there were really too many "pussy chasers" in the crews, since many of the guys were married, some of them with babies and small children already. And the single guys like me were mostly too tired to chase anything by the time we finished

35

work every night. I had been celibate as a monk since returning home from the army, and I'm not sure if I'd have recognized a real pussy if I'd fallen into one face-first. In any case, we all really liked Lloyd a lot, probably because he never abused his position of authority over us and treated us pretty much as equals. Lloyd was probably fifty-something, a small-ish, rather wiry-looking guy, with dark wavy hair streaked through with an iron grey, not an ounce of fat on him. He had a rather devilish, sly sense of humor, and enjoyed ragging us gently whenever he could. We all respected Lloyd for his quiet manner and sense of humor, and he seemed to genuinely enjoy our company too, to the point that he even held a couple of big cookouts at his home in Morley and invited all the guys, along with their families or girlfriends, over for barbecue and beer or pop and a good time.

Sometimes on those Saturday mornings there would also be a few other older fellows from the custodial staff, some of them regular, full-time workers like Ed Howe and Red McClain. But I remember in particular one guy of indeterminate age who would show up occasionally. His name might have been Will. I can't remember for sure, and perhaps that's for the best. Will was unmistakably an alcoholic. He always reeked of cheap liquor or wine. His hair was often uncombed and stuck up wildly in all directions. He had an underlying sour unwashed smell about him, an odor of B.O. and old thrift shop clothing. He was also missing his front teeth, and probably a few others too, and usually sported a two- to three-day growth of gray stubble on his face and chin. I suspect Will was probably a welfare recipient that the state would try to get a few hours of honest work out of from time to time. I doubt if it ever worked though, because the few times Will was assigned to one of my Saturday work crews, he rarely did more than stand off to one side and talk and smoke.

The real reason I remember Will though was one morning Lloyd (who I don't think appreciated having Will around much, but tolerated him) asked Will how his Friday night had been.

Will, obviously pleased to be included in the camaraderie and early morning banter, responded eagerly, "Oh, purty good, purty good! After supper we watched that there Andy Griffith Show on the TV. Ol' Andy and Barn make me laugh, an' that there girlfriend of Andy's, that Miss Crump? You know, the teacher? Well, she really makes my jaws tight, ya know? I shorely wouldn't mind slippin' her the meat, ya know? She's so sweet, ya know? Got me all horned up, so we sent the kids all upstairs to bed, an' then me an' the ol' lady, we was doin' it doggy-style on the livin' room rug right in front of the TV. We was really getting' it on, ya know? The ol' lady was pantin' an' moanin' an' I was humpin' away wid my eyes all squeezed up shut, thinkin' about that Miss Crump, ya know? Then, just as I let go and got my gun off, I opened my eyes, an' damned if them fuckin' kids wadn't all lined up in a row on the stairs watchin' us. *Hee-hee-hee!* Kids! They like to watch, ya know? They're cute that way."

Having made this astounding revelation of what apparently constituted a "family home evening" at his place, Will flashed a proud gap-toothed grin into the uncomfortable silence that momentarily filled the office.

We had already known by this time that Will had six kids, the oldest about ten years old, but still .... Hmmm, talk about *too much information*! But, hey, since I still remember this small, eminently forgettable incident, I guess it just goes to show that you get your "education" from a variety of sources. I wonder how many of the other guys still remember that enlightening moment. Good ol' Will, always willing to share.

Working on a scrub crew was pretty basic simple work. There were usually three or four guys to a crew, although two guys, or even one, could have done the job when you came right down to it. I was doing the same kind of stuff I'd learned to do the summer between seventh and eighth grades when I'd helped Fred Morris, our school janitor at St. Philip's, sweep, strip, scrub and wax all the floors in the school. If you worked alone, it was constant, fairly labor intensive work, but if there were two people, or even three or four, as was usually the case with the Ferris scrub crews, there were lots of opportunities for breaks, squatting in doorways watching someone else swing a mop or run the buffer, or maybe just standing around with your thumb up your ass waiting for the floor to dry. A few years of working over-manned army details while on casual duty had practically made me an expert at this kind of work and occasional goldbricking. But probably the best part of the job was that there was no "customer service" involved, and no bosses constantly looking over your shoulder. You got your work assignment in the morning and knew exactly what you needed to get done and how long you had to accomplish it. And Lloyd was careful to never overtax his crews with too much work or unreasonable expectations. In fact we quickly learned to pace ourselves on the jobs we were assigned. After all, we didn't want to get done too soon and have to go back to Lloyd's office and "bother" him for still *another* job that same day.

But probably the best perk of being on a scrub crew was the good company. I can't remember meeting any real goobers or pricks on any of the many crews I was a part of during the nearly two years I worked at Ferris. Nope. The guys were all pretty unassuming regular sorts who were just trying to make ends meet and get through school.

One of the first guys I met was a fellow named Larry Coffey, who was single like me, and hailed from Fowlerville. (I mention his single-ness for a good reason, which is that probably the majority of the guys were married, and I'll talk about of few of them soon enough.) Larry was a funny guy who talked in a gravelly sort of southern Michigan drawl. He was a little shy, but once he got to know you he could be fairly forthcoming and at our first meeting he showed me a wallet photo of his girlfriend back home. The girl was quite cute, which kind of surprised me, because Larry was rather average-looking, with a kind of overgrown crew-cut that usually had a flattened-out slept-on look, and often was complemented by a slight stubbly blonde growth of whiskers on cheeks and chin. Of course, that unshaven look was fairly common among the scrub crew guys. After all, it *was* Saturday morning, and we were going to spend the day filling buckets, wielding and wringing out mops, and running buffers. Why bother to shave for *that*?

In any case, Larry was an okay regular sort of guy, and the reason I remember him is he talked me into a blind date one weekend. Remember blind dates? They've always been kind of a joke among single guys – and probably girls too. Well, Larry had this cute girlfriend, like I said, who was coming up to Ferris for the weekend to see Larry, but she didn't want to drive up alone, so she was bringing her best friend along for company, also hoping, no doubt, that some "dream date" would magically materialize for her painfully plain pal.

I don't remember the girl's name, and I'm sure she doesn't remember mine either, so I guess we're even. She may have been plain, but I was no dream date either, so again – even. I mean I kind of knew what I was looking for in a girl, but I wasn't any too confident of my own drawing power. I had a car. I cleaned up fairly well. My complexion had cleared up some since the zit-plagued agonies of adolescence. I was over twenty-one. I wasn't a virgin exactly, but it had been a while. But this girl – I'll call her Patty, "Plain Patty" – just didn't arouse any predatory instincts in me. Truth be told, I was much more attracted to Larry's girlfriend, but, as it turned out, I didn't even see much of Larry and his date that night. We all went to a Saturday night mixer dance in the Dome Room of the Student Center, and soon after we got there, Larry and his girl disappeared. I found out later that they had gone back to Larry's off-campus apartment. In the meantime, I was left with Patty to stand around the edges of the dance floor, drinking punch and nibbling cookies and making polite small talk. It was all very proper – and much *much* too sober. After all, my most recent dating experience had been in Germany at a GI dive called "The Deuce", where the beer and liquor flowed freely, and where I had been a kind of second-hand celebrity as a "friend of the band." The girls at the Deuce were regulars, and not necessarily "good girls," but "B-girls."

The Student Center, Dome Room in foreground

So Patty and I passed a fairly uncomfortable evening, dancing occasionally to the popular tunes of the day, like the Stones' "Hey, You, Get Offa My Cloud", or the McCoys' "Hang On, Sloopy". I could dance a little, and enjoyed it too, but I was, by this time, looking hard for "*the* girl", and unfortunately Patty was not the one. What I did that night then, was precisely what I was intended to do – keep the girlfriend's girlfriend occupied elsewhere while Larry and the girlfriend consorted, or whatever, in his rooms. It wasn't a horrible experience, but I kind of learned my lesson about blind dates. Don't do 'em.

The blind date weekend did not, however, hurt our friendship. After all, Larry didn't set out to ambush me. He just wanted some quality time with his girl, and I guess he got it, judging by the pleased look he had on his face when we met up later that night for coffee at the Beacon Restaurant, an all-night diner overlooking the Muskegon River at the north end of town where guys often rendezvoused after they'd dropped off their dates. To compare notes, so to speak – a perfectly Pinhead-ed custom.

I guess the only reason I mention this "date" at all is to illustrate the fact that I was lonely those first few months at Ferris, al least whenever I had time to think about it, given my busy work-school schedule. I know guys aren't supposed to think about things like this, but I was hungry for not just sex, but simply for some female companionship. I was desperately seeking someone I could be comfortable with, someone who enjoyed some of the same things I did, someone – now don't laugh – I could touch and hold and who would return those touches and embraces. I didn't know much *about* love, I know, but I sure wanted someone to love, and someone to love me back.

* * * * *

6

FUN AT SCHOOL
WITH DICK AND JANE

There was plenty of guy-girl pairing off going on at Ferris. Unfortunately there was about a nine-to-one ratio of boys to girls there at the time – pretty poor odds for the guys. But amorous couples were all over the place and not just in the spring either. You didn't have to look very hard to notice that "love was in the air."

One of the places our scrub crews worked often my first year was in the Swan Technical Building, a brand new facility that was only partially operational. Contractors were still applying the finishing touches inside, painting walls and laying floor coverings

The Swan Trade-Tech Building under construction, President Victor Spathelf in foreground. Ol' Vic reigned at Ferris for 18 years, 1952-1970.

down over the poured concrete floors. As each room was completed, we would move in with our brooms, mops, buckets and buffers and put down wax and shine everything up. Because parts of the structure were still under construction, the whole place was coated with a thin film of cement dust, sawdust, and other unpleasant residues that got into your nose and eyes as you swept and cleaned, so it wasn't the most popular venue for a scrub crew that winter and spring. Then one Saturday afternoon we made a discovery that changed all that, that made the Swan a much more *interesting* work assignment.

We were scrubbing a hallway on the east side of the building when one of guys, I think it was probably Terry Karnitz, looked out the window and saw, down below in the alley that ran under the concrete ramp that connected the street to a large garage-type door on our level .... (This sentence is too damn long and complex and run-on, I know, and not even complete, but sometimes just setting the scene for even a *small* incident takes more work – and *words* – than the point of the scene itself. This writing shit is hard *work*, you know?) Anyway, there was this guy and this girl huddling together up against one of the supporting concrete pillars under the ramp, and they were in a classic make-out clinch. The guy had her pinned up against the post, their lips were locked together, and there was undoubtedly some tongue action going on there too, and her arms were laced up around his neck, and she even had one leg cocked up around his butt. And the guy's hands were busy fumbling around inside the girl's coat. It was a winter coat, one of those fat insulated car coats, but it was all unbuttoned or unzipped, and this guy had one hand up under the girl's sweater and the other one was pushed down the front of her jeans. And hey, it was *cold* out there that day, with the temperature hanging right around freezing, but these two were gettin' it *on*! I mean they were workin' hard at gettin' *busy*, if you know what I mean, so they weren't noticing what the *temp*erature was or anything as mundane as *that*!

So Terry, he was just leaning up against the wall and waiting for me to finish dry-mopping so he could lay down a coat of wax, and he looks down from the hall window and he sees these two and his eyes get a little bigger and he watches them a minute, and then he says in a loud excited whisper, "Hey, Bazzett, *c'mere*! You gotta *see* this! We got some lovebirds down here underneath the ramp!"

Now Terry was known for his practical jokes, so I figured he was just trying to lure me over there and then he'd lay a wet mop-head up against the back of my head or goose me with the mop-handle or something. So I was cool in my response, and just kept mopping, and replied with a laconic, "Yeah, sure. Whyn'cha quit fuckin' around? C'mon and get the wax, and let's get this done."

"No, *really*, come look! These two are gettin' ready to do the *deed*, I *swear*!"

More curious now than concerned about maintaining my cool, I leaned my mop up against the wall and walked across and joined Terry at the window and looked down into the shadows in the concrete alleyway where he was pointing, and was not disappointed, because by this time a pale pink-tipped breast had popped into view, but only for a brief moment before it was quickly blotted out by the back of our campus Lothario's head, as he fastened his mouth greedily onto it.

Let's call our loading dock lovers Dick and Jane. We had no idea who they were, after all, and they seemed so earnest and were so innocently absorbed in their play. Remember those first and second grade readers about Dick and Jane, and Mother and Father, and, of course, Spot? Well, our Dick and Jane were a bit more grown up now, Mother and Father were nowhere in sight, and the only Spot on the scene was a wet one that would soon be spreading across the front of Dick's trousers, inside of which one of Jane's hands was now working busily. And things were probably getting pretty damp inside of Jane's jeans too, where one of Dick's hands was now equally busy, as the two bent awkwardly over each other in persistent pumping pursuit of their mutual pleasure.

See Dick and Jane play.

Which is basically what Terry and I were doing, and also by now Bruce and Ted, the two other guys on the crew who had been scrubbing a section of floor a little further down the hall, but had come strolling over to join us when they saw us both peering so intently out the window and down into the gloomy shadows under the ramp.

Imagination is a powerful thing. It must be, because we really couldn't see squat down there, except a couple of college kids, mostly covered by heavy winter clothing, humping and bumping frantically against each other. Dick's curly-haired head was bent at an impossibly awkward angle to Jane's chest, and her head was thrown back, mouth partly open and eyes squinched tightly shut in total concentration as she *willed* herself toward orgasm under Dick's rough handling, her own hand on auto-pilot, pumping like a piston. What we were witnessing was raw, untrammeled, mutual manual sex in its most desperate manifestation, and it must have all worked, because after just a few moments everything shuddered to a satiated halt, and we could almost palpably feel the relief from our window perch a whole floor above them.

The young lovers sagged momentarily against each other, limbs tiredly entwined. (*See Dick run. See* Spot!) Then, disengaging themselves from each other, they briskly zipped and buttoned everything back up, and strolled, arms around each other, down the darkening alley and out of our field of vision.

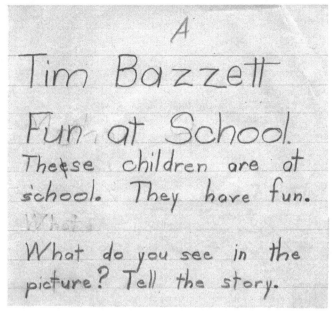

A paper I wrote at St. Philip's School, circa 1950-51, my own Dick and Jane years. I don't have a picture, but I have tried to tell the story.

Now I realize, in retrospect, that all this might seem rather seedy and perhaps even a bit reprehensible, this blatant voyeurism on our part. But I also figure, what the hell, there's a bit of the voyeur in everyone when you come right down to it. Ol' Will was right. Kids do like to watch. We all like to watch. It's in our nature as curious beasts. How else to explain the continuing trend towards more blatant sexuality in movies and television? (And I'm not talking about the smoldering hidden sexuality of Miz Crump, either – although I must confess that I too found Helen rather attractive, and often wondered when Andy was gonna finally get off the dime and *git* some o' that.) Not that I'm condoning that trend. I'm not. I can barely stand to watch most TV fare anymore, and I hardly ever go to the movies or rent videos. It's all become just a bit too crude for me these days. There's nothing left to *imagine* anymore. But perhaps I'm just getting old.

But I was still young and full of juice those years I spent on the Ferris scrub crew, so yeah, of course I found this little voyeuristic interlude – this *Fun with Dick and Jane* – interesting. (And I've also been told it's important to throw a little sex into the mix in any book, so I'll try to do that every now and then.) As a matter of fact, our friends Dick and Jane showed up a few more times in that same spot throughout that winter. I suppose Dick didn't own a car, so the poor kids had no place else to go. So every time we got assigned to work in the Swan building, either Terry or I would make it a point to go take a peek under the entrance ramp, even if we were working at the opposite end of the complex. Granted, we never did actually *see* much, but, as in any deed good *or* bad, it's the *thought* that counts. Once the weather warmed up in the spring, we never saw those kids again, so they must have found a more comfortable spot, maybe down on the riverbank below St. Paul's campus chapel, where the grass grew soft and grew tall, providing some small semblance of privacy, although you had to be careful of chiggers.

Those few times we bore silent witness to this furtive desperate sex, I inevitably would end up feeling more of a sense of loss than of lasciviousness. I felt more loneliness than lust. Watching these young lovers served only to intensify my already all-too-acute awareness that I was too much alone, that I was *not* part of a couple. It was, ultimately, an extremely sad and empty feeling. I doubt that the other guys on the crew felt the same way, especially considering the fact that most of them were married. Probably, if they were feeling or thinking anything, it was more along the lines of, *Hmmm ... Gonna have to get me some o' that when I get home today!*

* * * * *

7

MORE SCRUB CREW SHENANIGANS AND JEOPARDY

The married guys on the scrub crews probably outnumbered the single ones by at least two to one. Terry Karnitz was one of my closer friends on the crew. He was only twenty-one, but he had married right out of high school. His wife, Molly, was tiny, with a creamy, freckle-flecked complexion. She wore little rimless glasses and had an infectious smile. I developed an immediate and hopeless unspoken crush on her from our first meeting. Terry and Molly were both from the Muskegon area. They lived in an upstairs apartment in a big old house near the M-20 Bridge, at the corner of Maple and Ives, just a few blocks north of campus. The two seemed perfectly matched in their baby-faced innocence and with their smooth, rosy-cheeked faces.

That first summer, after my freshman year at Ferris, many of us on the scrub crews opted to work a full-time forty-hour, or sometimes even a forty-eight-hour work week, putting as much money as possible aside for the expenses

Terry Karnitz

of the coming school year. Most of us would carry a lunch with us, frugally hoarding our meager wages. Since Terry only lived a few blocks away, he would go home for lunch, and often invited me and another guy who commuted from Reed City, Bruce Jensen, to bring our brown bag lunches over to his place. Molly was usually at work in town, so the three of us would arrange ourselves around the coffee table in his tiny living room with our bologna or cheese sandwiches and potato chips, flip on the twelve-inch black-and-white TV, and indulge ourselves in our noontime guilty pleasure – Art Fleming and *Jeopardy*.

I don't think I had ever seen *Jeopardy* before that summer of '66 when I began watching it every day at the Karnitz apartment. I was hooked though, and probably the reason I enjoyed it so much was because I was *good* at it. A lifetime of reading and a mind that absorbed all sorts of useless information just like Bounty paper towels soaked up spilled coffee was finally paying off. All those state and world capitals that Sister Mary James had forced us to memorize in the sixth grade would spring unexpectedly from the back recesses of my brain where they had lain dormant for the last several years. And, after all those countless card games of *Authors* with my brothers and sister and mom, of *course* I knew who wrote *Ivanhoe*, or *Little Women*, or *The Scarlet Letter*. (That last one is a book I *still* haven't ever managed to finish, much to my shame, although the names Hester Prynne and Arthur Dimmesdale are well known to me.) Song lyrics from old tin-pan alley standards by composers like Cole Porter and Jerome Kern were easily recognizable to me, thanks to my mother's battered collection of 78 rpm records I had grown up with, and all those hours spent listening to Bing Crosby and Arthur Godfrey on the radio. I even found, much to my astonishment, that I still remembered some of the simpler geometric theorems and algebraic formulae that I had so detested learning in tenth and eleventh grade. The Periodic Table of Elements, or at least a few of its place settings, was still piled with some old furniture back in a dark corner of my brain. I amazed even myself when I blurted out words like Beryllium, Bismuth and Bromine when presented with their symbols. I had absolutely *hated* that kind of stuff when forced to memorize it in Mr. Kilmer's chemistry and physics classes. How could I have possibly *retained* it? I am reminded here of Paul Simon's song, "Kodachrome", with its line, "When I think of all the *crap* I learned in high school". Well, once I discovered *Jeopardy*, all that stuff ceased to be crap. It became instead the welter of winning, the junk of *Jeopardy* champions. For the next twenty years or so, I remained, at least in my own mind, the uncrowned *Jeopardy* king, amazing friends and family alike, with my seemingly unending hidden caches of trivial information that I could pull out of my ass and blurt out effortlessly without even having to think about it.

Unfortunately, key to *Jeopardy* king-dom are the twin elements of speed and good reflexes. Alas, those facilities have deserted me in recent years, and now I am reduced to being the archetypal old geezer who sits in front of the TV pondering Alex Trebek's latest answer and thinking, *I* know *that*, and then confirming the correct question once a much younger and faster contestant buzzes in and blurts it out. *That's it! He's right!* I'll think to myself, but there's not much pleasure in that acknowledgement.

I still watch *Jeopardy* on occasion, when I remember it. (*See?* It's not just that I can't remember the *questions* quickly enough anymore. Shit, I can't even remember to *watch the show*!) But I often think back fondly on those first competitions that summer nearly forty years ago, when the show was a noontime fixture, Art Fleming had all the answers, and I would pit myself against Terry and Bruce, as well as the TV contestants, and emerge victorious.

Bruce and Terry were friends before I met either of them. They were already on the scrub crew when I started working, and I think they may have both been juniors or seniors at Ferris when I was still a freshman, although we were all about the same age. Because of my hitch in the army, I was usually a few years older than many of my freshman and sophomore classmates. Bruce Jensen and I often car-pooled to work that summer since he too lived in Reed City. He and his wife, Sherry, lived in a rented mobile home situated near the west end of Osceola Avenue just a block or two down the hill from our house. As a matter of fact, I could see their place from our front yard up on Church.

Bruce and Sherry were yet another married couple whom I secretly envied for their apparent "wedded bliss" – for the simple fact of their together-ness, their membership in *couple-dom*. They seemed, like Terry and Molly, to be perfectly matched, and to be

Bruce Jensen

perfectly happy together. Of course, I might have been wrong in this perception, but then I was always on the outside looking in, and was very much aware of that fact.

Bruce was an interesting guy. In appearance he seemed to be all spheres – round head, round stomach, round butt, rounded leaning-towards-chubby arms and legs. His hair was usually cut close to his head in a buzz cut, and he wore round, dark-rimmed glasses. Sherry, not nearly as plump as Bruce, was a freckle-faced strawberry blonde, whose more softly contoured figure somehow managed to complement Bruce's boyish chubbiness. They were both from Ludington, and, somehow, like Terry and Molly, they made a matched set, leaving me the odd setting once again.

I think Bruce and Terry may have both been business majors of some kind, and even had some classes together, so they were pretty tight by the time I met them. The were, at any rate, close enough friends that they could kid each other easily, sometimes in ways that could appear cruel, at least to an outsider. Well, actually maybe it was mostly Terry that was the kidder, or practical jokester, and Bruce was usually the butt of the jokes, or the victim.

In addition to being a bit on the fat side, Bruce had one other unfortunate characteristic that could put him at a disadvantage. He had a rather high-pitched voice. Remember how Mickey Mouse sounded in the old Disney cartoons, when old Walt himself provided Mickey's voice, using an improvised falsetto? Well, Bruce's voice was almost that shrill, and consequently could easily be mistaken for a woman's voice. So one of Terry's favorite things to do, just to needle poor Bruce a bit, was to phone Bruce at home, and then when Bruce would pick up, Terry would disguise his voice and say, "Hello. Could I speak to your *husband*, please?" or sometimes, "Could I speak to the *man* of the house, please?"

Flustered and insulted, Bruce would sputter and stutter
something in reply, like, "Wh-, b-b-but th-, this *is* the husband!" or
"I *am* the man of the house!" all in his Walt-as-Mickey high-
pitched voice, which became even shriller in his outraged
indignation.

At this, Terry would crack up, effectively blowing his cover,
whereupon Bruce would catch on and start shouting, still in the
same Walt-as-Mickey voice, "Is that you, Karnitz? God-*damn* you!
Quit *fuckin'* with me, dammit!" and then *slam* down the phone.

If you just try to imagine Mickey Mouse, that lovable all-
American icon, shouting obscenities over the phone, then perhaps
you can see why Terry found this prank so amusing, and I'll admit
that I couldn't help cracking up myself the one time I was there
with Terry listening in. But it was, ultimately, a rather cruel joke on
poor Bruce, who, I should also tell you, always forgave Terry. They
were, after all, friends, and, as any guy can tell you, *real* friends can
fuck with each other with impunity – and they can get away with it
too. (Sometimes I just can't resist a good resounding redundancy.)

That summer we scrubbed countless classrooms, labs and
hallways in several buildings on campus, so many that after a while
they all began to blend together into one long endless stretch of
vinyl tile, bordered by the inevitable heavy wax buildup along the
mopboards at the edges. I remember one day we decided to
experiment with our wax removal methods. It seemed like it took
forever to strip that built-up scrim of heavy wax along the walls.
We'd scrub and scrub at it, and then scrub some more. One morning
one of the guys working with me decided to do something about
this. It might have been Larry Coffey, or it may have been this other
guy, I can't remember his name for sure. It might have been Donley
or Butler. Anyway, he was a trip, always whistling or humming, or
sometimes he'd sit on the floor and do the hambone, slapping his
hands in rhythm on the backs of his thighs and calves, and singing
along, buzz-cut head bobbing in time. Yeah, I'm pretty sure it was
this Donley guy. He was always looking for a "better way" to do
things. Actually, I think he was more interested in relieving the
boredom and the drudgery that the job couldn't help becoming at
times. So anyway, I was running the scrubber along this hallway
wall in the Automotive Tech building, bearing down for all I was

worth on this particularly stubborn strip of dark buildup, and Donley was leaning on his mop, studying the problem, and all of a sudden, he lets go of his mop, claps his hands, and exclaims, "More weight! *That's* what we need! More weight equals more pressure on the bristles! More *scrubbing power*!"

Meanwhile, I'm still bearing down on the scrubber, while looking at Donley, my mouth hanging slightly open, wondering, *What in the hell is he talkin' about?*

Then, before I have time to react, or even to let up on the handles of the scrubber, Donley walks briskly across the wet soapy floor and plops his broad ass right down on top of the housing of the buffer motor and quickly draws his feet up on the outer edges of the buffer, and hollers, "Scrub it, cowboy!" throwing one arm up into the air like a rodeo bull rider.

Well, that sudden extra two hundred-plus pounds of pressure mashes the scrub brush bristles nearly flat to the floor and throws the centrifugal motion of the machine completely out of whack, causing me to momentarily lose control of the scrubber, which careens crazily across the width of the hall with me hanging on for dear life and smashes Donley head-first into the opposite wall, *KA-WHUMP*! The impact knocks him off the buffer and sends him sprawling flat out onto the soap-spattered floor.

Finally managing to let go of the controls on the buffer handle, I turn the buffer off and stand staring, still startled, at Donley, who rises slowly up out of the soap suds onto his elbows, shakes his rock-hard head as if in surprise, and then looks up at me with a wry grin and muses, "Hmmm. Obviously a few kinks yet to work out. Back to the drawing board. Carry on, James."

I like to think that Donley went on to become one of those time-and-motion efficiency experts, like the father in *Cheaper by the Dozen*. Or maybe not.

There's no question that the guys I met while working on the scrub crews were the best part of the job, since the money certainly never amounted to much. No, it was definitely the camaraderie that made all that tedious drudgery worthwhile, working every day with guys like Terry and Bruce, Coffey and Donley. And there were a couple other slightly older married guys, Marsh Draper and a guy named Ted something-or-other, who had their own particular steady styles and personalities that I admired. There was something so eminently attractive to me about the lifestyle of these married students. They all had that special someone to go home to at the end of each day, and the concept of "home" took on a whole new meaning to me when they would invite me into their usually tiny, cramped and cluttered student apartments. They and their wives would usually apologize for "the

Marsh Draper

mess," but I never saw any mess. I saw two people who obviously cared for each other, and already had a good start on this exciting voyage we call life. I wanted onto this cruise in the worst way, but first I had to find a partner, a first mate. I know this all sounds a bit naïve and idealistic, but I was both in those days, and I was also, as I've already mentioned, lonely as hell and "lookin' for love."

One of the other single guys I met my second year on the scrub crew was Ken Sanford. Ken was a friendly easy-going guy with a high forehead and already thinning sandy hair, probably about my age. I can't remember where he was from, but we got along from

day one, and it wasn't long before he proudly showed me a picture of his girlfriend. I was surprised to discover he was dating a Reed City girl, a former classmate of mine, Linda Fleischauer. Although we hadn't been close friends in high school – Linda, a very attractive girl, had run with the "in-crowd" of jocks and cheerleaders – we had always been friendly. Actually we went back a lot further than high

Ken Sanford

53

school. Linda and I had both attended kindergarten at the Holdenville country school, or "beginners" as it was called there, way back in 1949. And we were sometime playmates outside of school too. Her house in Holdenville was just a "hoot and a holler," so to speak, from our house. I only had to cut across Leo Roggow's property, where my brothers and I often went to play in the driveway or garage with Kenny, and then across the road and up a gravel driveway to the Fleischauer house, nestled at the top of a thickly wooded knoll. Linda's place was newer and fancier than ours, a brick house that seemed to hold an endless supply of toys.

I think, at the age of five, I was probably in love with Linda. Sometimes she would come to our house to play too, and my mom can still remember how polite and serious Linda was, and how one summer afternoon she came to the kitchen door and lisped, "Mithuth Baththett, may I pleathe borrow your bathroom?" Such lovely manners. How could you *not* love someone like that?

My apologies here to Ken. I know I was writing about my scrub crew buddies here, and I do remember him well, but I was also using him as an excuse to recall a nearly forgotten childhood crush that I neglected to mention in my first book. Linda became a real freckle-faced beauty, and Ken Sanford was the lucky guy who won her heart.

Workin' on the scrub crew. I wonder what ever happened to all those guys.

* * * * *

8

OLD FRIENDS –
KEITH AND DIANNE EICHENBERG

In the spring of 1966 my Chevy, the by-then not-so-beloved Black Betty, began burning oil big-time again, despite the ring job, or valve job or whatever the hell you call that costly mechanical operation I had just had performed at Tucker's garage a few months earlier. In addition to her belching black oily exhaust and other mechanical shortcomings, Betty had also failed to fulfill the fleshy promise of her wide and inviting back seat. My just-in-case pillows and blanket stored back there were just gathering dust, and I was tired of shaking them out periodically.

It wasn't that I hadn't been trying. I don't think I was aggressive or "dangerous" enough to make an impression on the few girls I had half-heartedly pursued that first year at Ferris. During my last few months in the army I think I had actually mastered some measure of coolness and achieved that subtle air of danger, partly, I suppose, because I had been "with the band," and partly because the German girls who hung out at the Deuce and other bars frequented by GI's had sexual agendas of their own.

In any case, since my return home I had somehow lost that hard-won, predatory sensual edginess, and had reverted to my former good Catholic boy persona. I mean I suppose my momma and my grandma loved me that way, but the young women and girls were largely unimpressed. As far as dating was concerned, I seemed to be starting from square one again, and I wasn't even sure where to find that first square. I car pooled to class a couple times that first fall with Sharon Lindsay, who was Keith Eichenberg's sister-in-law, and about three or four years younger than me. Sharon was very cute, and as Dianne's sister, she held a certain charm for me, if only because I was so envious of Keith and Dianne's apparent wedded bliss. But even though we shared a car ride to Ferris a few times, I never did get up the nerve to ask her out, perhaps because I was afraid of having to face Dianne again if we didn't work out as a couple. Because I did spend quite a lot of time at Keith's place the first few months after I got back from overseas. Since we'd known each other since before first grade, we were comfortable together, and Dianne always made me feel welcome whenever I called, or came knocking forlornly at their door. Their apartment was always spotlessly clean and gleaming, the floors and furniture polished to the nth degree. I can still remember how proudly Keith showed me around the place the first time I came to call, starting at the front, where the tall, old-fashioned windows overlooked North Chestnut and provided a fine view of the alley and parking area behind the Osceola Inn just across the street, where his brother, Tom, was the head chef for the hotel's restaurant, which featured a monthly Sunday smorgasbord that was famous throughout western Michigan.

The small spare bedroom in the front of the apartment was soon to become the nursery (and, later, just "the kids' room" with bunk beds stacked neatly in place, as Mike, David and Sarah each made their subsequent entrances). The sparsely furnished living room seemed very spacious to me, at least before the kids started coming. Behind the living room was a kitchen and dining area with a washer and dryer too. And finally, *the piece de resistance*, next to the kitchen – the "master" bedroom and bath, with its meticulously polished vanity and chests of drawers and, finally, the bed, which Keith cavalierly pointed out as "the work bench where we build tricycle motors," a remark which caused Dianne to blush furiously, although she also laughed and remonstrated gently, "Oh, *Keith*!"

In retrospect, I recognize that Keith and Dianne's first home (where they lived for ten years before moving into a near palatial home out west of town, where their last child, Katie, was born) was nothing more than a tiny two-bedroom walk-up, but at that particular time, to my young and envious eyes, my old friend Keith had already died and gone to heaven. I didn't see how things could

Keith and Dianne (Lindsay) Eichenberg, 1964

possibly ever get any better than that. (And who's to say? Perhaps things *don't* get better; only more complicated and crowded as we blindly fulfill the procreative imperative prescribed by society.) He and Dianne had this "beautiful home" filled with lovely furniture and all the accoutrements of modern living, but most of all they had each other. They were a "whole," while I was still a "half."

So yes, I spent a lot of time hanging out at the Eichenbergs', hoping, perhaps, that some of that magical air of bliss would rub off on me. Alas, it didn't work that way, but I think both Keith and Dianne could sense my loneliness. On one occasion at their place, Dianne introduced me to a childhood friend of hers, a most attractive young woman named Jean Taylor, who, it turned out, was an Air Force nurse stationed at Wurtsmith air base. I won't say there was any immediate chemistry between Jean and me, but like I said, she was pretty and I was lonely. So, on the basis of our one short, informal evening spent together at Keith and Dianne's, a week or two later, on the spur of the moment, I took off on a Saturday night and drove all the way across the state to Oscoda, found the air base, then the base hospital, and went inside and found Jean. Of course, she was working, so could only spare me fifteen or twenty minutes over coffee, but in that time she managed to gently let me down, although I think she was a bit flattered that I had driven nearly two hundred miles in the snow just to see her. In 1965 my actions would probably have been seen as no more than a sweet, albeit naïve, gesture. In the paranoid tenor of today's times, however, I would no doubt be viewed as a crazed and menacing stalker. I offer this strange isolated incident strictly as an example of the extent of my desperate loneliness. Like the song says, I was "lookin' for love in all the wrong places."

You might wonder how it was that I didn't meet any girls just by virtue of being a college student. Surely there were girls in my classes I might have met and dated. But the truth is, when you're a townie, or a local student who commutes to school each day, and on top of that you work every night after school and all day on Saturday, there's not much time left over for socializing. By the time Sunday, your one day off each week, arrives, you need it just to catch up on sleep and homework. So my dating opportunities were pretty severely limited. I tried, but probably not very hard.

* * * * *

9

A NEW CAR AND A NEW START –
THE VET'S CLUB

A couple things happened in the spring of 1966 that were to change things for me socially. I bought a new car – my very first new car. It was a dark blue 1966 Volkswagen 1300 – a Beetle. This probably sounds pretty strange, considering how important that enormous back seat in the Chevy had seemed when I bought that car. But frankly I'd never had occasion to "use" that back seat, so perhaps that particular feature had lost some of its importance. And after pouring countless quarts of oil into Black Betty's hungry maw, I just wanted something mechanically reliable. I was ready for something bright and new and shiny, perhaps hoping it would change my luck.

On my daily commute to Ferris I would pass the VW dealership on the north end of Big Rapids and would often glance in at the shiny floor models in the showroom windows. One sunny Friday afternoon I arranged with Ed Howe to take the night off from work and drove back over to the VW garage, parked the Chevy and went into the showroom. I took a few minutes to look longingly at the sporty red Karmann-Ghia in the center of the floor, peeked into the windows of a VW microbus, then went over and opened the door of a bright blue 1300 Beetle and folded myself carefully into the driver's seat, pushing it all the way back on its tracks. I laid my left hand on the steering wheel, pushed in the clutch, and cautiously worked the floor-shift through its H-pattern

4-speed paces, then, after a moment of experimentation, discovered reverse gear, reached by pushing down on the lever, then over and back. Soon I was approached by a salesman, a small, dark-haired, smartly dressed young man in a coat and tie, who explained the synchromesh feature of the transmission and a few other features of the dashboard display, but he didn't pressure me in any way beyond that. I switched on the Blaupunkt radio and experimented with its pre-set pushbuttons. It produced a much richer sound than the cheap radio I had in my Chevy – a definite plus in my eyes … er, ears. This was, of course, before the advent of FM radio as a regular option in cars, so it was only an AM, but I was impressed by the fact that even parked within the glass and steel confines of the showroom, the radio pulled in WLS out of Chicago, one of my favorite stations, but one I could usually only receive at night.

After a polite interval of keeping a respectful distance, the salesman approached me again and told me he had an identical model out on the lot and asked if I'd like to take it for a test drive. I was ready, so I showed him my driver's license, which he examined briefly and, noting my name, asked if Ellis Bazzett was my dad. When I replied in the affirmative, he told me he knew Dad, and, giving me his business card, introduced himself as Rudy Grahek, aka Dynamite the Clown. I had failed to recognize Rudy minus his red bulbous nose and garish pancake clown makeup. Rudy, who had started clowning after returning from the Korean War, was already something of a local celebrity by the mid-sixties.

Rudy Grahek (left) on the showroom floor at the Big-R Volkswagen dealership

My first new car, a 1966 VW Beetle

I'm not sure if clowning or selling cars was his sideline back then, but he was, as it turned out, very good at both jobs.

Car salesmen in 1966, at least in small towns, must have been much more trusting than they are today, because after just a brief chat, during which Rudy learned I was an army veteran, a Ferris student, and employed part-time, he dropped the keys to a new Beetle into my hand and told me to take it home for the weekend and drive it before I decided anything. Astonished and quite pleased, I waved good-bye to Rudy and pulled proudly out onto 131 and headed for home in what would be my very first new car.

The base sticker price on that '66 Beetle was just $1666. With the addition of dealer prep, taxes and a few options, some already on the car and some I requested (radio, whitewalls, gravel guards and mud flaps), it rounded up to about $1800. I didn't have that much money, but, in the grip of new car fever, I was ready to finance it and make payments. Instead, Dad lent me the cash to buy it outright and then set up his own payment plan at a token interest rate, which saved me a considerable amount of money over the next year or so. Finally then I was equipped and ready to roll with a new and reliable set of wheels.

The other event that spring that was to lead to an improvement in my social life and status was my re-connection with another old friend from high school.

Gary Perdew was a year older than me and was a good friend and classmate of Jerry Whitman, one of my best high school buddies. Jerry had dated Gary's younger sister, Fran, who was in my class, the last year or two of school. In fact, shortly after my return home from the service, I had attended Jerry and Fran's wedding at the Methodist church on Higbee and the reception held in the church basement. Jerry was living in Flint and working for GM, but he was a long-time and ardent fishing and hunting enthusiast and self-styled outdoorsman and was even then probably plotting his move to the remote Kenai Peninsula in Alaska where he planned to build a cabin and homestead. I can still remember, much to my chagrin, my wedding gift to the newlywed Whitmans: two full cases of assorted Campbell's soups. It seemed like a very practical gift at the time to me. I mean, gee, what if the hunting and fishing weren't very good? Sorry, Fran.

But I was talking about Gary Perdew, not Fran or Jerry. I think I may have just accidentally run into Gary one day on campus, where he was a student in the refrigeration and air conditioning tech program. I hadn't seen Gary in probably four years. He had left home after high school to join the army just as I had. Now, in addition to his class schedule and working part-time, Gary was also very active in the campus veterans' organization.

The FSC Vet's Club (or Veterans Association, as it was formally named) was still a fairly new group in 1966. It had started in 1963 with just ten members, but by the time Gary introduced me to the club it was the fastest growing and largest sanctioned student group on campus, with nearly a hundred members, a number which would eventually more than triple before the Viet Nam war finally ground to a painful and shameful halt in the mid-seventies.

When I first met Gary again he was living here and there, rooming with assorted other guys in no permanent sort of arrangement. His family had re-located from Reed City to West Branch while he was away in the service, so he didn't have the luxury of living at home like I did. When he first came home, he lived for a while with the Noder family in Holdenville, and then he made do with various rental houses and trailers in Big Rapids or Paris. About the time I met him, Gary was looking for another place to live, and, after consulting with my folks, I offered him temporary

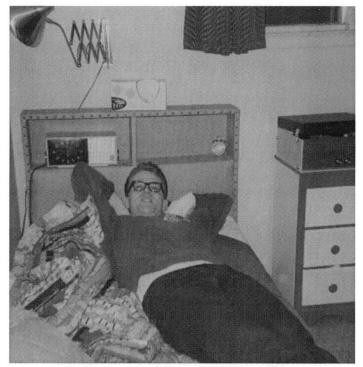

Relaxing in my basement bedroom at home on West Church, 1966

accommodations at our house, so he moved into my basement bedroom with me for a short time.

It was during this period and at Gary's urging that I joined the Vet's Club, albeit probably with some reservations, wondering how I would possibly find time for it in my already busy work-school schedule. I needn't have worried, because I did find time, and also made a number of new friends.

The Ferris Vet's Club was in a kind of transitional stage when I joined. Because it was growing so quickly, it was like an adolescent boy, tentatively trying out his new height and weight, lurching about in an uncoordinated fashion and trying to figure out what he wanted to *be*, and how to use his newfound strength and size.

By the end of 1965 the Viet Nam conflict was an inescapable fact of life. Tens of thousands of American troops had already been deployed into the jungles of Southeast Asia. Every night the six o'clock news featured combat footage and toted up the latest figures of dead and wounded until we became numb and inured to the carnage and suffering such reports represented. But we couldn't close our eyes to the war, because even a small community like Reed City was personally touched by its tragedy. About the same time I joined the Vet's Club, nearly a year after I had returned home from the army, I attended the funeral of a former friend and schoolmate who was one of the first Reed City casualties of the war.

Ron Mis had been an altar boy with me at St. Philip's. He was a grade behind me in school, but I think he was close to my age, and by the time we were in high school he was hanging out mostly with the kids in my grade, usually the jocks and the "hoods." Ron was one of those "dangerous" types that girls just naturally gravitated toward. Even while he was still at St. Philip's he began to develop and perfect his rebel look, combing his nearly black hair into an oily-looking DA, often with a careless curl or two overhanging his forehead. Except for his horn-rimmed glasses, he had the Elvis look pretty down pat by the time he was fourteen or so, right down to the curled lip sneer. Soon after he started high school he had his own car, which only served to increase his status, particularly among the hoods and greasers, those dark and moody kids who hovered near the school entrances between classes with burning cigarettes concealed in their cupped hands, the same guys who never seemed to wear a coat, even in the most frigid weather. Ron's father, Henry Mis, was the owner of Henry's Bar, one of just a few drinking establishments left in town. I don't personally know if Ron ever took advantage of this fact by getting beer or booze for his pals. Probably not, but the very fact that his dad owned a bar couldn't have hurt his carefully cultivated image among his contemporaries. I call it an "image" because I think it was just that. Ron had successfully re-invented himself in the course of his adolescence. I remember Ron mostly from our mutual altar boy days, when, garbed in our black cassocks and white surplices, we moved in quiet unison about the sanctuary of the church, genuflecting, ringing the bells, or fetching the water and wine, and the person I remember was a good kid.

Ron Mis,
Reed City High School heartthrob,
1963

Ron Mis, US Army Paratrooper,
1st Cav Div (AM). KIA Viet Nam
October 2, 1966 22 years old.

Ron came back in a box from Viet Nam and brought the war home once and for all to the people of Reed City, who turned out in force for his funeral at St. Philip's, where, only a couple of short years before, he had still been serving Mass. That same year another local boy, Randy Totten, was killed in Nam too. The names of both of these Reed City boys are inscribed on The Wall in Washington. I made it a point to find them and whisper a prayer of gratitude when I visited the memorial over twenty years later. *Requiescat in pace*, Ron and Randy. Reed City remembers you.

By 1966 it had become apparent not only to the American people, but also to the Johnson administration, that this war would not be easily won, and that we were in it for the long haul. The country had been torn asunder by protests against the war, and it was becoming increasingly difficult for armed forces recruiters to fill their monthly quotas to supplement the military draft. So that summer new legislation was pushed through congress that authorized a new GI Bill for education which I think was retroactive to the time the old bill had expired. In other words, anyone who signed up for the military was guaranteed financial assistance towards a college education upon discharge – *if* he survived his term of service.

I don't really know if the new GI Bill fulfilled its intentions of bolstering enlistments, but I know I was certainly happy with its immediate implementation. What it meant for me was a monthly government check for the princely sum of one hundred dollars, which in effect nearly doubled my monthly income. It was a completely unexpected windfall, like found money, to me and to thousands of other recently discharged veterans across the country. The new GI Bill was then undoubtedly a major factor that contributed to the unprecedented rapid growth of the Ferris Vet's Club, as its paid membership soared suddenly to over a hundred in the Fall Term of '66 and continued to grow steadily in subsequent terms.

When I joined the Vet's Club it was still kind of floundering, trying to find its rightful niche on the campus and in the community. Rick Waldchen was the president that term, and the faculty advisor was Hugh Griffith, an English professor, who remained the club's quiet mentor for all of the years the club was in existence.

Gary Perdew introduced me to a lot of guys when I joined the club, and I quickly found the group to be an easy and comfortable fit for me. There was a nearly immediate bond of brotherhood that sprang from the shared experience of simply having served and survived.

And there was the beer and the booze. Yes, rivers of the stuff, as the vets, most of us newly assimilated to civilian life, got to know each other, swapped lies and told our endless "war stories." The most natural setting for this was, of course, a bar, and the club members had a regular one, located just across the Maple Street Bridge, first joint on the right. It was called The Red Rail, and was right across the street from a tiny log cabin restaurant, which we all called *EAT*, after the large neon sign that hung on the front, dwarfing the smaller sign which indicated the real name of the place, the *A la Mode*.

Unfortunately, because of my night work schedule, I seldom had time to frequent the bar myself. But there were frequent weekend parties, Saturday nights to remember – or not, since so many of us got too blasted to recall much later. The club members

These are just some of the vets from 1966-1967. I was always working when they took photos, so I never showed up in the group shots.

ROW 1: *Richard F. Waldchen, president; Roland New, secretary* **ROW 2:** *Doug Colwell, Harry Tellman, Luther Lessard, Walter Len, Gary Perdew, Robert Steen, Mike King, Dale Pero* **ROW 3:** *Rodney Mosier, Mike Mullendore, Larry Thornton, James Clabuesch, Daniel Fuller, Bob Maihofer, Frank Perry* **ROW 4:** *Wayne Shook, James Roddy, Mack Gaut, George Bryant, Arnold Morgan, Dan Bittner, Paul Keltner, Richard Sanborn* **ROW 5:** *Donald Blough, Edmund Feeney, Thomas Hart, Richard Reed*

ROW 1: *Hugh Griffith, advisor; William Ott, treasurer; Ronald Savage, vice-president* **ROW 2:** *David Allshouse, Lawrence Stubbs, Jan Fokens, Tony Marcindewciz, Sam Gilbert, Loren Sibilla, Kingston Applegate, Brian Cavern* **ROW 3:** *Douglas Hura, David Morrison, John Cook, Thomas MacQueen, Richard Hawk, Donald Vincent, Dennis Whitney, Carl Pinard* **ROW 4:** *Terry Telder, Patrick O'Connor, John Finn, Harold Fredrickson, David Weakly, Michael O'Meara, John Nibbelink* **ROW 5:** *Kenneth Frambes, Richard Simonelli, Carl Ziegler, Miles Van Orman, Danny Campbell*

often pooled their funds to rent a hall, or any empty building would do, like the old country school house on the west side of Paris. A couple guys would bring a portable stereo and some records and everyone would bring their own liquid refreshments, and most were very generous about sharing their liquor or beer with buddies who were temporarily short of funds – a common curse among the vets. The music provided served a dual purpose, for background, or mood music, and for dancing.

No, we weren't dancing alone, or with each other. There were always girls around, sometimes even a few extras. My first date as a vet came from this pool of extras, or hangers-on. Her name was Ellen, and she was a tall, willowy redhead with a cute freckled face, a Dutch girl from Grand Rapids. She liked to drink and she liked to *Par-TEE*! When I met Ellen she was on the rebound from another vet. I'm not sure if she was the dump-*er*, or the dump-*ee*, but she was available and I was looking for a date.

I should probably explain here that Vet's Club parties were very popular among the party girls at Ferris, who understood that if you were a vet, you were old enough to get into bars and to buy beer and liquor. There was no fake ID finagling involved. Everything was legal and above board, at least as far as *buying* the stuff was concerned. Supplying it to minors was, I suppose, an entirely different matter, but it was a technicality that not many vets stayed up nights worrying about.

I dated Ellen maybe two or three times, and I use the term "date" rather loosely, since a couple of those occasions didn't involve much more than driving around in a car with another couple and a brace of six-packs, or perhaps a few imperial quarts of Blue Ribbon. *PAR-TEE*!

* * * * *

10

ICE SKATING –
PARTIES AND MEMORIES

My first real date with Ellen, however, was an actual party, an ice-skating party. Doesn't that sound Currier-and-Ives picturesque and wholesome though? Well, it *could* have been, I suppose, if either one of us had taken *skates*, but we didn't.

The party was at Horsehead Lake, several miles east of Big Rapids. One of the vets I had just recently befriended was John Nibbelink, whose parents had a summer cottage on the lake that normally stayed closed up and empty during the winter. John, who was a veteran of the Coast Guard, probably figured it would be a good idea to take a landing party of about a dozen vets and their dates to reconnoiter the cabin area and its contiguous shoreline to make sure that all was secure for the winter. I'm sure his commander would have been proud of him for taking such a sterling initiative, although I'm not sure how his folks would have felt about it, had they known.

In any case, it was, I think, early December when we set out on our secret mission of "drink, dance and debauch." There were already several inches of snow on the ground the Saturday of John's party, and it snowed like blazes for much of the day. I felt pretty invincible in my new VW, however, with all the traction supplied by its rear-mounted engine. Gary and I were double dating, so around 11 that morning we stopped in at Grunst Bros. Party Store on North State Street and loaded a couple cases of beer into the front hatch of the Bug (more traction) and added a couple fifths of Kessler's whiskey ("smooth as silk") to keep us warm, then headed on down to Ferris where we picked up Ellen and Gary's date at one of the dorms.

It was probably noon by the time we crossed over the Maple Street Bridge and headed east on M-20. The Blaupunkt was blaring – "Mah bay-bee does the Hanky-Panky" – and the windshield wipers were slapping away on high, keeping time with the garage band sound of The Shondells, as the snow continued to blow and swirl around us. By the time we got to Rodney where we got off M-20 and headed toward the lake, I was beginning to wonder if this was really such a good idea, because the snow was collecting in drifts at random intervals all along the road. I must have voiced my concern, because Gary, ensconced cozily under an army blanket in the back seat with his date, a girl from Evart named Pat, shouted, "Go *faster*, Tim, and you can just *blast* through the drifts!"

So I did. I blasted through and surfed over those drifts, and by God it *worked*.

Upon arriving at the cabin, I parked the Bug behind four other vehicles already lined up in the drive. Gary and I unloaded the beer from the front hatch and carried it up a narrow path that had been shoveled around the side of the cabin and stashed it near several other cases already stacked on the enclosed but unheated front porch. The temperature was hovering somewhere around freezing, so no refrigeration was necessary. There was a wide variety of beers represented on the porch – Stroh's, Pabst, Hamm's, Blatz, Goebel, Old Milwaukee, and even a case of Tudor Ale, an A&P budget brand of rotgut that could just barely lay claim to *being* beer. (Almost all of the vets shamefacedly admitted, however, to having sampled the stuff on occasion. After all, when you're nearly broke, you have to consider the price.) In those days before all the designer and imported beers, Bud and Stroh's were considered "premium" beers, at least among the financially challenged members of the Vet's Club.

Gary tucked the brown paper bag containing the Kessler's underneath one arm and grabbed a couple beers and disappeared with his date into the cottage. I only caught occasional glimpses of them throughout the rest of the afternoon and evening. He and Pat already knew each other pretty well, or at least it seemed so to me, judging by the way they had so quickly and cozily melded together under that backseat blanket on the ride out to the lake.

I pulled two cans of Hamm's out of the case I had contributed and handed one to Ellen and we walked down the steps to the lake shore where several people were already gathered and a couple guys were clearing snow off the ice with shovels and scrapers, creating a crude skating area. Some of the partygoers had actually brought ice skates. I saw Wayne Shook and his date, a luscious-looking blonde I didn't know, sitting on the edge of the dock, which had been pulled ashore, and lacing up their skates. George Bryant, a friend of John's, already had skates on and was pushing a wide snow blade back and forth across the ice, stroking gracefully from side to side in a scuffed-looking pair of long-bladed hockey skates.

Those old skates with the long blades reminded me of the hand-me-down skates I had worn several times as a kid when our whole family would pack a big picnic lunch and head for Indian Lake for a rare day of winter family fun. Dad would bring his fishing gear, which included a heavy long-handled steel tool called a spud, which he used to cut a hole through the inches-thick lake ice. He also had a small wooden nail keg in which he kept his short ice-fishing pole and other tackle, a kerosene lantern and hand warmer, extra mittens and a few other things. Once he'd made a satisfactory hole in the ice, he would bait his hook and select a suitable sinker, and then he would light the lantern and turn the keg upside down over it and use it for a seat. The lantern kept his butt warm for the long hours he would sit gazing at the red and white plastic bobber floating in the dark hole in the ice, waiting for a fish to bite. I don't remember him ever catching a lot of fish on these winter expeditions, but he seemed to enjoy the ritual, sitting and dreaming his own thoughts, occasionally removing a mitten to pick his nose as he alternately watched his line and also us kids as we raced each other awkwardly about over the bumpy uneven lake ice, often pushing a metal lawn chair in front of us as a kind of "ice walker."

My oldest brother, Rich, always had the newest and best skates, quite simply because as the oldest he had the biggest feet and had to keep moving up to the next size. I remember my hand-me-downs were usually a bit large, a problem Mom would solve by adding extra pairs of socks to my feet until the skates were reasonably snug. My skating skills were never very impressive, especially in the earliest years when I was only seven or eight. I would lurch uncertainly about on the insides of my ankles until I hit a rough spot, then fall forward, throwing my mittened hands out in front of me to break my fall. Or, forgetting to bend my knees and lean forward, I would fall backwards, arms flailing wildly to no avail. It was all great fun, being out in the brisk winter air and blindingly bright sunshine, but you get the picture, I'm sure. Perhaps some of you have been there, done that, so to speak.

As I got a bit older, say eleven or twelve, I won't say my skating improved exactly, but I became a bit bolder on the ice, particularly if there were a few girls around that I wanted to impress.

Back in the fifties, Reed City had a public skating rink every winter, in a manner of speaking. It was located on the ball field at the southwest corner of Church and Higbee. Early in the winter, some city workers would scrape up a low earthen berm around the edges of the ball field. Then, as soon as the weather turned frigid and snowy, a fire department truck would come over and the firemen would employ their high-pressure hoses to flood the field, and – *VOILA!* – we had a municipal ice rink. And it got used plenty too. Kids from all over town would come trekking over to the rink, skates slung over their shoulders. And, since the rink was superimposed on top of the ball field, at night we turned on the "stadium" (*ha*!) lights, and – *VOILA* again! – we had *night* skating. After heavy snowfalls the city would usually try to send a snowplow over to clear off the rink, but only after all the roads had been cleared. Of course, if the snow were heavy enough to cause a school closing, a lot of kids would flock to the rink to skate and bring snow shovels and scrapers to clear the ice themselves. We couldn't wait for the snowplow to get there. We wanted to skate *now*!

Our house was less than a block from the rink, so I went skating often, particularly during the winters when I was between the ages of ten and twelve. Like I said, I never got very good at it, but I got braver. I never quite mastered the art of stopping gracefully, but I loved to get going full speed ahead, so I would race across the rink and aim myself at the snow banks that encircled the ice, and then, jumping into the air, I would launch myself over the banks and into the deep snow, which quite effectively stopped me. It was an exhilarating daredevil feeling, racing around the ice and diving into snow banks. My brother Bob was a much better skater than me by then, and he and his friends would usually engage in more sophisticated skating activities, like forming a "crack the whip" line, or even an occasional game of pick-up hockey.

I thought briefly back on those long-ago days as Ellen and I stood sipping our beers by the lake shore, watching as George and Wayne and a few others began gliding about over the cleared space on the ice. We didn't linger long however, as it was pretty damn cold and neither one of us were dressed very warmly. I was wearing my newly acquired status symbol, a navy blue Ferris Vet's Club jacket with its "Old Bill" logo emblazoned on the left breast. Unfortunately, the jacket was nothing more than a thin nylon shell, and even with the cable knit ski sweater I wore under it, I was still shivering.

Vet's Club crude logo –
"Old Bill."
Designer unknown.

So, having paid our token respects to the frozen lake, we made our way back up the wooden steps, through the porch and into the cabin, where we greeted John and his date, who were feeding a couple more logs onto an already roaring fire in the stone fireplace. More vets and their dates continued to come and go throughout the afternoon and evening, some of them actually going down to the lake to skate (it was a "skating" party, after all), but most of them congregated in the cabin's great room or spilled over into the two or three bedrooms that opened off to the sides. It was a large and lively group, and many of us danced to the stereo, which was cranked up to the max, strains of the Stones' "Satisfaction" alternating with other pop groups and sounds of the day, like the Buckinghams' "Kind of a Drag", the Beatles' "Norwegian Wood", or, an enormously popular dance band that year, Mitch Ryder and the Detroit Wheels. The frenetic screaming and booming bass beat of "Jenny Take a Ride" or "Devil with a Blue Dress" would never fail to fill the small dance area with sweating gyrating couples.

If you're waiting with bated breath for a sweaty sex scene here, you're going to be disappointed. Oh, I'm sure there were varying degrees of sexual activity going on in the bedrooms and other dark corners of the cabin, from furtive frustrated groping of brassiere-clad breasts beneath heavy sweaters, to perhaps slightly more satisfactory mutual manual manipulations performed under the cover of coats or blankets. But, as for any real, full-bore bare-naked boffing going on, nope, I doubt it. Too many people packed into too small a space. And all that alcohol being consumed tended too to lessen the libidinal forces at work.

* * * * *

11

THE VETS, ALCOHOL
AND A SPODEE-ODEE

Alcohol, incidentally, appeared to be the drug of choice among the members of the Vet's Club. In fact, there was a notable precedent of hard-drinking guys at Ferris even before the Vet's Club formed. The "Turtles" were an informal but legendary underground group of drinkers around campus throughout the sixties. According to their custom, if one of their members were asked, "Are you a Turtle?" he was honor bound to reply with the set phrase, "You bet 'cher sweet *ass* I am!"

I got to know quite a few of the vets during my one year of club membership, and I never saw any evidence of drug use, not even marijuana. I could be wrong in this, of course. It was, after all, the mid-sixties, a time when experimentation with drugs was supposedly rampant among the ranks of young people and college students all over the country. But the guys in the Vet's Club had been old-fashioned enough to serve their time in the military, most of them enlistees, so perhaps it was only natural that their drug of choice would be the same as their fathers, many of whom were WWII era veterans. I think we vets thought of alcohol more as a relaxative or a social lubricant than as a means of "getting high" or expanding our consciousness.

Our old-fashioned-ness extended to all the areas of our lives. We studied hard, we worked hard, and we partied hard. We filled up all our time. We were older than most of our fellow students and felt we were a few years behind, and needed to catch up as soon as possible and get on with our "real lives." College seemed to many of us to be just another obstacle we needed to overcome to get to the "good stuff." At least that's the way *I* felt at the time. Recently, however, I read somewhere that real life, or the good stuff, is what happens while you're waiting for it to happen – or something to that effect. If this is true – and I believe now that it is – then I was living the good stuff – was smack in the *middle* of it during my Ferris years, and particularly during my short time in the Vet's Club.

That skating party at Nibbelink's place was the first of several vets' parties I attended my last year at Ferris. They all tended to bleed into each other after a while, as there was a sameness to them: crowds of guys and girls looking for some fun, and maybe for love too; lots of loud music and dancing fast and slow; rivers of alcohol consumed, and very sketchy, fragmented memories of what exactly happened at these parties, wherever they took place. I have only vague recollections of most of them, and of their various venues – a VFW or American Legion Hall in Howard City or near Rogers Heights, the old Paris schoolhouse, the Paris Bar, or small crowded apartments or rented houses in and around Big Rapids.

Only one other party stands out in my memory, and probably only because of its novel "theme." Gary Perdew organized a gala "Spodee-Odee" party at the ramshackle furnished rental house he shared with a couple other guys on the east side of the river on M-20. It was a green-shingle-sided house that seemed to lean slightly to the south, and its only memorable feature was a "religious icon" that Gary had added and kept prominently displayed on the fake mantle in the living room. Gary's "Saint Peter" was carved from wood, was about ten inches high, and wore ornate colorful bishop's robes and a tall miter headdress with a curved crest – a very impressive figure. Gary liked to show it to his dates and would tell them that if they rubbed his old "Saint Pete," they would most certainly be lucky in love, perhaps even that very night. When the girls eagerly picked up the icon to comply, they would inevitably turn it around and would find that when viewed from the reverse side, the icon was actually an erect penis of impressive proportions.

Yessir, Gary's ol' Saint Pete was a real conversation starter – or *stopper*.

I'm not sure exactly where the term "Spodee-Odee" came from, although years later I did run across a tune by Jerry Lee Lewis called "Drinkin' Wine Spodee-Odee". Maybe that's where it came from. I don't know.

But, getting back to Gary's theme Spodee-Odee party, I think I may have helped him clean up the place to prepare it for the event. Then we went to a hardware store and bought a shiny new galvanized steel garbage can and brought it back to his place and scoured it out with hot soapy water, then rinsed it repeatedly with more hot scalding water. If you've never been to a Spodee-Odee party, then this takes a bit of explaining. The garbage can would serve as a kind of giant makeshift punch bowl. The price of admission to the party was a contribution to this communal watering trough – something hard and something soft. A pint of bourbon, a can of Hi-C. A little vodka, a little orange juice or tomato juice. Unequal mixes of scotch, gin, wine, whiskey, beer, Coke, 7-Up, and other assorted mixes, juices and sodas, and maybe even some Kool-Aid snuck into the equation as the evening progressed. Gary or one of his roomies usually presided over the can, mixing everything together with a new equally sterilized canoe paddle bought specifically for the purpose. What you ended up with was a reddish-brown-colored non-descript-tasting cocktail with a foamy head on it that was probably near lethal in its alcohol content. There were dozens of people at the party, as Gary had announced it at the last Vet's Club meeting, so it was a much-anticipated social and cultural occasion. And I think it was a resounding success.

Of course, there *was* a lot of puking going on in the bathroom, and out in the yard and driveway, and in the street, so you had to be careful where you stepped as the evening wore on. But since no one died, or was even hospitalized, at least as far as I know, then, yes, I would have to say that it was, if not the social event of the season, at least a real success. I can still remember that shining galvanized grail filled with all that foaming unrecognizable goop, and Gary grinning and paddling with his varnished oar as he greeted each new couple, who would pour their particular alcoholic and fizzy offerings into the rainbow mix, then dip out a cupful to sip. It was

ALL COLLEGE STUDENT GOVERNMENT ROW 1: James S. Young, advisor-Assistant Dean of Students; David Fershee, housing chairman; Mike Busch, speaker; Nancy Dailey, secretary; John Cook, chairman-Committee for Campus Improvements. ROW 2: Lynne Strong, Carole Meyers, Gary Perdew, DiAnne Janus, Jacques Almasian, Joel Black, Patty Knapp. ROW 3: Patrick Vollmar, Stuart Wall, Ronald DeMerilt, Judicial Chairman, George Klepser, Allan Hulbard, Sam Denn, Milt Kley, Bob Schultz.

FSC Student Government – John Cook, bottom right, and Gary Perdew, third from left in second row

a uniquely novel and impressive display, Gary, the likes of which may have never been seen again at a Ferris gathering. In retrospect, however, I would offer this warning to my readers: Don't try this at home without a trained medical emergency response team and an ambulance standing by. *Geeze*, were we *stoo-pid*! Perfect pinheads.

I don't mean to give the impression that the Ferris Vet's Club was nothing more than a bunch of rowdy irresponsible drunks, although it's true there may have been a few of those in the mix with such a large group. No, as I said earlier, the Vets were an organization in transition around the time I joined. That year, 1966, there was an election of club officers, and one of our new officers, John B. Cook, was a truly exemplary young man who really helped turn the club around, getting its members involved in worthy campus and community projects, and into fund-raising and volunteering. John was an extremely personable fellow, liked and admired not just by other vets, but also by faculty and administration and the student body at large. He was also a very handsome guy, something that did not go unnoticed by all the girls around campus, and probably helped considerably that year when he ran for a vacant seat on the student body council and won. So the Vet's Club stock soared that year. We were becoming respectable. The club formed its own intramural volleyball and softball teams. In the spring of '67 John even arranged for an inter-

The Vet's Club supporting a worthy cause, with Gary Perdew holding the sign

collegiate softball game with the CMU Vet's Club at a ball field on School Section Lake. I don't remember who won, but there was plenty of beer for everyone. Some things never change. Nevertheless, organizationally speaking, the Vets had arrived. They became involved in campus government, and were movers and shakers, at least as much as students can be, given their primary aim of getting an education.

Probably what most former Ferris students remember about the Vets from that era, however, is the club's annual entry in the Homecoming Queen contest. I know, you may be thinking, *doesn't he mean the king?* Nope. Every year our entry in the pageant was the same, a guy in drag who was always named Zelda "Godiva" Gurch. He-She was the centerpiece of the Vet's Club float in the Homecoming parade every year, except for those rare times when he-she was actually elected queen or a member of the court. (Yes, it *did* happen!)

The Vet's Club at Ferris will always be intertwined with some of my best memories from my college years. It gave me a sense of belonging, and made me, even if only peripherally, a part of the campus community. As a townie, or local, I didn't live in a dorm, or even in Big Rapids. I drove down from Reed City every morning, attended classes, and holed up here and there around campus in between classes, studying and doing homework, then put in my four hours of sweeping, mopping or buffing in the Science Building every night and drove home again. For much of my first year at Ferris I felt nearly invisible and alone in the crowd. It was not, in any sense of the word, a "complete" college experience. I suspect there were many other local students who commuted back and forth to Ferris and worked nights and weekends like I did and never developed any real connection with the school. It was nothing more than a tedious means to an uncertain end, cramming and slaving and skimping to just get that degree in hopes of a better life. This is not a criticism of Ferris; it's simply a statement of fact. Thirty-some years later my daughter, Susan, moved to Reed City to act as a caretaker-tenant for our retirement home, and while she was here she completed her last year of college at Ferris, commuting back and forth just like her father had in the sixties. Because she was a commuter, she made very few friends, and had practically no involvement in campus life. She feels very little connection to Ferris now, although she did manage to graduate with high honors in the spring of 2002. (Suzie holds the distinction of being the very first recipient of a Bachelor of Arts from FSU, and was an English major to boot.) She has since moved back to Maryland where she grew up and where many of her closest friends still reside.

* * * * *

12

DRINKIN' AGAIN
AND SMALL TOWN JUSTICE

While my association with the FSC Vet's Club finally gave me a much-needed sense of belonging and a connection on campus, it also precipitated my slipping back into some rather bad habits, namely binge drinking. During my tour in the army I had indulged in some prodigious and dangerous drinking bouts. A lot of young GI's away from home did it, which doesn't excuse the practice, I know, but it was a fact of life in the service.

When I returned home, however, I had immediately cleaned up my act. I had quit smoking. I did my best to refrain from the use of foul language, another GI habit I had lazily picked up on, *and* I had pretty much quit drinking too. In other words, I worked hard at being a good son. I was after all living in my parents' house again, and there was an unspoken expectation that I would provide a good example to my younger siblings, who were just fourteen and twelve when I came back home. I did my level best to "be good" and to help out around the house whenever I could, given my already full schedule of school and job. I pitched in and helped with mowing the grass in summer and shoveling snow in winter and tried to keep my basement room picked up and neat, in exchange for the room and board I was getting free of charge.

Mom usually packed me a lunch to take with me to school, and it was usually a good one too – a sandwich or two, with perhaps some chips and cookies and a thermos of milk, or, on cold days, some hot soup or cocoa. I probably didn't properly appreciate these wonderful lunches until one Monday when Mom had gone for a few days to Owosso to visit her mother, so Dad decided to pack my lunch for me. I know I didn't really look at it, but just grabbed the sack out of the fridge that morning and hurried off to school. Later that day, famished, since I'd skipped breakfast, I settled into my car in the Student Center parking lot and opened the sack, anticipating a delicious olive loaf or PB&J sandwich, with maybe some chocolate chip cookies for dessert. Instead, I discovered in the bag: two uncooked wieners, a carrot, a piece of celery, and, for dessert (I guess?), a cold rolled up pancake left over from Sunday breakfast filled with strawberry jam. And in my thermos cold, leftover cocoa. It was such a strange and unexpected combination of "delicacies" that I remember laughing out loud as I sorted through it all, and continued to chuckle as I proceeded to eat every last bite and drained my thermos, as I studied the lines of "My Last Duchess." Robert Browning, cold wieners and flapjacks – an interesting and unique literary and culinary conjoining. Dad must have been pretty proud of that inventive lunch package and his ingenious recycling of leftovers ("waste not, want not"), because he even asked me that night how was my lunch. I told him it was great. Thank God, Mom had gotten home that afternoon.

Yeah, yeah, I *know*. I'm digressing again. So where was I? Oh yeah, playing the good son.

Well, it wasn't an act, actually. I *was* being good, but it wasn't always a lot of fun, and it could get pretty damn tedious and lonely too. So when the Vet's Club came along my second year at Ferris, I was more than ready to have some fun again. And I did. I tried to make it to as many parties as I could, and Vets' parties meant drinking, so I was back at it again. I'm not particularly proud of my drinking and often irresponsible behavior during that period, because there was a lot of "driving under the influence" that occurred after those parties. Again, we all did it. In retrospect I am horrified at how thoughtlessly I climbed behind the wheel of my Bug and drove home after those parties, navigating the fifteen miles back to Reed City in a kind of drugged "reptile mode" auto pilot. I would often wake up in my bed the next morning with absolutely no memory of the drive home. I remember once even rushing upstairs to look outside to see if my car was in the driveway. I knew I had somehow made it home, but wanted to be sure the car had survived the trip too. Like I said, I'm not at all proud of these habitual lapses in good judgment. In fact I am completely horrified at my irresponsible, dangerous, absolute *asshole* behavior. But there it is. *Mea culpa*, Lord, and thank You for looking after me in those days of my darkest stupidity.

I was living, then, a kind of Jekyll-Hyde life for several months after joining the Vet's Club. During the week it was business-as-usual as the good son did his school-job thing, but come Saturday night I would morph into my Mr. Hyde persona and often drank myself stupid at parties that I attended with various girls I had met at Vet's Club functions. Most of these girls were party girls who liked to drink themselves, so my prodigious drinking and half-hearted fumblings and gropings in dark corners of dance floors or badly-lit bar booths were unremarkable to them – all part of dating a vet, the price of admission. I vaguely remember how one of these girls, Kathy, a short freckled redhead whom I dated several times, gently admonished me once as she fended off my awkward octopus advances. She was, I think, a biology major, because she tried to distract me from groping her admittedly modest melons by blithely pointing out to me that breasts were really nothing more than a concentration of fatty tissue, and she didn't understand why men were so obsessed with them. I had to agree with her that it was indeed a mystery, but one I was trying desperately to solve. That line didn't work either.

I was groping in more ways than one in those dark days. I was literally looking for *THE* girl, the one who would fill that empty space inside me and assuage the ache I felt in my heart whenever I was in the company of my married friends like the Eichenbergs, the Dobsons or the Karnitzes, whose shared lives seemed so infinitely more complete and satisfying than my own.

I almost got myself in trouble and blew my nice guy "good son" cover one night after leaving Keith and Dianne's place, where we'd spent a couple hours watching TV and talking and killing a six-pack. Well, actually I'd probably killed most of it, because I had a mild buzz on by the time I left around 10:30, feeling even more unattached and glum than I had when I got there. It was still early, so I though I'd go make the circuit at the A&W on the north end of town. I cruised across the bridge and up to US10 where I glanced both ways and then continued across the highway and up the hill. Suddenly my rear view mirror was ablaze with flashing red, white and blue lights, and a siren whooped briefly behind me.

A sinking scared feeling arose in my stomach. *Shit! Did I stop at that stop sign? Probably not. Maybe one of those rolling Michigan stops like my dad used to make at corners.*

I pulled my car carefully over onto the shoulder near the Miller Industries parking lot, by this time in full view of the A&W stand just across the road.

Great! My traffic stop would be the featured entertainment for all the A&W patrons tonight. And it looked like the place was pretty full too.

A burly Michigan state trooper appeared at my window and politely asked for my driver's license and registration, which I managed to produce without too much fumbling around, saying as little as possible, lest my beery breath waft his way. I wished desperately I had a breath mint. The trooper took my license and registration back to his cruiser. After several minutes he returned and handed them back to me, and then asked, "Sir, did you know you failed to make a complete stop back there at the highway?"

I mumbled something rather unconvincing about how I thought that I *had* stopped. I was walking a very thin line here. I was concentrating on my enunciation, doing my darndest to sound stone cold sober, but at the same time I was also speaking more into the front of my shirt than towards the officer. The officer assured me that I had not made a complete stop, and he was going to have to cite me for this infraction. Then he questioned me a bit further about where I had been and where was I headed. I must have mumble-enunciated satisfactory replies, because, after shining his flashlight briefly around the interior of my car, the policeman tore off the citation and handed it to me with a warning to drive carefully on my way home, looking me meaningfully in the eye. I had a sneaking suspicion that he could tell I'd been drinking, but chose not to pursue that more serious offense. He was giving me the benefit of the doubt.

As he strode back to his vehicle, I released a long shuddering beery sigh of relief, realizing I'd practically been holding my breath through the whole exchange. Even in my intoxicated state, I knew full well how lightly I'd just gotten off, and how lucky I was. I sure didn't want to have to explain any DWI to my folks. Running a stop sign, while stupid, was at least understandable. Dad had been nailed himself for that at least once that I could remember.

No longer interested in cruising the root beer stand, I made a careful U-turn under the curious gaze of dozens of eyes, and headed back down the hill for home, carefully stopping and even counting to five at each stop sign along the way. *Too late*, ass*hole*!

The following week, following the instructions on the ticket, I telephoned a Justice of the Peace to arrange for my "hearing" and payment of the ticket. At that time, I think there were only two JP's in town. One was Percy Conrad, who had also been for a time the Reed City Chief of Police. Hell, he may have been the whole damn force at the time for all I know. Reed City rarely ever had more than two full-time officers for most of the time I lived there.

The officer who had pulled Dad over some years before for rolling through the stop sign at Church and Higbee was Fay Ziegler. Dad had been lost in thought about his upcoming Saturday morning at the mill, and obviously hadn't even realized his infraction, so he was suitably startled and then equally embarrassed when Fay pulled him over right in front of the Trinity Lutheran Church, the lights flashing on the city's police cruiser. (Ain't it funny how one story leads to another? And if you grew up around here, they're all kind of interesting, so you hate to leave them out. An enterprising editor would no doubt just red-pencil this whole story right out, but I don't have an editor, so you get to hear the rest of this little story.)

Anyway, the thing is, Fay used to work for Dad at the elevator before he became a city cop, so he seemed just a little embarrassed too when he realized whom he'd pulled over.

"Mornin', Ellis. Did you know you didn't stop at that stop sign?"

"Didn't I? Gee, I'm sorry, Fay. I guess I was thinking about what I needed to do after I opened up the office this morning."

Fay looked down at his shoes, then back over at the neglected stop sign, his lower lip puckered in thought, then replied, "Well, I'll let you off with a warning this time, Ellis, but them signs are put there for a reason, ya know."

Nodding his head, Dad acknowledged this small admonishment, his neck turning pink with embarrassment, probably because he was suddenly and acutely aware that my brother Bob and I were bearing silent witness to this whole scenario. We were probably about fifteen and fourteen at the time, riding to the mill with Dad to put in a morning's work. In the backseat, I was nearly pop-eyed with wonder at this spectacle of my father being bawled out by his former employee. Bob, in the front seat next to Dad, had a tight-lipped barely suppressed grin spread across his face as he gazed straight ahead through the windshield.

"I appreciate that, Fay. I'll be sure to stop from now on," Dad replied, his whole face flushed now.

Small town justice.

And now it was my turn for a taste of the same. So I didn't call Percy Conrad, thinking perhaps that, as a former police officer, he might be a bit too severe in how he viewed my small infraction. Instead I called the town's other JP, Bertha Stafford.

I didn't really know Mrs. Stafford. I mean I knew who she *was*. Her late husband, Norris, had been the owner-manager of the local movie theater for all the years I was growing up. He had also been the mayor for a short time too. Her son, Jeff, had been in my brother Bob's class in high school, and her daughter, Sally, had been one of those pretty little freshmen girls I used to eye guiltily from afar when I was a senior.

Yes, I knew who Mrs. Stafford was. Mostly to me she was just someone's mom, and as such I suppose she seemed less threatening as a JP than a former city police chief. So I made an appointment to have my traffic ticket adjudicated and arrived at the appointed time at Mrs. Stafford's "chambers," which was really just the front parlor of the Staffords' neat yellow house at the corner of State and Slosson.

Justice was swift – and fair. After showing me into her parlor, Mrs. Stafford sat down at her desk and quickly read through my citation, then looked up at me and asked what I had to say for myself. Under her steady scrutiny I was suddenly ten years old again, when this elegant and proper lady used to sell me popcorn from the concession counter at Saturday matinees at the Reed

Theater. Flushing, I ducked my head and, actually scuffing one foot nervously from side to side across her carpet, I mumbled something about how I guess I hadn't been paying attention, and I was sorry, and it wouldn't happen again.

Apparently satisfied at my obviously genuine show of remorse, Mrs. Stafford replied crisply, "Well, I should hope not! Shame on you, Tim." Then she scribbled something into a ledger on her desk, stamped my ticket, and said, "I'm fining you ten dollars plus two dollars court costs. Can you afford that?"

"Yes, Ma'am," I said, and fumbled my wallet out of my back pocket and thumbed out a ten and two wrinkled ones and placed them on the corner of her desk. Shame on me, indeed. And that was that.

* * * * *

13

STILL LONELY
AND TRYIN' TO BE GOOD

Following my brush with the law, I made a conscious effort to cut back on my weekend drinking, so I briefly even distanced myself a bit from the Vet's Club and their parties – and even all the "regular" girls who seemed to gravitate toward these alcohol-fueled events. I tried dating "nice" girls for a time and doing normal things, like going to a movie or out to eat. I made an effort to try to get to know the girls in some of my classes. I met Linda, a Big Rapids girl who was active in the drama club and also a concert pianist. I attended a recital she gave and was a bit intimidated by her talent. She was very nice to me, but not terribly interested. I briefly dated an honors student named Karen. We had interesting talks about our favorite authors and about movies and music, and I really enjoyed her company, but whenever I tried to get "serious" or talk about more personal things or future plans, she would draw back, or put me off, until finally she told me she had a boyfriend from back home, who was attending the University of Michigan, and "couldn't we just be friends?" Well, any guy knows that those words are the kiss of death to any hopes of a serious relationship (or even to just getting laid), so I said good-bye to Karen, and withdrew from dating altogether for a time, and slunk away to lick my wounds.

Around this time I made a quick weekend trip to the Chicago area, to visit Bob and his fast-growing family in Roselle. He and

Bob and Maureen Bazzett with babies Laura and Mike
at home in Roselle circa 1966

Maureen had two little ones by then, who were happy to see their Uncle Tim, and climbed all over me, clamoring for me to play with them or read them a story. Babies were a pleasant change from my unhappy dating experiences, but both little Laura and Mike were both so sweet and beautiful that they made me even more lonesome and more acutely aware of what I didn't have. Laura was a toddler at the time, and Mike was still in diapers and they were almost as much fun as a pair of new puppies.

I remember especially one incident that made me laugh and also horrified me just a little, but was apparently business-as-usual stuff to Mama Maureen. I'd just finished breakfast and had gone to look in on the kids, who were playing together on the floor in the nursery, surrounded by toys. Just as I peeked in through the open doorway, Laura picked up something small and brown off the floor, looked closely at it, then proffered it generously to her baby brother, who took it from her in his chubby hand, and then, as babies are wont to do, put it carefully into his mouth to taste it.

Omigawd, NO! I lunged forward, and with a curled index finger, I gently removed the mystery treat from Mike's mouth. Yup, just as I'd feared, it was a tiny, perfectly formed turd, which had apparently dropped out of Mike's drooping diaper. Mike gave me a startled look, his mouth puckered, and he began to cry loudly. Maureen came strolling casually in from the kitchen, coffee cup in hand, and assessed the situation. Holding out my hand to show her the offending, nearly-recycled turd, I started to explain the horror of what had nearly occurred, but Maureen ignored me. Putting her cup down on the dresser, she scooped the wailing baby up from the floor, wrinkling her nose and exclaiming, *"Pee-YUU!* Mikey. You *stink!"*

As she laid the baby on the changing stand, I adjourned to the bathroom to flush and wash, feeling perhaps just a bit indignant that I hadn't gotten enough credit for my heroic role in saving little Mikey from the horror of actually eating his own shit. After all, as anyone who has ever watched television knows, "Mikey will eat *any*thing."

Actually, I had nothing but admiration for Maureen and her equanimity and ease in handling such messy situations. You might think that this scene of crying babies and poopy diapers would have turned me off the whole idea of love and marriage, but it didn't. I still envied Bob and Maureen for what they had together, dirty diapers and all. I wanted this kind of domesticity for myself. I wanted someone to love who would love me in return and would give me babies, poopy pants and all. I realize that all this sounds most unmanly, but it's true. I was ready to be married. I just needed to find the right girl.

My single-ness and sense of being left behind were only emphasized by the weddings I attended my first year or so after returning home. Besides Jerry and Fran Whitman's nuptials in Reed City, I also traveled downstate twice for the weddings of a couple of my army buddies. Tom Gordon married his high school sweetheart, Charlotte, in Hazel Park, a Detroit suburb, and Larry "Dusty" Sanders got married over near Port Huron.

My old army roommate, Joe Capozzi, flew in from New York for both occasions, and the second time he came back to Reed City with me and stayed for a few days. There wasn't a whole lot to do, but we holed up in our basement recreation room and listened to music and reminisced about our army days, a time which, even after only a year or two, was already rapidly becoming "the good ol' days." I think Joe was feeling lonely and displaced too and was looking for love in much the same way I was. Our old pals' weddings only served to exacerbate those feelings. We smothered our sorrows with Mom's homemade chocolate chip cookies and milk, and speculated and dreamed aloud in a desultory fashion about what the future might hold for us. Joe was studying business administration at Pace College and working part-time as a key-punch operator for IBM. I was an undeclared English major in a General Education program at Ferris, which didn't even offer a Bachelor of Arts at the time, so I knew I would have to transfer somewhere else after a couple of years. And my job scrubbing floors, while comfortable and simple, certainly didn't offer much in the way of future opportunities.

* * * * *

14

GIRL-WATCHING AT THE PUG

Although my "love life" (*HA!*) was rather unsatisfactory and frustrating during this period, my membership in the Vet's Club at least alleviated somewhat my feelings of being an outsider on campus. The vets even staked an unofficial semi-permanent claim on two or three tables in The Pug, the central cafeteria and snack bar in the Student Center. On any given day between nine and eleven o'clock there would be a group of anywhere between six and twelve vets occupying a few tables, which we sometimes pulled together to form a long single surface which would be littered with coffee cups, half-filled ashtrays, textbooks and dismembered newspapers. There was a core group of five or six guys. John Nibbelink was usually there with his roommates, Harold "Gomer" Frederickson, and "Rank Frank" Perry. They would claim the crossword puzzle from *The Detroit Free Press* and make completing it a group project. Everyone who came by the tables would usually take a casual stab at the unsolved words. Frederickson's nickname, Gomer, derived, of course, from his being an ex-Marine. Why Frank Perry was "rank" was less clear. It may have resulted from some particularly disgusting display at a drinking party, but most of the vets could be pretty rank in various ways, so probably Perry was no nastier than anyone else. "Rank Frank" did have a rather distinctive ring to it though, and no doubt served to elevate Frank's status in an already pretty groaty group. Jim Roddy and Larry Miller, other friends of John's, would often show up for a while, as did Gary Perdew and a couple other vets I came to know well and count among my close friends: Patrick O'Connor and Wayne Shook. John Cook, our more respectable club "diplomat", would even make an occasional appearance at his constituency's tables, and I would try to make it to the vets' "long table" at least a couple of times a week between classes.

Harold "Gomer" Frederickson

I call it a "long table" not just because of its shape, but to distinguish it from the round table of King Arthur's knights. Because we vets were no knights, not by any stretch of the imagination. Probably chivalry and upholding ladies' honor were the last things on our minds. In fact, the open textbooks and the smudged-over crossword puzzles and the scattered sports and entertainment sections of the newspaper were really just a cover for the real reason we gathered in The Pug every day – girl watching.

It's hard to even know where to begin in describing this age-old ritual of male bonding. Girl watching is such an ancient sport among boys and men. Its origins are lost in the mists of antiquity, but I can easily imagine, say, a couple of Neanderthal or Cro-Magnon men with their sloping foreheads and dragging knuckles, hunkered together by a cave entrance, mouths hanging slightly ajar as they watched a female of the species go by, probably on her way to "freshen up," or perhaps to readjust the decorative bone fixed in her hair or septum.

"*Ti-its!*" one would mutter appreciatively, eyes glazing over as all the blood from his tiny brain sluiced suddenly south.

"*Ya-aah!*" his hairy companion would agree, nodding and drooling and reaching down to adjust his own bulging blood-engorged bone.

You guys know what I mean, I'm sure, because the scenario hasn't really changed all that much, though thousands of years may have passed. Our "cave" was The Pug, where we hairy males hunkered at our casually conjoined tables, mouths ajar, swaying slightly to the booming jungle bass beat of the Four Seasons' "Let's

Sign outside The Pug in the Student Center

Hang On" as it jolted forth from the jukebox, the amplified sound waves jarring and jittering the paper Coke cups that sat scattered across the tables' sticky surfaces.

The guys at the table would even employ a crude rating system, using a scale of one to ten, as they watched the girls enter and exit the cafeteria. A "ten" was, of course, the highest possible score, and rarely awarded. Scores were arrived at rather arbitrarily, but always took into account front end ("headlights"), rear end ("bumpers") and overall chassis condition. It was, as I said, a very "crude" system, and it wasn't as if we ourselves were such fine specimens of our own sex either. I didn't say it was fair or equitable, or even very nice, just crude – in every sense of the word. And this was years before the successful film entitled, incidentally, *10*, starring Bo Derek and Dudley Moore. I think our Pug pastime may have also pre-dated Bobby Bare's hilarious tune, "Numbers," which pokes fun not only at the rating system, but also at the somewhat repulsive raters themselves.

In order to fully appreciate the truly complex crudity of our rating system, you have to realize that the era of the middle sixties at Ferris was still a very much "covered up" time, as far as female fashion was concerned. Foundation garments were an important element of what constituted anything above a rating of, oh, 7, say. Remember girdles? Well, they *worked*, by golly! A good one could sometimes reduce the width of a woman's rear end from a full axe handle to maybe one and a half hatchet handles, a significant reduction that could raise a rating from a 5 to a 7, or maybe even an 8! Of course, there were different schools of thought regarding this matter. (If you can call thinking from below the belt "thought.") Some guys preferred the unfettered female form, while a few others liked to see things all cinched up tight and neat. Of course this would all become a moot point just a year or two later, when girls began shedding their bras (and certainly girdles) on campuses all over the country, with the advent of flower children, hippies and "free love."

But that was later. During my short stay at Ferris there was still actually a dress code in force. Students who lived in the dorms were expected to "dress" for classes, and for meals in the student cafeterias in Masselink and the other food commons up on "the Rock" on south campus. Women were required to wear dresses or skirts with blouses or sweaters. Most wore nylons too. For men shirts and ties were de rigueur, usually with a sweater or sport coat. This will probably sound unbelievably strict to today's students, many of whom look to me like homeless vagrants, especially the men, but that's the way it was back then.

I need to insert just a small personal footnote here in regard to women and nylon stockings. As a kid growing up, I remember that women always wore nylons when they went out in public, shopping or out to eat or church services, and this was before the advent of panty hose. It was all a very complicated web of buttons and straps and hooks and eyes involving girdles or garter belts and, of course, the stockings themselves. I never really gave all of this much thought throughout my childhood and adolescence. It was all just part of the female uniform. Then, in 1964, my last year in the army, I went to Germany. I had just completed a tour in northern Turkey, where I hardly ever saw any women at all, and the few that I did catch glimpses of were shrouded in tent-like affairs from head to foot, so I certainly didn't see any women's legs, nylon-sheathed or not. So, by the time my buddy Joe and I got off the plane in

Frankfurt, in August of '64, we were eager to see some real live women again. Of course we'd seen some already in the airports in Ankara and Rome, and on the plane, but now we would actually be seeing and mixing with females on a nearly daily basis again. And we were *ready*, and we were *looking*! Maybe *gawking* would be a more accurate term here. It sure was great to finally see members of the opposite sex again, and dressed in normal women's clothing – skirts and sweaters, suits and dresses, and nylons and heels. Some of these women looked great, as we shamelessly ogled their legs and bodies like a couple of rude goobers fresh off the farm. But by the time we got off the train in Kassel, we noticed something odd about many of the women we encountered. They were wearing hose, true, but there was a bumpy, unevenly textured sheen to their legs, a kind of spotty, unhealthy look. It was a mystery, and one which puzzled and troubled us. It wasn't until a week or two later when we finally got a pass to go back into town that we solved this mystery. We were window shopping along the *Steppenstrasse*, the main business district of Kassel, on a bright Saturday afternoon, and also ogling the girls and women as they hurried up and down the street, when we realized why many of these women's nylon-clad legs looked strange. Those bumps and spots weren't really bumps or spots. They were *hairs*! Long hairs that curled and coiled and caused unsightly protrusions where they were smashed down under the nylon sheathing. *Eee-YUUU*!

Joe and I were both stunned, and perhaps even somewhat horrified at this discovery. These women *didn't shave their legs*! And then they compounded this flagrant breach of female grooming by just pulling hose right on over their hairy legs! I mean this wasn't just a couple days' stubble we were seeing. No, it was long mature hair that coiled and whorled under the pressure of the stretched stockings. Now I know I'm getting dangerously deep into female territory here, but Joe and I were American boys who had been brought up on lots of TV commercials and advertising which included, quite prominently I might add, countless ads for things like Lady Schick and Lady Gillette, and other hair removal products like Neet and Nair. To us there was absolutely no earthly excuse for this, this ... I'm at a loss. I mean what in the *hell was this*?!

Luckily for us, we learned that this particular grooming deficiency was not endemic to all German females, but was limited primarily to women slightly older than our generation, women in their thirties and forties and older. We also found out fairly quickly that underarm deodorants were a pretty new concept among the older adult population of Kassel too. All it took to find this out was one ride on a crowded municipal bus. The B.O. smell was overpowering.

In any case, we were most relieved to learn that girls our own age, at least the ones we met in the local clubs and bars, were for the most part much more civilized and advanced in regard to these things. Their legs were smooth and they smelled *good*!

And the same was true of the girls at Ferris, which made the aforementioned girl-watching a favorite sport, not just among the vets, but for all the guys on campus. I still believe firmly that there is something to be said for dress codes. If you don't agree, take a look through the Ferris yearbooks of the early and mid-sixties. The students pictured therein *look* like ladies and gentlemen. They are dressed up. Appearances *are* important.

<u>DRESS</u>

The young women on the campus of Ferris State College take pride in their appearance. They practice the essentials of good grooming, their attire is inconspicuous and appropriate for the occasion. For class and in the Library they wear sweaters and skirts, tailored dresses or suits; afternoon or "date" dresses are worn for dances, banquets and church. While relaxing in the residence hall, pug or South Food Center Snack Bar, they may wear slacks or bermudas. Tennis shoes are an essential item in a coed's wardrobe but she has "dressy flats" for wear to the dining hall for dinner; "heels" are reserved for special occasions.

Excerpt from the AWS (Associated Women Students) Handbook 1965-1966, p. 16.
(It doesn't specifically tell the young ladies to keep the young men's hands out of their sweaters and skirts, but by God it's implied!)

I should probably admit here that the vets, as a group, were often the groatiest-looking guys on campus, as many of them often wore their old well-worn field jackets or pea-coats, and some of them even wore old, frayed odd bits of uniforms – camouflage or khaki trousers or fatigue pants. But they cleaned up well as a group too. Witness the group photos of the Vet's Club from that era, everyone clean-shaven and in coats and ties. By the end of the decade this had all changed, and such formal dress became a rarity, even for group photographs. But the FSC Vets were, all things considered, a fine organization, and I am extremely proud to have been a member.

* * * * *

15

CLASSROOM MEMORIES – COLLEGE ALGEBRA, KITTENS AND RECURRING DREAMS

I've been struggling for some time now with the problem of writing at least *something* about my *academic* experiences at Ferris. It seems like there is a real paucity of memories from the classroom. So let's see what I can dredge up, okay?

I have always been a worrier. Even when there doesn't seem to be much to worry about, I can always find something. Well, the thing I was really worried about in the fall of 1965 when I first started school at Ferris was how *long* it had been since I'd been in school. I know. It had only been a few years. But when you're only twenty-one, three years away from anything seems like an eternity. What I was particularly concerned about were the minimum math and science requirements for the School of General Education, which I was enrolled in. I had already at least vaguely decided that I would major in English, even though I knew there was no such thing as an English major at Ferris, which was an institution which leaned heavily toward practical programs and preparing its students for the world of work and business. Ferris had a national reputation even in the early sixties for its fine School of Pharmacy. Its other Schools included Commerce, Technical and Applied Arts and Sciences (divided into the Collegiate Technical and the Trade and Industrial Divisions), and General Education, as well as a small

Department of Education. You could earn a teaching degree and certificate at Ferris, but only in Math and Science, Business, or Trade Technical Education – *not* in English or the arts.

I suppose you might be wondering why I chose to go to Ferris then, if I wanted to major in English. Well, it was a decision based strictly on practical and financial considerations. If I went to Ferris, I could live at home and save what it would have cost me for room and board (or rent and groceries) at another more distant school. And I also recognized that no matter what your major was, you still had to take nearly two years worth of "required" courses toward any Bachelor's degree. And it was also a plus to me that I could take all of these more onerous courses, along with some I might even enjoy, and end up with an actual degree after just two years (in my case, an Associate of Arts). I figured what if something happened and I never got my Bachelor's? At least I would have *some* kind of a degree to show for my time and efforts. The final consideration was that if I chose my courses carefully and coordinated with a faculty advisor, all my Ferris course work would transfer to practically any other college in the state where I could complete my Baccalaureate. I can't really swear that I thought all of this through so carefully at the time, but I know I tried to figure it all out – how to get the most bang for my buck, so to speak – and I know I had help from a few trained counselors at Ferris. In any case, things did work out well for me when I transferred to Central Michigan University (CMU) a couple years later.

So what was I so worried about? One word. Math. I had always hated math, and for the usual reason. I was lousy at it. I had absolutely no natural aptitude for anything mathematical. It's true I had completed the college prep curriculum at Reed City High School, and had taken the full program of math, which included Algebra I and II, Geometry, and, in my senior year, even an introductory mix of Calculus and Trigonometry and fooling around with a slide rule (remember *those things*?). But I had never been any good at any of those courses, and retained only vague unpleasant memories of struggling with ever-increasingly complex equations, memorizing theorems, and being almost completely bamboozled by logarithms and square root shit. I also guiltily remembered copying a lot of homework assignments from my more mathematically-savvy and sympathetic friends, like Art Gerhardt, Rex Dolley or Don Truax.

I was very surprised to learn, then, that my math score from my freshman week placement tests had catapulted me directly into a course called (*GULP!*) College Algebra. My initial reaction to this news was: Wait a minute. Shouldn't I be taking some kind of refresher course first, or, better yet, isn't there some alternative easier course I could take to satisfy the math requirement? You know something like Long Division or Addition and Subtraction? Those things I figured I could probably handle, but *College Algebra*?! My advisor, however, was quite unsympathetic to my barely concealed panic, and pointed out to me once again that my math placement score was really quite respectable. The only thing I could figure out was that some of my guesses on that math test must have been pretty lucky. I think I had been using the "when-in-doubt-mark-C" method that day.

So I took College Algebra. Here's what I remember most about that course. First of all, I was absolutely sure that I couldn't possibly pass a course called "College Algebra." I didn't really know any of the other kids in the class, so there was no one to copy homework from. My only alternative was to actually do it myself, so I did. The only way I could accomplish this, I figured, was to take copious notes in every class, so I did. Whatever the instructor wrote on the board, I wrote it into my notebook. Whatever he said, even what he didn't write on the board – into my notebook, scribbling furiously. I was scared shitless that if I didn't do this, I'd sit down to try to do my homework some hours later and wouldn't be able to remember how to attack this particular problem. I was so terrified of failure that I would often still be sitting in my desk copying final notes from the blackboard into my notebook long after the teacher and all the other students had left the classroom.

When I would finally get home each night, usually around 9:30, after putting in my four hours of sweeping or buffing floors and emptying waste baskets, my first homework chore was always algebra. First I would review all of my notes from that day's class. Then I would make my way painstakingly through each of the several or so problems assigned. Then I would attempt to double check and prove each solution. Once I was satisfied I'd done the problems correctly (and I found, much to my surprise, that I usually *could*), I would neatly re-copy each problem, including all the steps, into *another* math notebook to keep for review purposes before exams.

My algebra teacher was a young guy named Bob Kosanovich. With his wide shoulders, crew cut and bull neck, Mr. Kosanovich looked more like a football or wrestling coach than a math instructor, but he must have been a pretty good teacher, because I earned a solid mix of B's and A's on my exams that quarter, which finally translated into a final grade of B. I was still worried that I could blow my grade right up to the final exam. My math phobia was still working overtime. I remember going to see Mr. Kosanovich in his office the day after the final to find out how I'd done, even though I thought I had understood most of the problems on the test. No, wait. Perhaps I should re-phrase that. I don't think I *understood* the problems. It was more like I *recognized* either the problem itself, or at least the pattern it followed. Because my ultimate success in that course was a result not so much of understanding, but of recognizing what I had *memorized*. My short-term memory was definitely working overtime during that class and during each test. And I knew that, but my teacher didn't. I had *aced* my final exam, which gave me a solid B for the course! Mr. K was very impressed, and even apologized that he couldn't give me an A for the course, because of averages and exam weights, and so forth, but I was absolutely *ecstatic* and even dumbfounded that I had received a *B* in College Algebra! Mr. K commended me on my "fine work," and even tried to talk me into taking the next semester's math course. But *oooh, no*! I was not going to press my luck. I had fulfilled my math requirement and I was *done* with math!

Fear of failure can be a powerful incentive. I think I may have been prouder of that B than any other grade I received at Ferris. I remember walking away down the hall from Mr. K's office that December day, feeling immensely relieved and very pleased. Smiling to myself, I was reminded of the favorite expression of an army buddy of mine back at Fort Devens. Kowalski had been from Chicago, and anytime something genuinely pleased or surprised him, he would exclaim, *Well, fuck ME*! I think I must have uttered this phrase aloud, because a gaggle of girls passing by me in the hallway suddenly recoiled and stared as I strutted happily toward the stairwell. A *B* in College Algebra. Fuck me, *indeed*!

I never took another math course during my undergraduate years, and I remember absolutely nothing from College Algebra, except what I've already told you. It terrified me, but I survived it. Survived, *hell* – I kicked *ass*!

The science requirements at Ferris were slightly more extensive. I struggled through two terms of Biological Science (Bio Sci 101 and 102), and then two terms of Physical Science. All of these were large freshman and sophomore survey courses, so the lectures were held in Pearson Lecture Hall in the Science Building and then the students were broken up into smaller lab groups which met once or twice a week in the laboratories.

Lemme see. Do I remember anything from those courses? Well, I do remember that in one of those Bio Sci labs we dissected, or at least studied, cat cadavers. Yeah, all you cat lovers. You'd better keep close tabs on your pussies or they could end up as cold stiffs on a college lab table.

I earned a certain distinction in my lab, due to the fact that when I opened up my cat, it contained a whole carton of kittens, each one curled up inside its own individual opaque envelope. I think it was an eight-pack. I remember clearly being struck with conflicting feelings of awe and pity.

I had seen and played with my share of cats and kittens while growing up. There were always a few barn cats around my grandpa's farm, both in Wayland and, later, in Reed City, and more than once my brothers and I had discovered new litters of tiny kittens tucked away in dark places up in the hay mow or behind stacked bags of cow feed, their hiding place given away by their shrill, hungry mewling. These still-blind newborns were not nearly as interesting as the lively, darting, half-feral kittens they would become over the next several weeks, their huge dark eyes filled with wonder and curiosity. I would often spend hours playing with them in the barn, and sometimes I would even smuggle a kitten into the house, sneaking it by Mom under my shirt or tucked into a coat pocket. In the room I shared with my brother Bob, I would take the kitten out. Bob would look up from studying his scouting handbook, or from reading his *Boy's Life*, and say, "Hey, you know we can't have cats in the house." But then, inevitably, he would get down on the floor and join me, often even suggesting new devices to entertain and tantalize our tiny, illegal guest – a string dangled from a Tinker Toy stick, or an open paper sack to explore. Finally, exhausted from its play and our attentions, the contraband kitten would fall asleep, and I would lift it carefully onto my bed, where it would curl, purring, in the crook of my arm.

Fragmented memories of those times flitted through my mind in the minutes after my student's scalpel opened the abdominal area of this unlucky feline and revealed her secret. Although I had seen my share of small and even nearly newborn kittens, this was first time I had ever seen any in their original packaging, so I was momentarily immobilized with a sense of wonder as I looked down at these impossibly tiny yet anatomically perfect "near-cats." The outlines of the kittens were clearly visible through the nearly translucent membranes that enveloped each tiny feline fetus.

The magic of the moment was shattered when the lab instructor came by and, looking over my shoulder, saw what I had, which he immediately announced to the whole class as an "unexpected bonus." The whole lab group then crowded quickly around with a chorus of soft *ooohs* and *wows*. The instructor suggested I open up one of the membranes to display a kitten, but I respectfully demurred, then slowly moved back and melted into the rear ranks of the group as another student did the honors. I had already seen newborn kittens. I was not particularly anxious to see one that would never be born. My eyes suddenly stung with unshed tears, and I was overcome with sadness at this so-called "bonus" discovery.

I took four terms of science and lab courses, and that is one of my only surviving memories of all those hours. Odd, isn't it? Or maybe not.

I also remember one classmate from those science courses. He may have been a lab partner, I'm not sure. Bob's hair was red, but his name was Green, and I think perhaps the reason I remember him was he was always so well turned out – dress shirts and ties, nice sweaters and sport coats or blazers. I always felt poor and under-dressed around him. Well, in comparison, I suppose I probably was. Bob Green was a fraternity man, a "Teke," if I remember correctly, as the members of Tau Kappa Epsilon were called. I was always a bit wary of fraternity types, who represented money and leisure to me, both of which were scarce commodities in my own student days. We were never exactly friends, although Bob was always nice enough to me – a gentleman, and perhaps that's why I still remember him all these years later.

"Frat rats," which was how some members of the Vet's Club referred to the Greeks on campus, were not often known for being gentlemen. Of course neither were the vets, and there was a kind of restrained and subtle tension between our groups that would occasionally flare up and erupt into open hostility, expressed in chest-bumping or shoving matches, or even exchanged blows, usually at places like The Red Rail bar, where the two groups would sometimes mix.

But I digress. The other thing I remember about my required science courses was a final grade I received for Phy Sci 101 in the fall term of 1966. I got an A, but I'll never understand how, because I had never received anything higher than a C on any of my tests. There may have even been a D or two in the mix. It was the only A I received that term, and I was absolutely astounded. I knew something was wrong, that a mistake had definitely been made, and probably some solid-A student, who may have been on either side of me alphabetically on the class list, had received my shaky-C grade (or worse, since the final had been a mystery and a horror). I felt vaguely guilty for a while, but certainly not guilty enough to go and seek out my instructor and point out a possible error in his final computations. In the end I decided it must have been an act of Divine Providence, and mine was not to question why. The ways of the Lord are often mysterious indeed.

Perhaps my penance for simply letting that grade ride has been a recurring dream that I have had aperiodically ever since. In this dream I am back in college again, although the actual setting can change crazily, because sometimes I recognize the hallways and classrooms of Reed City High, and other times I might be wandering the halls of the Starr Building at Ferris or Anspach Hall at CMU. The settings, however, are not as important as the central premise of the dream, which is that it is late in the semester (or quarter, or marking period) and I have suddenly remembered that I had registered for a math class – calculus, algebra, trig, or statistics; it doesn't matter which – and *have never attended the class*! It's nearly time for the final exam and I am in an utter panic, rushing up and down a maze of hallways and staircases, trying to find either my instructor or the registrar's office, hoping desperately that I can still drop the course. In this dream I never find either, because I always wake up first, often in a cold sweat.

I often wonder if this kind of dream, which I call my "math phobia" dream, is one of those common dreams that lots of people suffer from. You know some of the other common dreams, I'm sure. One of the most famous of these is the one where you're back in high school, sitting in class, and you suddenly realize you're naked from the waist down. You have no idea how this happened, but it's almost time for the bell to ring and you'll have to get up to change classes. And on top of all this, you have an erection, and you know there will be no hiding it, because it's a real Louisville Slugger kind of a boner that you can't even hide under your geography book. (The setting for *this* dream, interestingly enough, is *always* high school. *Hmmm* …) You are first in line for a really *major* mortification scene in this dream. Then, of course, you wake up, because you really have to pee in the worst way. *Whew*!

And then there's the "falling" dream, which comes in an infinite number of variations, but popular wisdom says that if you should ever actually hit bottom before waking up, you will *die*! My own recurrent version of this one places me in the backseat of a speeding automobile on a winding mountain road and I suddenly realize that *no one is driving the car*! I lunge desperately over the seat and grab at the wheel, but I can't get to the brakes, which doesn't matter, because the car has already plunged over a cliff and is *falling, falling* … Ever had this dream, or one like it? Scares the hell out of you, doesn't it? You try to scream and nothing comes out, remember? Then you wake up – or you crash and die, pick one.

I probably should have gone to the library and checked out one of those books on dreams before exposing myself in this way, but it's too late now. I'm already in free fall. I have actually looked up some of these dreams and read the various interpretations by so-called experts, but I don't put much stock in them. I think most of these dreams are caused by a full bladder. They wake you up so you can go empty it.

Or maybe not. In any case, this math phobia dream is a real nightmare for me, because I've always been the kind of person who tries to get things done on schedule or even ahead of time. So perhaps it really is just that unearned A in Phy Sci coming back to haunt me.

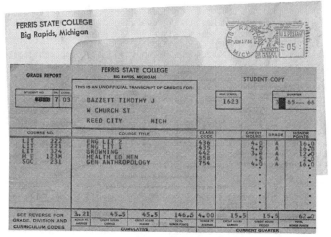

All-A Grade Report

I reached what was to be my academic zenith at Ferris in the third quarter of my freshman year when I earned A's in all five of my classes. This was no small achievement in view of the fact that four of these classes involved a very heavy reading load.

The fifth class was the only "required" course that term – Health Education for Men. Health Ed was a ridiculously simple and probably a completely unnecessary course dealing mostly with personal physical hygiene. I guess Ferris wanted to be sure that its students bathed on a reasonably regular basis. The course was a joke, and a frequent target of nastiness by the men who were required to sit through it. Many of the vets, in particular, took great delight in coming up with unusual suggestions for improving the class when they filled out the end-of-term course evaluation forms. We would ask things like, "Shouldn't there be a unit on how to best deal with the unpleasant male problem of smegma?" Or, "We never really discussed merkins for men. Are they readily available in stores, or only by mail order from specialty firms?" (*Smegma*? *Merkins*? Look 'em up.)

Three of my classes that term were literature courses. Against the best advice of my academic advisor, I took English Lit I and II concurrently instead of sequentially. I can't really remember much anymore about the courses themselves. They were probably typical of such survey courses, but I must have enjoyed most of the reading, or I couldn't have possibly kept up. I do remember that one of my favorite lit teachers at Ferris was Dr. Herbert Carson, who may have taught one or perhaps even both of the English Lit courses. Carson was a fascinating lecturer, who obviously loved his subject. (He was also famous for his bow ties.) I'm pretty sure I took at least two or three courses from him. I remember that his wife was also a teacher, and she would occasionally fill in for Herb when he was ill or otherwise occupied, and she was an excellent and engaging teacher too. What are the odds of *that* happening? After my experiences with the Carsons, I used to daydream that a perfect career scenario would be one in which I would teach college literature and would marry someone who did the same thing and we could take turns going to work at a single job.

I took an anthropology class that term too, which was actually an advanced sociology course. I must have enjoyed it, because I went on to take several more "soc" offerings, and sociology eventually became my college minor. My pal, Donnie Dobson, actually majored in sociology. Recently I asked Don how he came to pick soc as his major. Without even thinking about it, and in typical Don fashion, he laughed and replied, "Hell, sociology is about 98% bullshit, and I was always a good bullshitter. It came easy to me, so I figured, *why not*?"

Well, I'm not a half bad bullshitter myself (but I don't have to tell *you* that; you *are*, after all, reading this book), so it was fairly easy for me to gravitate towards sociology as a secondary path of least resistance, academically speaking.

Because choosing English as a major was no struggle for me. I can't even remember actually ever pondering what I would major in. That it would be English was just a given. I'd been reading since I was four years old. I loved to read. Path of least resistance?

Probably, although I was to find out in the next few years that I didn't necessarily enjoy *all* kinds of literature.

The fifth course in my all-A term was – yup, you guessed it – another English class. It was called, simply, Browning, and was actually a junior level course, an in-depth examination of the works of Robert Browning, the nineteenth century English poet who is perhaps best known for his love affair with and subsequent marriage to another English poet, Elizabeth Barrett. I had never read Browning before taking the class, and had to get special permission from the instructor just to enroll.

My teacher and guide in exploring Browning's work was Dr. William Wolfinger, who also happened to be the husband of my tenth-grade English teacher, Dorothy Wolfinger. I can't remember ever telling Dr. Wolfinger of this earlier connection, or even that I was from Reed City, so I'm pretty sure I didn't get any "points" for this. I don't think I was a particularly stellar student of Browning, but I was very interested and enthusiastic about the poet's work, and I answered, or *tried* to answer, many of the questions Dr. Wolfinger posed, and also asked a lot of questions of my own. So if I earned an A for the class, it was probably at least partly due to my obvious pure enjoyment of practically everything we read and discussed. Since the goals and interests of the student body at Ferris leaned heavily toward business and science or trade and technical skills, a guy who was truly interested in literature was something of a rare bird, one which teachers like Wolfinger and Carson would no doubt appreciate and cherish, and perhaps even reward with an A grade.

Having bragged about my best academic term at Ferris, I should probably also fess up to what was my worst. It wasn't really all that bad, actually, but my attention to things scholastic was obviously slipping by the second term of my sophomore year, the year I joined the Vet's Club. I earned C's in all of my classes except one that term. My only B was for a class in Shakespeare, which was taught by Mr. Hugh Griffith, the Vet's Club faculty advisor, and I strongly suspect that Hugh had a soft spot for his veterans, and had no problem with slightly skewing the curve to insure that we received good grades and stayed in school.

The reasons for my falling grades weren't too hard to figure out. More time drinking and partying left less time for serious studying. I've already gone into the major reason for my backward slide into boozing and carousing – I was desperately and miserably lonely. But all of that would change in an instant, because I was about to meet the love of my life.

* * * * *

Here are a few of my teachers that I can remember. William Wolfinger, English and Philosophy; Gordon Lindland, Geography; Robert Kosanovich, Math; Frank Curtis, Political Science; Hugh Griffith, English; and Philip Clugston, Humanities. (I received my only D at Ferris in Poli Sci (yawn) from Mr. Curtis.)

PART II

Finding Love –
or Something Like It
(The Love Story Stuff)

Someday I'm gonna write
The story of my life.
I'll tell about the night we met
And how my heart can't forget
The way you smiled at me.

"The Story of My Life"
recorded by Marty Robbins
written by Hal David & Burt Bacharach

16

"THE NIGHT WE MET"

I met her on March 17, St. Patrick's Day. It was final exam week of the second term. (Ferris was on a "quarter" system in the sixties, which means that a normal school year consisted of three terms, or "quarters", rather than the usual two semesters of most colleges.) We like to tell our kids that we met "in church," which is only a small deviation from the actual truth. But now I'm going to try to tell "the truth, the whole truth, and nothing but the truth," as they say in court, so *help* me, God, *please*. Of course I don't have either hand on a Bible, so there may be some degree of literary "licentiousness" (heh-heh) in my story.

Okay, so here's the way I remember it. Of course, you have to keep in mind at all times that *she* probably has very *different* memories of how we met. Well, perhaps not so very different, but any time I try to tell my version, she can come up with any number of subtle variations, usually to soften or clean up my memories. Can you tell I'm stalling here? ... You *can*? I mean is it *really* that obvious? ... Oh, well. Here goes nothing.

It was just after nine o'clock when I punched out from work at the Science Building. I'd gotten my work done early that night and had spent nearly two hours of the shift studying for my Geography and History exams, both scheduled for the next day. All that crap to memorize, and what *for*, I'd kept wondering. Both courses had turned out to be a lot harder than I had expected, and I was desperately hoping to pull at least C's in them (a hope that was, thankfully, realized). I knew I should probably head for home and try to get in a couple more hours of study time, but I'd had enough, and I needed a break, a diversion of some sort. And *dammit*, it was St. *Paddy's* Day, for cripes sake, which should have been a *holiday*, if there were any real justice in the world, and all I'd done all day was work and study. So I walked across the street and up around the corner to Carlisle Hall, the men's dorm where Pat O'Connor lived. Ed Howe, my boss at the Science Building, had told me they were serving green beer in the bar at the Casa Nova in honor of the Irish holiday. I figured who better to celebrate with than someone who actually bore the saint's name?

Patrick O'Connor

I had met Pat at a Vet's Club meeting a couple months earlier and we'd hit it off immediately. Pat even looked like an Irishman with his prematurely thinning sandy hair and freckled, fair complexion that flushed easily, especially when he was drinking, and, like most of the vets, he did enjoy his brew now and then. The meeting where we'd met had been in a room at the local American Legion Hall, and had been followed by a real relic of a stag film, which featured a couple of skinny guys clad only in black socks and Lone Ranger-type masks and a tired-looking middle-aged whore. The grainy black-and-white texture of the film was unflattering and unforgiving to its "stars," particularly the woman, whose shiny appendectomy scar kept flashing into view as she gracelessly bent herself this way and that, attempting to accommodate the probing members and tongues of the two masked men. Although the film was silent, there was no lack of commentary, since a number of the vets in the smoky darkened room had already had several drinks before the meeting. Some of these kept up a running critique of the performance, while others offered helpful suggestions or shouted encouragement or disparaging insults at the two tired uninspired cocksmen. This sad scenario finally faded to black, and another began; no subtle segue here. The next segment apparently featured only a young-ish Asian-looking woman, quite naked, and a Pepsi bottle. I decided I didn't want to know how this "storyline" would develop. I'd had enough, and made my way out of the room and back out to the bar. Several other guys decided to leave then too, and Pat was one of them and he joined me at the bar. We both agreed that the film was pretty disgusting and lame, and, chuckling and shaking our heads, we sat and talked for a while over beers. Pat was an accounting major and a junior, I think. We didn't have any classes together, but had seen each other in The Pug and elsewhere around campus. He sometimes studied in the lounge annex of the Catholic chapel, and so did I. It was a quiet, out-of-the-way place on the eastern edge of the campus where you could usually get some serious cramming done.

Over the next several weeks Pat and I became pretty good friends, and even double dated a few times, always in Pat's car, since my VW's tiny back seat would have been pretty uncomfortable for Pat, who was close to six feet tall. Pat's car, on the other hand, was perfect, a huge old Mercury with a wide, date-friendly back seat.

We'd both had our ups and downs on the dating front, but by the time that St. Patrick's Day rolled around, Pat had struck gold, or so it seemed to me, since I was still looking. He had started going out with a very attractive girl who'd recently pledged with the Delta Zeta sorority. Marilyn LeRash was a strikingly beautiful girl, with a dazzling smile and a mane of thick, light brown hair distinguished by a natural streak of silver that started at her hairline near the middle of her forehead. The DZ's were an

Marilyn LeRash

impressively good-looking bunch of babes that year and I had even dated one new DZ myself, Bonna Holmgren, who was from Reed City. She was a very sweet girl, but for some reason we never got beyond that first date. I had known both Bonna and her older sister, Carla (also a DZ), in high school, but not very well, as they were

119

both younger than me. Maybe I was subconsciously still looking for a nice Catholic girl, like Marilyn.

In any case, I was definitely between girls that night as I went looking for Patrick at his dorm. He wasn't in, so, since I figured he'd be cramming for finals, I cut back over to the Student Center parking lot to get my car and headed for the chapel, where I thought he might be holed up to study.

St. Paul's Catholic chapel is located at the bottom of a hill at the end of Damascus Road, on the banks of the Muskegon River. I knew I'd found Pat as soon as I pulled into the parking lot and spied the massive brown bulk of his old Merc parked near the sidewalk that led up to the double glass doors of the annex. I could almost taste that cold green beer as I pushed through the doors and scanned the main lounge area, where a couple of guys were engaged in a desultory game of bumper pool, one of them bent over the small table, cue poised carefully, while the other leaned lazily against the nearest wall, chalking his cue and watching. At a long table near the door I saw Frank Bozek, deep in study, one hand splayed over an open Pharmacology textbook while the other busily jotted notations into a spiral notebook. Frank and I had been ninth-grade classmates at St. Joe's Seminary in Grand Rapids during my short-lived stab at a "religious vocation." He'd lasted a little longer than I had, but not much. Now he was a fourth year pharmacy student and quite active in the Newman Club here at the chapel, where I'd first run into him again my freshman year at Ferris. Frank had tried to recruit me into the Catholic group, but I had successfully resisted. Since my stint in the army, I had become very selective about "joining" anything. Now Frank looked up from his notes and

Frank Bozek, deep in study

sum

The FSC Newman Club, 1966. I was not a member, but there I am, second from left, with Frank Bozek on my left, in the St. Paul's Chapel lounge.

nodded at me. I asked him if he'd seen O'Connor, and he pointed his pen and inclined his head toward the closed library door over in the corner of the lounge.

The chapel "library" was largely a collection of old religious texts and tattered tracts and pamphlets, and I think there may have been a worn set of Catholic encyclopedias too. There were two walls of bookshelves and four small study tables that could each accommodate four students. Before I even opened the door, I could see, through its long narrow window, Pat's head, facing my direction and bent over one of the tables. Two girls were facing him across the table, their backs to the door. One I recognized as Marilyn by the silver streak in her wavy brown hair. The other one was a blonde.

Wait a minute. No. She wasn't just "a blonde." She was *the* blonde. She was, she was … I'm really stuck here, I have to tell you, and I've *been* stuck for over a *week* now. Because how do you even *begin* to describe meeting someone who will irrevocably change your life forever. "Love at first sight" is such a dumb overused cliché, I know, but if it wasn't love, then it was lust. Yeah, that's probably what it was all right, *lust*.

Remember that famous *Playboy* interview with former president Jimmy Carter? The one where he "confessed" that he had "lusted in his heart" over women? Well, shit, Jimmy, that ain't nothin' to be ashamed of. It's just *human*, and, as near as I can figure out, it has to be part of the Divine Plan. Hell, if men didn't feel that strong physical attraction toward women, there wouldn't be any human race. I figure there's probably a good reason for man walking upright on his hind legs too. I know it can sure play hell with the spine and can cause all kinds of back problems eventually, but it also affords the male of the species a much better view of the mammaries of the female of the species, and aren't tits just the grandest things on God's green earth to *look at*, guys? I mean, come *on* now. Let's be honest. I know that probably the politically correct answer these days whenever someone asks you what first attracted you to your wife (or girl friend) is some bullshit like, "Oh, she had the most beautiful eyes," or "she had a great sense of humor" or "we shared so many common interests," but you can't *tell* me you didn't check out the headlights first thing too. I mean it's part of the natural order of the male stimulus-response mechanism. And I'm not dwelling on this just for the sake of a little gratuitous crudeness either. I guess what I'm trying to say – to *illustrate* – here is that love begins with lust. Guys in their teens and twenties are just not naturally wired for love. That will come later – *may*be. What they are wired for is sexual stimulation and gratification, as *soon* as possible and as *often* as possible. They want to get laid, first and foremost – and then, as John and Placido so beautifully phrased it, "Perhaps Love."

Terri's Delta Zeta photo

So let me tell you about my last love, the love of my life, and how it all began – with true lust. Her name was Terri (although there's a whole 'nother story just about that, which we'll get to later on). Marilyn made the introductions, as I stood staring none too subtly, I'm afraid, at this stunning stranger. A back-combed blonde helmet of hair softly framed strong regular features and the softest brown eyes I had ever encountered. I know I just got through calling the "beautiful eyes" bit bullshit, but I may have to recant already, because I could have gotten lost in those eyes. My mouth was probably hanging slightly open, and I must have been a bit too obvious with my staring, because the girl, who had been meeting my eyes quite boldly, suddenly ducked her head demurely and blushed in the most beautifully becoming fashion. It's entirely possible that I was a goner from that moment on, whether I knew it or not at the time. If I can stretch a religious simile here, just like St. Paul on the road to Damascus, I was knocked clean off my horse and instantly converted to the religion of love, or lust, or perhaps an exciting combination of the two, and it happened, interestingly enough, at St. Paul's chapel, at the end of Damascus Road.

St. Paul's Chapel

I should probably add, in the interest of continuity and honesty, that I *did* check out the whole package, so to speak, and all the necessary equipment seemed to be there, including a *fine* set of headlamps.

After meeting Terri, I damn near forgot why I'd come to the chapel in the first place, but then I saw Pat grinning at my stunned discombobulation and I remembered. It was St. Paddy's Day! I blustered something to him about what the hell was he doing studying on the feast day of his namesake, and suggested we all adjourn to the Casa Nova to hoist a few of those aptly-colored green beers. Pat readily agreed. Marilyn pointed out that she and Terri were underage, but quickly added that they could have Cokes, and it sounded like fun. Pat and the girls quickly packed up their books and papers and put on their coats, and, while the ladies made a quick trip to the powder room, I pumped Pat for information on Terri, namely, did she have a boyfriend? But Pat didn't really know much, except that she was one of Marilyn's roommates and had just tagged along with them that evening to study for her finals. In any case, when Marilyn and Terri emerged from the ladies' room, freshly combed, powdered and lipsticked, they appeared to have decided something themselves, and were ready to go. I cast a sideways appraising and appreciative look at Terri, who smiled shyly back at me, and *I* was *definitely* ready to go.

* * * * *

I want the world to know
The story of my life
The moment when your lips met mine
And that first exciting time
I held you close to me.

17

SAME NIGHT –
FIRST DATE, FIRST KISS

Our first "date." Where do I start? And how do I "delicately" describe what went on, knowing our kids, our families and our friends will probably be reading this? Delicacy may not be possible, unless I lie, or leave a lot of stuff out. I would like to be able to preface this by explaining just how I was "wired" in those days when I was searching so hard for someone to share my life. My mind is simply roiling with all the things I'd like to say, but the thoughts are for the most part inchoate and unformed. Crudeness and romanticism are all tangled up in an enormous Gordian knot, and I'm afraid I haven't the verbal skills to undo that knot, but I need to try, because that girl, that same lovely brown-eyed girl, is still in my life, still here nearly forty years later, and – and here's the most *won*derful part of this whole story – she *loves* me. Yes, she still loves me. I've grown old in the interim, of course. My hair has thinned and gone gray. My muscles have gone slack, and I suffer from many of the usual pains, weaknesses, complaints, and sometimes disgusting habits of advancing age. And yet she *loves* me. So you see why I have to try to get this right. Because I believe – and I know I'm digressing, but I *need* to say this – I believe that finding someone you love, someone who loves you back, is the single most important thing that will ever happen to you in your lifetime. Tears have sprung to my eyes as I write this, and I feel a little silly, but I'm not ashamed. I am humbled and grateful that this wonderful thing finally happened to me all those years ago, and that we found each other and have made this life together.

Okay. (Big, weepy, snuffly sigh here.) That said, I now have to try to find my way back into my callow, clueless, twenty-three year-old skin and tell how I felt on that first date. Horny. That's how I felt. Spring was in the air and the sap was running high. I was horny as hell and had been living like a monk and this girl was one of the juiciest-looking pieces I had ever laid eyes on. "*Yee-HAW*! Let's go git some *beer*, Patrick!" I may have even said that, or something like it.

We all piled into Pat's big boxy brown Merc, Terri and I into the back seat – no awkward shyness about pairing off – and headed out for the Casa Nova.

I find it rather interesting that the venue of our "almost" first date was a place called the Casa Nova. Casanova was, of course, a legendary eighteenth century rake, lover, and notorious deflowerer of virgins – a very smooth and polished Lothario. No, wait – Lothario was *another* one of those guys. Too many literary references here could spoil my broth, or pudding – or fix my hash, or whatever. What I started to say was that I was no Casanova – *or* Lothario. Nope. I was more of a clueless klutz when it came to courtship. But that will become quite apparent as my tale unfolds.

The Casa Nova (which, as two words, just means "new house") was a bowling alley and bar on the south end of Big Rapids, just over the hill from the southernmost dorms of Ferris, a cluster of housing affectionately known as "The Rock." The Vet's Club had a bowling team that year. My pal and "roommate" at the time, Gary Perdew, was on the team, and I had subbed for him a few times at the Casa Nova, so I was pretty familiar with the place, and so was Pat. The bar, or "lounge," was really a pretty nice place, with soft lighting and carpeting, with several booths and some tables, in addition to the bar itself, and you could also order food there. Of course part of the bar's "ambience" was the constant thudding, whirring and clattering of bowling balls, automatic pinsetters and flying pins that came through the doors from the adjacent lanes.

All of the usual noise and then some greeted our small group as we pushed open the outside doors and entered the bar. Every

The Casa Nova

booth and table were taken, and patrons were two deep along most of the bar too. The smell of hops and hot grease from the kitchen wafted through the room as the jukebox against the far wall blasted out a nasal chorus of "Hang On Sloopy." It appeared that every erstwhile Irishman in the area had converged on the Casa Nova that night to celebrate. There was absolutely no place left to sit, and – still another disappointment – there was no more green beer either. It had sold out, and the bar had no more green food coloring to mix more. After receiving this bleak news from one of the bartenders, Pat and I went into a brief huddle and decided to quit this mob scene and go make our own party of four. So, bundling ourselves and the girls back into the car, we headed north up State Street, past the college campus and through town. Pat pulled into the parking lot of Grunst Bros. Party Store and I hustled inside and grabbed a

Grunst Bros. ad

six-pack of Pabst from the cooler, and then as an afterthought a six-pack of Coke too. After all, I had no idea whether this girl was a drinker or not.

As it turned out, she wasn't. A drinker, that is. Or at least she didn't like beer. But, wonder of wonders, she did seem to like me. I could tell by the shy way she kept sneaking glances at me and smiling as we exchanged information in the darkness of the back seat while Pat drove north out of town. I learned that, like me, she was in her second year of a two-year program at Ferris. She was in the cosmetology school, which offered its students the opportunity to earn a two-year college degree and learn to be a beautician all at the same time. (The cos program at Ferris finally died a natural death in the early eighties, probably because it was a lot cheaper – and quicker – to get certified at countless small beauty schools scattered around the state.) Terri was from Belleville, which I'd never heard of, but I learned it was located downstate near Detroit.

She also confided that her flaxen blonde hair was "new." It seemed that, in the cos program, bleaching or coloring hair was so common among the students as to be nearly a kind of rite of passage. Turning to face me on the back seat and reaching up with both hands, she patted tentatively at the carefully sprayed and back-combed blonde bouffant that was so in style at the time, and asked me what I thought.

I don't know if girls are conscious of this, but anytime they reach up and back like this with both hands to fix or adjust their hair, or perhaps a hat, the motion causes their breasts to rise in the most irresistible and delicious manner, two perky protrusions practically crying out for attention – *Hi there. Aren't we cute? Don'cha just wanna squeeze us?*

Uh-HUH!

See, guys just can't help noticing these seemingly innocent gestures, and some recessive Neanderthal gene in the frontal lobe kicks in, rendering them, at least momentarily, nearly incapable of speech. Once those high beams are flicked on, we're like deer caught in the glare, paralyzed. Most guys are not naturally poetically inclined, but we can recognize the beauty – and the poetry – of a brace of upturned breasts. (Talk about a cupcake couplet!) The problem is that same Neanderthal gene blocks out all possible efforts at eloquence and replaces them with the rude but honest reaction of *Ti-its*!

But if I may chance a metaphor here, I would say that if a woman's eyes are the windows of her soul, then her breasts are the billboards of her body.

No? Doesn't work? Okay, then. How about this: Her "breasts are like two fawns, twins of a gazelle, that feed among the lilies." (*Song of Solomon*, 4:5). I've always liked that metaphor myself. Fawns. *Bambi*. Don'cha just wanna reach out and pet 'em and cuddle 'em?

Well, I did – *wanted* to, I mean. But somehow I managed not to, as my eyes flicked nervously up and down between her deep, soft, doe-like brown eyes and the tautly stretched fabric of her pale yellow blouse.

"Um, yeah. I like 'em. (Oops!) I mean, I really like your hair. It's really purty."

Yeah, I think I actually *did* say "purty." I was that discombobulated, so much so that it caused me to talk like an illiterate hillbilly hick.

My *gosh*! I actually just *sali*vated all over the page as I re-read this, so I must be getting it right. Because I'm pretty sure I was salivating in the back seat of that old Merc that night, and there were probably a few other glands kicking into high gear too, as I reached over to touch Terri's hair and she obligingly slid in a little closer to me, ducking her head ever so slightly as my fingers grazed the back of her hair and the softly furred nape of her neck. And then, when she raised her face to look up at me, it seemed the most natural thing in the world to kiss her, so I did, ever so carefully at first. My hands were already automatically cupped (that recessive caveman gene again), but I somehow managed to bring them up and placed them gently on either side of her face, instead of where they really *wanted* to go. It must have been just the right gesture, because her hands slid slowly up my chest and around my neck, and suddenly she was kissing me *back*!

Oh, that *kiss*. That first indescribably *delicious* soft kiss. Remember? That unfor*get*table first kiss that just stopped you dead in your tracks and set your heart to hammering and your mind to racing, and planted that first small seed of suspicion, an *ex*quisite suspicion, that *this* girl just could be the one you've been searching for. Do you remember that moment, and the way your heart leaped crazily out of its normal rhythm and did a special little dance of joy and thanksgiving that was both frightening and exhilarating all at the same time? *I* do. *I* remember it. Across a lifetime of memories I remember. I know it may sound trite, but my life began again with that kiss. I probably didn't realize it at the time, apart from a small inkling that something very special was going on here, but *that kiss* ... I remembered that kiss all over again several years ago when Faith Hill, the country singer, came out with her smash crossover hit, "This Kiss", with its line, "It's that pivotal moment." I could relate. The memory – the *taste* – of that first kiss Terri and I shared was still vivid, over thirty years later. The first time I heard that song on the radio, I had to run out and buy the CD. I brought it home, slapped in onto the player and cranked it up, and we danced in the kitchen. And remembered.

In all honesty, I should probably confess, admit to myself at least, that all these feelings and the way I've described them here are unavoidably colored by everything that has happened to us since that night in the back seat of Pat's car, by that same "lifetime of memories" – for we have been through a lot together, and I have come to love this woman in ways that my twenty-three year-old self could never have conceived of.

But I was telling you about that first "date," and I want to try to be honest about it, or as honest as I *dare* to be, knowing that the love of my life will read these pages, and, as she is constantly reminding me, "We have to *live* in this town, and maybe *you* don't care what people think, but *I* do!" Point taken, dear.

As first dates go, it probably wasn't very typical. So many of the usual preliminaries were skipped. There was no dinner, no movie, no meeting the parents, no elaborate preparations. Nope. It was all spur-of-the-moment. Nearly a pick-up, as a matter of fact, except there was another couple present, and proper introductions were made. And don't forget that this near pick-up was made in extremely close proximity to a church. And don't forget St. Patrick and St. Paul and the road to Damascus and all that stuff. I mean I've done my level best to lay a respectable, and even religious, veneer over that first date.

If I've made it sound really romantic so far, well, I suppose that depends on your point of view. *I* remember it that way, but Terri remembers it as something more like "attempted sexual assault." I don't really understand why she remembers it that way, and yet I do, I guess. That first kiss was indeed so very lovely, and I suppose I took it, in a typical male fashion, as an invitation to the goods. Yeah, it set my heart racing all right, and all the blood raced south. My *Gawd*, she made me horny! I mean I knew, I suppose, that I wasn't gonna get laid that night. I mean, after all, we'd only just *met*. I knew instinctively too, that this was a nice girl, and that I should hold myself back and slow down, but I guess the raging hormones took over, and the beer I was guzzling in between the clinches probably served to further break down any of the minimal inhibitions I might have normally felt. There are probably really no good excuses for my quite *in*excusable behavior, however. It was purely animal instinct taking over, that basic urge to procreate.

Terri remembers that night as exciting and embarrassing all at the same time. After all, Pat and Marilyn were just a few feet away in the front seat, and she didn't want her roommate to think less of her, to think she was "easy," so she essentially spent most of the evening fending off my aggressive and crude advances, and yet trying to do it in such a way that wouldn't offend or discourage me *too* much. I suppose it really was something of a dilemma for her. In retrospect I understand, but at the time I just wanted what I wanted, and was none too subtle or gentlemanly about it.

Pat had pulled the car off the road and parked at a secluded turnaround on the west bank of the Muskegon somewhere north of town. The radio was tuned to WLS out of Chicago, and I could hear deejay Dick Biondi's irreverent patter between tunes as he took requests. (Rumor had it that Biondi was later fired for his inappropriate sense of humor. He supposedly took a call one night from a young listener and asked if she'd like to play a kissing game called "baseball." She said okay, so he continued, saying, "Okay, sweetie, here's how it works. I'll kiss you between the strikes and you kiss me between the balls." Good ol' Dick. No wonder all the kids loved him.)

Before long all the car windows were fogging over. I should probably note here that I have no idea what Pat and Marilyn were up to in the front seat. I was much too intent on what *we* were doing in the back seat, or, maybe more accurately, what *I* was *try*ing to do and what Terri was tactfully trying to *prevent* me from doing. In any case, she finally suggested, perhaps out of sheer desperation, that we get out of the car for a while and get some fresh air. Sounded like a good idea to me, so we did. She has since told me that her suggestion was prompted mostly by embarrassment at all the noise we were making – i.e. the struggling and thrashing around, the heavy breathing, and the panting and gasping when we'd come up for air. Terri was torn in what she was feeling at the time. One the one hand she was very flattered by all my strenuous attentions, but on the other hand she was also just a bit terrified, not only by my amorous enthusiasm, but also by her own quite unexpected physical response to these attentions. In other words, she was frightened not so much of me, but of her own mounting sexual excitement. She has since described those physical sensations in much more graphic terms, most of which I have been sworn not to disclose under pain of emasculation and/or death. Use your imagination, ladies. (Does the expression "wet panties" mean anything to you?) I'm sure the guys know what I'm talking about. And lest anyone get the wrong idea, we both remained fully clothed throughout this blissful if frustrating evening. Any groping that went on (and there was plenty of it, all on *my* part), was done through layers of clothing.

So we clambered out of the car, literally *gasp*ing for breath. I would like to be able to say something here like, "it was a beautiful evening, a soft spring breeze was in the air, and a full moon hung in the sky above the river, casting its reflection on the water, providing a soft ambience on the graveled bank where the car was parked under a huge old willow tree." But the truth is, even if all that had been true – and maybe it *was* – I wouldn't have noticed. I was just too darned excited by this girl. I couldn't get enough of her kisses, and I knew that was pretty much *all* I was going to get that night, but I didn't care. I couldn't keep my hands off her. There was an immediate and palpable physical tension between us that I had never felt before in my admittedly limited sexual experience.

I'm not saying, as I mentioned earlier, that our budding "relationship" was a case of love at first sight. It probably wasn't. I mean she was nineteen and I was twenty-three. What the hell did *we* know from *love*? What the hell do *any* kids that age know about love? But it was most certainly a case of *lust* at first sight, from that first kiss, that first touch. I may not have quite realized it yet, but I was, from that moment on, a definite goner. I. Was. Hooked. Gut me and filet me. Wash me off and cracker meal me. Slap me in a pan and fry me up and squeeze a little lemon on me. Hooked. Caught. Dazed. Stunned. But dumb-and-happy dazed and stunned.

To describe the rest of our first date would be merely redundant, although if I were allowed to go into more detail it certainly wouldn't be dull. Does the old expression "dry-hump" mean anything to you? Oh, well …

When I ask Terri what she remembers about that night these days, she usually rolls her eyes and sputters something about my "impaling" her across the trunk of O'Connor's car, and I usually point out to her – ever the semanticist – that "impale" is a very suggestive and probably inaccurate word in this context, but she usually insists that that's what it felt like to *her*, so who am I to correct her terminology. Memories are selective, and also, I suspect, gender specific. I have mine and she has hers, and perhaps that's just as well.

I don't remember how long we stayed there by the river that night – or if there were actually soft breezes and moonlight. If there weren't, there *should* have been. But the girls had a curfew, and we managed to get them back to Helen Ferris Hall just before they might have turned into pumpkins. I know Terri and I exchanged one last excruciatingly long and lovely lingering kiss, our lips bruised and tongues tired, just outside the dormitory doors, part of a crowd of lust-struck couples reluctant to let go for the night. Old William really was right, you know? "Parting *is* such sweet sorrow."

So there you have it, kids – as accurate a picture as I can give you of how it all began, way way back before we became "just your parents." Because this book, like my first two, is still, more than anything else, a letter to my children, to *our* children. This is who I am, who I was. And, from this point on, at least a little, if I tell it right, you may also get a small glimpse of who your momma was too.

As I Beetled my way home from Ferris, balls aching, I think I knew that something very special had begun that night, because I just couldn't wait to see this girl again, to look into those bottomless brown eyes, to kiss those lovely soft lips, and to lay hands on that luscious lush body. In the parlance of the old Baltimore Catechism of my childhood, I was definitely having "impure thoughts" about this sweet girl, and was perhaps a bit bothered by that old bugaboo, Catholic guilt. She would definitely qualify as a "near occasion of sin," but I didn't care. I would have readily risked the fires of hell to hold her close again.

Pretty mushy stuff, huh, kids? Well, that's the way you feel when you're in love – or lust, or whatever the hell it was I was in.

I called her as soon as I got home that night. It couldn't have been more than a half hour since we'd parted, but I just wanted to hear her voice again, to "tuck her in" for the night.

Making a "private" phone call was not as easily accomplished back then as it is now. It seems like most of the kids in college now, and even in high school, have their own cell phones, which provide instant and intimate access to anyone they want. In 1967 our house, however, had one telephone. (Yeah, kids, just *one* phone!) It was the standard noisy rotary dial type, and was mounted on the wall of the entry hall near our front door. The only way you could achieve any privacy while using the phone was to pull the receiver to the limits of its curling cord and retreat into the hall closet and pull the sliding door shut and crouch among the coats and galoshes and dust bunnies. Or you could go in the opposite direction, around the corner and down the stairs leading to the basement. I chose the latter, first enduring with clenched teeth the chirring chatter of that damn dial as I pulled each number around, hoping like hell it wouldn't wake up Mom or Dad or Mary or Chris, all sleeping just a few yards away down the hall. And to make things worse, I had to place the call several times, as I kept getting a busy signal for the one hallway phone on the third floor in Terri's dorm. I wasn't the only guy trying to say good-night, obviously. I can't remember what we might have said to each other that night as I crouched at the top of the basement stairs with the folding door pulled shut, the phone cradled against my cheek. I just knew I had to hear her voice and to feel her near me again, even if it was only through the phone wires.

There were just two more days left in the term and I had exams scheduled for both days, but I don't think I was able to study much from that night on. I managed to see Terri again the next evening. We drove around campus and into the nearby countryside where I parked, and we had a repeat performance of our first night together, with much breathless kissing and frantic groping (me groping *her*, of course) across the gearshift and emergency brake assembly that separated the bucket seats. *Damn* bucket seats! Neither one of us could bear the thought of being separated for nearly two weeks, but spring break was upon us, and we both had previously made plans, so we said our reluctant good-byes that night outside the dorm, because she was leaving for home early the next day.

I, on the other hand, was leaving the next morning on a trip that would turn out to be my last time to run with the boys.

* * * * *

18

HEADIN' SOUTH –
WHERE THE BOYS ARE

Do you remember the 1960 film, *Where the Boys Are*? It wasn't a *great* film, but it did, I think, have far-reaching cultural repercussions. It was a fairly simple and standard plot-line of "boy-meets-girl, boy-loses-girl, boy-gets-girl-back." But the film's special twist on this old story was its setting. It took place on the beaches and in the motels and clubs of Fort Lauderdale, Florida, during spring break.

The normally sleepy little town of Lauderdale had been discovered by college kids, and every Easter week thousands of them converged on the place, somewhat to the dismay of many of its retired citizens, and much to the consternation of its limited constabulary. The local merchants and motel owners, however, made out like bandits. Hundreds of thousands of dollars, perhaps more, swelled the coffers of the little community during this seasonal influx. The aforementioned film had other things going for it too, of course. The lead love interests were played by Dolores Hart and George Hamilton. Hamilton was a brand new star in the Hollywood galaxy in 1960, and could be found on the covers of all the movie magazines. While it's true that *Where the Boys Are* was essentially a piece of film fluff, it also afforded George his very first opportunity to display what would become his most important asset as an actor – his tan. That same year Hamilton co-starred in another film that received a great deal of favorable attention from the critics. *Home from the Hill* was a serious drama, one of the season's so-called "blockbusters," which starred Robert Mitchum and Eleanor Parker, and dealt with such gritty themes as infidelity, illegitimacy, and suicide. George Hamilton played the tormented legitimate son and heir to Mitchum, and another movie newcomer, George Peppard, played his more self-assured bastard brother. It was, in many ways, a west Texas version of *Peyton Place*. I know I'm digressing again, but *Home from the Hill* was one of my personal favorite films back in high school, one which intrigued me enough to seek out the book it was based on (by William Humphries) and read it. I often think of it as the "two new Georges" movie.

Dolores Hart, Hamilton's love interest in *Where the Boys Are*, was one of those dewy-eyed innocents, the kind of girl that made a guy feel more protective than predatory. She was *way* too good for that oily snake Hamilton, with his superior sneer and Technicolor tan. As a matter of fact (or maybe it was just more Hollywood hype?), she found Someone much better when she shocked the movie business and her many adoring male fans by chucking it all and entering a convent. Good for you, Sister D.

But *Boys* boasted a fine ensemble cast too. I'm sure everyone remembers Jim Hutton and Paula Prentiss, the comedian-impressionist Frank Gorshin, and, of course, last but not least, songstress Connie Francis, whose heartfelt rendition of the film's title tune was one of the biggest hits in a hit-filled career, and was most instrumental in making *Where the Boys Are* one of the biggest box-office successes of 1960. They were all great and aptly cast in their particular roles.

This is all by way of a lengthy introduction to where I was going for spring break in 1967. Yup, you guessed it – Fort Lauderdale. Now this was not an idea I would have normally come up with on my own. I'm more the cautious type when it comes to long road trips and "adventures." I think the idea for the trip originated with Gary Perdew, who was living with our family at the time, bunking with me in my basement bedroom. My initial reaction had probably been something like, "I don't know, Gary. That's a hell of a long drive."

Whereupon he would have prompted me, "Yeah, but think about all those *women*, Tim, and they're all on the prowl. It'll be easy pickin's, man. Come on, let's *do* it! Let's *go*!"

I can't believe I fell for that "easy pickin's" crap, but I guess I must have. Or at least the seed of hope was planted. From that small exchange in early March the idea snowballed.

We talked about it a few times with Pat O'Connor and his pal, Wayne Shook, and they both wanted in. Everyone would kick in for gas money and we'd take my car, since it was still new, hence the most reliable, and also would get the best gas mileage. This in an era when gas was still only around a quarter a gallon, but we were all pretty money-poor and two bits was two bits. Over the next couple of weeks, our plans for the trip slowly came together. Shit, four unattached guys don't really need to make any very elaborate "plans" for a week-long trip. You just threw a few changes of clothes into a small grip and you were ready to go.

As it turned out, Gary didn't go. I can't remember exactly why, but I think someone offered him a job during the break where he could make some serious money, something he was always short of. So it was just the three of us: Pat, Wayne and me. Three caballeros. The Three Musketeers. Hell, we were probably more like the Three Stooges. But we were all game for the "adventure," at least in its planning stages. In late February, and even in early March, when the Michigan snows still stood deep in most areas around Ferris, the warm sunshine and sandy beaches of southern Florida sounded pretty damn good. And there were other Ferris kids planning to make the trip too. At least one other carload of vets was going – John Nibbelink, Jim Roddy, Gomer Frederickson and Larry Miller. But they were making their own plans for the trip.

The thing was, I had been pretty excited about the trip, I mean really psyched up, actually. But then I had met Terri just two days before our planned departure date, and my whole world kind of turned upside down – in a *good* kind of way, I mean. Here was this girl, suddenly in my life, and after just one evening and a couple of days with her, I wasn't so sure I wanted to go *any*where anymore. I mean I just wanted to be with her. Every waking moment I was thinking about her and wondering where she was and what she was doing and wishing I were there with her and doing the same things. Was this *love*? Hell, *I* didn't know. I didn't know *any*thing! I'm not sure I managed to have even a single coherent thought in those last two days – not a good state of mind to be in when you're taking final exams, I might note.

In any case, Terri had already caught her ride home to Belleville and D-day was upon us, so off we went as planned. The beaches were beckoning, and so, we *hoped*, would the blondes, brunettes and redheads.

The drive from Reed City to Fort Lauderdale is no Sunday stroll in the park. It is in fact one hell of a long-ass haul, over 1500 miles. And we planned to drive straight through without stopping. Overnight stays at motels would have been cost prohibitive for poor vets like us, and we were very conscious of the need to carefully hoard our meager funds for the essentials once we arrived in Florida, for things like room and board, beer, and – hope always springs eternal – *babes*.

It was still quite dark when I left Reed City that March morning, my minimal luggage stowed in the front boot of the Bug and a bulging bag of sandwiches and cookies lovingly prepared by my mom tucked behind the back seat. I'm sure she and Dad had their doubts about this quite unnecessary and foolhardy interstate expedition, but they managed to limit their advice to multiple "be carefuls" during the days preceding my departure. It wasn't like I didn't have my own misgivings. After all, I had never made a trip this long under my own power before. Probably my longest independent car trip up to that time had been to Chicago to visit Bob and Maureen. So I was pretty revved up when I left the sleeping populace of Reed City behind me that morning and sped south to Ferris.

Pat and Wayne were waiting eagerly for me when I pulled up to the side door of Carlisle Hall. I popped open the front hood and they put their small pieces of luggage in between mine and the spare tire, and then Wayne climbed into the back seat and settled in among the extra pillows and blankets I'd brought along, and Pat slid into the shotgun seat beside me, setting a large thermos of coffee on the floor between his feet. The Blaupunkt was blasting a brand-new tune by the Supremes called "The Happening," which we would hear about a jillion more times as we passed through six states. I think this may have been the very first time we had heard the song though, and it was such an infectious and upbeat little ditty that all three of us were rockin' and boppin' in time along with Diana and her pals as we circled the Student Center and got back onto 131 and headed south. We were off on our joint adventure, and felt like we were all a unique part of "The Happening." By the time we were passing through Georgia, however, some twenty hours or so later, and the song came on *again*, we were all groaning and shouting, "Not *that* fucking thing again! *Change* it!" Oh, the fickleness of pop music fans.

Let's see. What memories can I dredge up about that long-ago journey? Well, it was a long trip, that's for sure, but at least the navigation itself wasn't too complicated. From Grand Rapids we aimed east towards Detroit, where we picked up I-75 south. Once you get on 75, all you have to do is stay on it, all the way to Fort Lauderdale, where 75 ends, about 1300 miles later. I think we made the trip in about 28 hours, stopping only for fuel and bathroom breaks, and taking turns at the wheel. I vaguely remember some of the highway interchanges around the bigger cities getting pretty confusing, with multiple expressway signs and numbers and overpasses and exits. It wasn't always as easy just staying on the same road as you might think, especially when you're passing through or around metropolitan centers like Dayton and Cincinnati in Ohio, and then Lexington, Knoxville and Chattanooga in Kentucky and Tennessee, and, finally, Atlanta. Sometimes it took all three of us watching the signs to successfully emerge from the maze of exits and turnoffs that surrounded these cities.

I'm pretty sure none of us got any real sleep during the trip. Did you ever try to "stretch out" in the back seat of a Volkswagen? The driver's seat is probably the most comfortable seat in a Beetle, but not a great place to relax. I have only vague memories of driving through the mountains in Kentucky and Tennessee, and the momentary terrors of fleeing at dangerous speeds down precipitously steep downgrades with huge eighteen-wheeled monsters in seeming full pursuit, roaring and rumbling fiercely and belching great clouds of oily diesel smoke as they downshifted with a dissonant clashing and grinding of gears. All I could think of at these moments were the many "runaway truck ramp" signs I had seen posted throughout these hills. Of course there was never one of these gravel-covered safety ramps anywhere in sight when you felt you really needed one, only a rocky mountain face on one side of you and a yawning chasm on the other, as a barreling behemoth bore relentlessly down on you from behind, air horn blaring loudly enough to scare the blasted bejeezus out of you. This is an experience guaranteed to snap you out of your trip-tired road reverie, especially if you're driving a Bug. Bugs are, after all, so easily squashed.

Fortunately, I found out on that trip that my Bug could fly, and not just going downhill either. When we finally left the mountains behind us and emerged onto the long flat stretches of highway in southern Georgia, our excitement mounted as we drew ever closer to our goal. Pedal to the metal, we flat *flew*, crouched in the cockpit of our small craft, risking the wrath of the infamous Georgia Highway Patrol as we tested the limits of the tiny air-cooled engine and its sixty horses, sometimes burying the speedometer needle well past its top limit.

We were munching the last of Mom's soggy sandwiches, the jelly, peanut butter and soft white bread all congealed into a gummy sticky mass, when we passed the outskirts of Valdosta and sighted a sign announcing that Florida was just fifteen miles ahead. I think the three of us erupted in spontaneous cheers. *Hot DAMN! Florida, here we come*!

As I do my best to remember those long-ago days, I've been studying the map of Florida, and I can't help but note its resemblance, as I always do, to a large flaccidly pendant penis, hanging from the bottom right-hand corner of the rough rectangle that is the map of our beloved United States of America. If Michigan is an upright mitten, then Florida is a nearly limp dick. Its capital city, Tallahassee, as the state's political power base, is safely situated at the base of a scrotum which is strangely shrunken, as if from cold, although it dangles delicately into the warm waters of the Gulf of Mexico. Indeed, the bump where the balls should be is so minimal that one wonders if perhaps they have been surgically excised (or maybe never descended), leaving Florida forever young, a sterile castrato singing its siren song and luring unsuspecting tourists and fun-seekers onto its sandy shores.

The song that Pat, Wayne and I heard as we crossed the state line, however, was, once again, "The Happening." We didn't curse it this time though, but instead wondered what sorts of "happenings" awaited us as we continued to speed south down the middle of the giant member towards Gainesville, historically the winter home of Barnum & Bailey, Ringling Brothers, and dozens of other smaller traveling circuses.

I'm sure I didn't think of that at the time, or if I even knew it back then. Nor did I give any thought to Florida being the home of the notorious Seminole war chief, Osceola. And I'm still not clear on how my own home county in west Michigan ended up named after this same Florida Indian chief. I mean I can understand why there might be an Osceola County in *Florida* – and there *is* – but why in *Michigan*? Anyone?

I'm sure we passed by a host of historical sites, not to mention a multitude of sun-seekers' Meccas on our journey southward, particularly as I-75 edged westward and gently skirted the bulging boil on the backside of the big bonker that was the built-up area of Tampa, St. Petersburg and Sarasota. We never once considered stopping at any of these beautiful Gulf-side beaches, so intent were we on reaching our agreed-upon goal of Fort Lauderdale. We pressed on, ever southward, until finally, barely brushing the base of the frenum near Naples, we turned due east and accelerated down Alligator Alley, crossing the Everglades at the top of the Florida foreskin.

* * * * *

19

FORT LAUDERDALE –
AND HOLLYWOOD TOO

I-75 finally petered out rather anticlimactically as we entered the outskirts of Fort Lauderdale and turned north up Route 1 to look for lodging. Nevertheless we had arrived! It was late in the morning as we drove slowly up the strip, bleary-eyed and exhausted, but high on adrenaline at just being there. We drove slowly through town, rubbernecking at the throngs of college students who milled slowly about along the streets and beaches attired in colorful bathing suits, Bermuda shorts and Hawaiian print shirts. There were so many stunning-looking girls in two-piece suits, their carefully pre-browned skin beckoning to hungry male eyes, that it was all just a bit overwhelming. I had to keep at least one eye on the road, since I was driving, but poor Pat and Wayne damn near got whiplash as they goggled back and forth from one side of the street to the other and fore and aft, trying to take it all in.

"Omi*god*, Bazzett, lookit that blonde in the blue bikini!" – Pat.

"*Geeze*! Check out those two redheads in front of the hotel! Are they *twins*?" – Wayne.

My own head was whipping back and forth like windshield wipers on high, as I tried my best to see everything, and I unconsciously drifted across the center line, but was brought rudely back to earth by the blaring horn of an oncoming car.

"Holy *shit*!" I exclaimed, as I pulled the wheel to the right and jerked sharply back into my own lane. "Dammit, you guys. Stop lookin' at girls and find us a *mo*tel!"

There were plenty of motels, of course. In fact the strip along the beach was made up mostly of motels, but it seemed like every one of them had a NO VACANCY sign prominently displayed out front.

Of course we didn't completely stop ogling all the girls, but we also peered anxiously ahead at each motel as we advanced slowly – traffic was moving at a crawl due to the milling crowds of kids drifting up and down the strip – hoping against hope to spy a VACANCY sign. No such luck. We must have reached the northern city limits of Lauderdale, because suddenly we were seeing signs for Oakland Park and Pompano Beach. I hung a careful left turn into a motel parking lot sporting still another NO VACANCY notice and pulled back into the slow stream of traffic, heading south this time. More rubbernecking and ogling ensued as we crept slowly along on the blisteringly hot blacktop, all our windows open to let in the cooling sea breeze. There was no question about it. The film *Where the Boys Are* hadn't lied. This place was flat out jam *packed* with college kids. They were walking in waves of brightly colored brief clothing and tanned bodies all up and down the strip, from storefront to water's edge, spilling off the curbs and into the street, often stopping traffic completely, as they surged along the beach in both directions, the two sexes checking each other out so obviously that they might as well have been sniffing each other's butts. There was so damn much testosterone in the air along the beaches of south Florida that day that it was a pure wonder the whole prick-shaped peninsula didn't just rare up into a full-blown erection and ejaculate a copious clot of Coppertone-coated jocks and co-eds all the way up past Cape Hatteras and the Carolinas and out into the Atlantic.

Yes, boys and girls, Fort Lauderdale was indeed the place to be in the spring of 1967. That much was obvious just from the sea of tanned young bodies that surrounded our blue Bug as it crawled slowly back down the coast highway. NO VACANCY signs continued to flash mockingly at us as we searched in vain for a place we could moor our small craft. Fort Lauderdale finally petered out again, and gave way to Dania Beach, and then to

Hollywood and Hallandale Beach. *Noo-oo VA-cancy*. When we started seeing signs for Miami, we turned around and crept north again. Back through Hallandale and into Hollywood again.

Finally, out of sheer desperation, I whipped the car left and into a motel parking lot just as the traffic slowed and parted to allow a station wagon packed with luggage and small children to emerge into the northbound lane. The NO VACANCY sign was lit here too, but *dammit*, my legs were cramping from all the constant clutching and braking, and I had to *pee*! I parked the car carefully in the only vacant space, and we all clambered creakily out, stretching our arms wide and bending over and touching our toes, trying to get the travel kinks out of our tired aching backs and limbs. Straightening slowly, I looked up at the simple rectangular sign mounted on top of a post at the motel's entrance. In bold black letters on a white background it stated simply, BADGER MOTOR COURT. The Badger was one of those old-fashioned motels that once peppered the highways and small towns of America in the forties and fifties. It consisted of about a dozen small cabins placed in a roughly rectangular pattern with a blacktop parking area in the middle, adjacent to the road. There were weathered-looking wooden picnic table set in the small grassy intervals between the cabins, and a pair of Adirondack-style wooden lawn chairs flanked the doors of each cabin. Outside cabin three a family of five were gathered at the picnic table having lunch, the three little boys all attired in bathing trunks, and the mom and dad in shorts and tee-shirts. There were a few other adults relaxing in the lawn chairs in the sun outside some of the other cabins, most of them probably in their forties or older.

I turned towards the office and pushed my way tiredly through the door. A balding grey-haired man in an open-necked sport shirt was standing behind the counter writing something into a ledger, but he looked up with a smile when I came in. I asked if I could use the bathroom and he nodded and pointed to a door on my left. I went into the bathroom, and after a minute or two of splattering blessed relief, I zipped up and came back out into the office where Wayne and Pat were both waiting for a turn. While they took turns in the toilet, I talked with the motel manager.

"I know you don't have any rooms," I said, "but maybe you could tell us where we might find one."

The manager looked me over in a friendly enough fashion, scratched his head, and said, "Well, rooms this week are gonna be a problem, what with spring break and all. Where're you boys from?"

I told him we were from Michigan, which seemed to interest him, and he asked whereabouts in Michigan. I explained that I was from Reed City, Pat was from Jackson and Wayne was from Sturgis, and we were all students at Ferris State and belonged to the Vet's Club there. The manager's smile widened as he nodded. He knew all these places. The long and the short of it was that he and his wife were from Ann Arbor, and this motel was a second career in their retirement. And then things *really* got better. He told us that he did indeed have an empty cabin. That loaded station wagon that had just pulled out when we turned in had freed up unit two. The manager looked us all over once more, which made us a bit nervous, since we didn't look any too good after nearly thirty hours in the car. Then he told us he didn't normally rent his cabins to college kids. He'd had some bad experiences with them in the past. But since we were all from his home state and veterans too, he guessed he could trust us, and we could have number two as soon as his wife got finished cleaning it up – that is, of course, if we wanted it.

If we *wanted* it? Holy *shit*! What a serendipitous gift from heaven! Not an empty room for *miles* up and down this strip of beaches and we fall into this!

Of course all three of us put on our best, most respectful GI manners, and fell all over ourselves assuring the manager that, "Yessir, thank you, sir. That's so great, sir. You won't be sorry, sir. You can depend on us, sir. We'll take good care of your place, sir."

I can't remember the names of this kind old couple who ran the Badger (I wonder if the previous owners had been from Wisconsin?), so I'll just call them Fred and Ethel, because they had that bluff and hearty friendly manner of the Mertzes. We got our bags out of the car and carried them over to number two, where Ethel was busy stripping and re-making the two double beds and a rollaway single. Poking my head in the open door, I asked if we could help, but she just laughed and waved us off, saying she'd be done in a "jiffy." Yup, she was from Michigan, all right.

And just like that – in a jiffy – we were in. We were on spring break in Fort Lauderdale. Well, Hollywood, actually, but it was close enough, all things considered.

* * * * *

20

VETS ON VACATION – SUNBURN, BUDGET BEER, AND MISSING TERRI

I may as well confess right up front that our stay in Florida was somewhat less than satisfying, and certainly nothing like the movie. We didn't run into Dolores Hart, Paula Prentiss, Yvette Mimieux, or even perky, slightly pudgy Connie Francis. And we didn't find true love – or heartbreak either, for that matter.

What we did find were literally *thousands* of horny college kids, more guys than girls (well, the film was called *Where the Boys Are*), all wandering aimlessly up and down the beaches and sidewalks of Lauderdale strip, the crowds creeping sluggishly and formlessly like monster amoebae, dividing, re-forming, and dividing again, sliding and sluicing sloppily to and fro in a liquid medium of beer and booze – and, oh yes, the ocean was there too.

There were some beautiful girls around to be sure, but to me they seemed simply unattainable. It was the old sigh and stare syndrome all over again, just like high school, only skimpier clothes and more exposed flesh, which made for more staring, but didn't assuage the ache in my heart.

But I've spent all this time getting us to Florida, so let's see what I can remember about our week-long sojourn in the sun. Well, the sun itself was definitely a factor. A major player, in fact, for none of us Michigan boys had ever experienced the particular rays

Spring break, Fort Lauderdale, 1967

of the Florida sun. The first thing we did after depositing our bags in unit two of the Badger was to get into our swim trunks and troop across the highway to the beach. We were all totally exhausted from our trip, running mainly on adrenaline, but we figured we shouldn't waste any precious time. We could "rest" on the beach, and do some heavy-duty girl-watching at the same time. So we spread our towels and ourselves on the sand and relaxed and took in the sights, occasionally dipping ourselves in the surf to cool off. We may have even dozed off a few times on our towels, made dopey by the soothing and radiant rays of the sun – that treacherous and devious semi-tropical sun.

We probably stayed on the beach for four, maybe five hours that first time, on our first day in Florida, turning ourselves fore and aft to get a nice all-over even bake. *BIG* mistake! Finally, feeling rather parched and prickly – and hungry – I decided I'd had enough, and the other guys agreed. Well, Pat did. Wayne had fallen fully asleep and was snoring, sprawled across his towel like a dead man. We had to wake him up. He seemed totally confused at first, trying to figure out where he was, but then he remembered – *ah,*

151

yes, the great Florida adventure. We gathered up our towels, my little Sony transistor radio, empty pop bottles and keys, and trudged tiredly up the sand and then back across the blacktop. *Ouch! Ouch! Ouch!* That pavement was *hot* on our bare feet as we darted across the street to the motel.

While I was unlocking the door to our room, Pat looked at me and exclaimed, "*Jesus*, Tim, you're as red as a *lob*ster!"

"I *am*?" I asked, looking down at my chest and legs. Then I looked at him and said, "My *God*, so are *you*!"

Pat, who is very fair-skinned, with freckles and light sandy-colored hair, was indeed a very par-boiled lobstery-looking red.

We both wheeled around and looked at Wayne, who stood drooping tiredly behind us, his mouth hanging slightly open. *Also* decidedly lobsterish-looking.

"I don't feel so good," he blurted suddenly, then rushed past Pat and me into the room and made it to the toilet just in time. We heard a quick retch, and then the gush and sustained splash of vomit, followed by gasping, a low moan, and then more puking sounds. Poor Wayne. Welcome to Florida, kid.

Pat and I didn't feel so great either, especially after we'd taken a closer look at our new "tans" in the big mirror over the sink. The unfamiliar ultra-violet rays of the southern sun had really done a number on all three of us. We were dangerously over-done, and Wayne was obviously suffering the effects of acute sun-poisoning.

Finally, apparently all puked out, but still on his knees, Wayne draped himself over the side of the tub, turned on the cold water tap and splashed some over his face, then gulped cold water greedily from his upturned hands, trying to get some fluids back into his badly dehydrated skinny frame. He was really hurting and in bad shape. Pat dug a bottle of Solarcaine out of his bag and told Wayne to spread some all over him. Wayne had by this time staggered back out of the bathroom and lay down on the rollaway single bed. He was so sick and exhausted he could barely move. I got him to sit up while I turned back the spread and top sheet, then I rubbed some Solarcaine into his badly-burned back where he couldn't reach, and gave him the bottle to do his face and the rest of him.

Pat and I took turns taking showers – *cold* ones. By the time we were finished, Wayne was passed out and snoring, and obviously feverish. His brow was *very* hot to the touch. Hell, his whole *body* – and probably ours too – was giving off heat. After taking turns with the Solarcaine and doing each other's backs, we put on some shorts, tee-shirts (*ouch!*) and flip-flops and set off for the supermarket just down the road to get in some food and supplies for our stay.

Our room was what you call an efficiency unit with a kitchenette. In addition to the beds and bathroom and a bureau, it also had a small combination appliance that incorporated a four-burner stove over an oven and a stainless steel sink over a small refrigerator-freezer. We could cook and we could keep stuff cold. There was also a small dinette table with two chairs.

At the market we were a bit overwhelmed by all the choices, but we decided to try to stick to the bare essentials, so we went first to the beer display, a veritable mountain of cases of beer, including many brands we had never seen before. Ever practical and mindful of our limited resources, we worked our way down the mountain, from the top premium beers to the rock-bottom cheapest brands. These turned out to be local brands totally unfamiliar to us. One was called Orbit, probably so-named because of our relative proximity to Cape Canaveral. Another brand was called Dorf, or maybe it was Dwarf, I can't remember for sure. We put a case of each of these exotically-labeled brews into our cart.

Since we were already in the alcohol aisle, we lingered briefly, pondering the rich variety of liquors and wines on display, thinking we might want a break from a steady diet of beer. Again, we worked our way down to the inexpensive end of things and settled on a rather robust-looking red table wine, attractively packaged in a clear glass gallon jug with an equally attractive price of just ninety-nine cents. It was obviously our lucky day, at least shopping-wise.

Thus suitably supplied with at least a two- or three-day stash of alcoholic beverages, we moved on to foodstuff shopping, throwing in a loaf of cheap white bread, some store-brand peanut butter and jam, some processed P&P loaf sandwich meat, and a giant jar of kosher dill pickles. In the frozen foods aisle we found Banquet pot pies on sale at six for a dollar, so we splurged on a dozen of those. I looked longingly at the ice cream, but figured with all those pies there wouldn't be room in the tiny freezer. We added some faux Oreo-type cookies and a gallon of milk. (Beer goes badly with sweet stuff like PB&J sandwiches or cookies.) Finally, at the checkout we threw in some Coppertone, more Solarcaine, aspirin and a tube of zinc oxide, having wisely decided, I suppose, that we needed to nip this sunburn thing in the bud. *Too late*!

I'm putting all these grocery-shopping details in here mostly for my mom. She was always worried about whether I was getting enough of the proper things to eat when I was away from home. Not to worry, Mom – all the food groups accounted for, as you can see.

By the time we got our groceries put away and had awakened Wayne just long enough to get a few aspirins and some more water into him, it was nearly eight o'clock, so, after refreshing ourselves briefly with a couple of ice cube-cooled Orbits (hmmm, not all that bad, actually), Pat and I finally called it a day and fell into our beds – the end of our first day in Florida. It had been approximately thirty-eight hours since we had departed the dirty, melting Michigan snow banks at Ferris. Those fresh sheets on our turned-down beds felt wonderful. We slept.

For the most part, the next several days passed in a sun-soaked blur of drinking beer and daily walks up and down the strips in Fort Lauderdale, and also in Hollywood and Hallandale Beach. We became part of the amorphous mob of kids, who, beer cans in hand, noses and cheekbones smeared with white zinc oxide ooze, wandered aimlessly up one side of the strip and then back down the other, looking for *some*thing – *love*? *Excitement*?

The truth is there wasn't all that much excitement to be found, other than the occasional cock-of-the-walk chest-bumping and shoving matches that frequently erupted between strutting males in attempts to impress the females who lay basking and baking on beach towels along the sandy thoroughfare. I think probably many of these "fights" were actually staged, in an attempt to startle some of these nearby face-down, top-untied bathing beauties into jumping up from their towels and unwittingly flashing their goodies. It seems perhaps a bit ironic when you think about it. Acres and acres of exposed, healthy brown flesh all around us, and yet we yearned to see those few round cubic centimeters of the soft white skin that societal rules forbade showing in public. All those tempting, delectable-looking cleavages and tight, bouncing bottoms just crying out for a cupped hand, for a subtle squeeze. But *no-oooh*! You can *look*, boys, but you can't *touch*!

I don't know about the other guys, but I never saw a single bare breast the whole time I was in Florida. It seemed almost criminal. Do I just have really bad luck, or what?

You could only stand so much of the eternal traipsing up and down the beach. The sun sucked your energy quickly from you, and the nearly constant imbibing of beer also tired you out. So – and this is a bit embarrassing – by late afternoon we often retreated to our room at the Badger, drew the shades, and napped – or, perhaps more accurately, we passed out for a few hours.

Nights we would bar hop or head for one of several huge cavernous night clubs where the same mob of kids finally mixed a bit more, only *in*doors instead of out and danced to the booming over-amplified sounds of live bands or deejays. There was undoubtedly some pairing off that resulted from these club nights, but I never quite became part of a pair beyond a few scattered dances. I don't think Wayne had much luck either, but Pat did disappear for a few hours on a couple nights, so I don't know about him.

One of the Ferris vets who probably did find a little action, or at least he undoubtedly *could* have, had he been feeling more himself, was Larry Miller. He and John Nibbelink showed up at our door at the Badger our second night there. They had stopped at the beaches on the Gulf side over around Fort Meyer on their trip south and sampled the sights there and slept on the beach. By the time they reached Fort Lauderdale they'd had enough of beach-bumming and were craving a real bed to sleep in again or at least a roof over their heads. They found us by spotting my blue Bug at the motel and recognizing the Osceola County plates. (Back in the sixties Michigan still used a system of letter prefixes on license plates that equated to particular counties.) There was still no room at the inn when they came knocking at our door, but they slept on the floor that night. The next day we checked with Fred and Ethel, who were, once again, most generous and understanding. They gave us some extra towels and told us one of the units would be vacant in another day, so John and Larry spent one more night on our floor and then moved into a cabin of their own for the rest of the week. Their first days on the Florida beaches had taken a toll too. Both were badly sunburned, especially Larry, whose normally dark good looks were marred by sun damage, his lips grotesquely swollen and blistered. Like Wayne, he'd gotten a bad case of sun-poisoning, and needed a day or two of rest and a regimen of forcing fluids and taking aspirin. Even with those measures, it took quite a while for his mouth to heal, and the disfiguring effects of his sojourn in the sun were still visible when we all got back to Ferris the following week. We didn't see a whole lot of John and Larry after they got their own digs, but I doubt if Larry did much making out that week with that mutilated mouth.

By the time we'd been in Florida for four or five days and seen no action on the dating front, I think we all finally recognized the Fort Lauderdale hype for what it was, and decided to just relax, hang out and enjoy ourselves. Our sunburns came and went – and came again – despite our daily regimen of Coppertone in the daytime and Solarcaine at night. I remember going to Easter Sunday mass at a nearby church wearing flip-flops because the tops of my feet were so badly burned that I couldn't bear to put on socks or shoes.

We passed our last couple of days in Hollywood sitting in lawn chairs in the shade outside our cabin, sipping from our dwindling supply of Orbits and Dorfs and watching the crowds mill up and down the Route 1 strip, sometimes engaging in desultory girl-rating games. That gallon of bargain red wine proved to be completely unpalatable, at least to us, so we gave it to the family with the three boys in number three, who turned out to be Italians from the Bronx, and they thought the wine was just fine, and drank it from plastic cups with their meals at the picnic table, often raising their cups in our direction with much lip-smacking and smiling and exclamations of *Grazie, grazie*.

During those last few less hectic days in the shade I got to know Wayne a bit better. Like me, he was a small-town boy, from Sturgis, down near the Indiana line. He was studying to be a teacher, and was a bit more sober and reserved than many of the vets I'd met. We talked about the Vet's Club and the guys we'd met there, and both agreed that it had its pros and cons, and how it had definitely been helpful to us in meeting girls. One afternoon I started telling him about this great girl I had met just before we headed south, this beautiful blonde named Terri, and how I couldn't stop thinking about her and couldn't wait to see her again as soon as school started back up. Wayne frowned thoughtfully, and then asked me what this Terri's last name. I told him it was Zimmer, and he chuckled ruefully and shook his head. It turned out he knew Terri and had even dated her a few times. They had attended a Ferris football game together back in the fall, and had gone to Nibbelink's skating party that winter too, the same party I had been at with Gary and our "party-girl" dates. At first I was a bit flustered at learning I wasn't the first to discover Terri, but then I quickly rationalized that well, sure, she was a gorgeous girl, so of course other guys had noticed her and even gone out with her before I came along. Still, my male ego felt a bit bruised.

Wayne, however, didn't seem to mind, and wasn't particularly surprised to learn that Terri had moved on to someone else. He hadn't seen much of her for the last few months, and had been dating other girls himself. He quite readily agreed with me that she was indeed a beautiful girl, and he hoped that she and I could have some fun together.

Just talking about Terri made me miss her even more acutely than I had been up until then. I wished suddenly that I could write her, and must have even mused aloud about this, because Wayne replied, rather matter of factly, that he had her home address, and got out his wallet and handed me a small folded piece of notebook paper which did indeed have Terri's name and address written on it.

"Keep it," he said with a wry smile, when I started patting my pockets for a pen and paper to copy it down. "Sounds like you've got more use for it now than I do."

A bit stunned at this sudden and unexpected turn of events, but very happy, I thanked Wayne and tucked the scrap of precious information into my shirt pocket. Later that afternoon I went into the motel office and selected a post card from a rack on the counter and penned Terri my first "love-note." I wanted to remind her of our last meeting, so I think I wrote something romantic and witty like, "Look, Ma, no *hickey*!" I'm sure I never gave any thought to the fact that whoever got the mail could read my note, since it was a post card. So I think Terri's mom got her first inkling of a new guy in her little girl's life when the post card arrived in Belleville – and she couldn't have been any too impressed. I mean I know I must have written something *sweet* in that note too, about how I just couldn't wait to see her again, and how much I missed her, but it's the "hickey" comment that Terri remembers, and how embarrassing it was for her trying to explain it to her mother. Because she *did* have one, a real doozy, and had been covering it up with turtlenecks ever since she'd gotten home – and it wasn't a turtleneck time of year. Even today I'm still embarrassed to recall this first epistolary faux pas, but such is love – or lust. In any case, it was, I think, the beginning – albeit a rather awkward and juvenile one – of a commitment, of a "relationship."

Once my missive was mailed, my mind stayed fixed on its recipient. Even though we spent a couple more days at the Badger, I might as well have been gone. I sleepwalked through more of the motions of spring break, quaffing beers and roaming the beach, but I wasn't hunting anymore. I was just biding my time until I could launch myself back up I-75, and finally that blessed day arrived.

While it may sound like our great Florida adventure was a bust, it wasn't, not really. I think it was like a lot of carefully planned and much anticipated "adventures." It couldn't possibly have even be*gun* to live up to the extravagant Hollywood hype, or to the hazy and impossible expectations or sexual fantasies we might have concocted for it. The important thing was we had *gone*. We had *done* it. We had actually made it to that fabled place *Where the Boys Are*. There just hadn't been enough *girls* to go around. But we had ogled and gawked and gaped at all the brown bikini-clad bodies. We had looked, but we hadn't touched. (*DOH!*) We came, we saw, we got schnockered. And then we went home. And for a couple weeks afterwards we proudly displayed our sun-damaged lips, peeling noses and ears and our quickly-fading "jiffy-tans" (because our burns *did* turn into a sort of mottled brown) as we lounged casually at the vets' table in The Pug and tossed off carefully rehearsed references to Florida and Fort Lauderdale whenever we could manage to work them into the conversation. I mean, it was no big deal, but yeah, *sure* we'd been there over spring break. Hadn't *every*one? We were cool, man. We were *with* it. We may have missed "The Happening," but we were happenin' cats, man.

* * * * *

158

The Courtship

21

"SOMETHIN' STUPID" – A GOOBER IN LOVE

Upon my return to Ferris in the third quarter of 1967, I launched a serious courtship campaign. I probably wouldn't have called it that at the time, because it wasn't like I ever sat down and planned my strategy, or even thought much at all about things like commitments, relationships, or marriage. I just knew, at a gut and gonad level, that I wanted to be with this Terri, this gorgeous girl I barely knew, and I wanted to be with her *all* the time. And the really incredible part of all this was that *she* seemed to feel the same way – about *me*. That part of the equation I couldn't quite understand, but I wasn't going to question it too closely either.

I was waiting in the lobby at Helen Ferris when Terri arrived back at school after spring break, and helped her carry her bags up to her room. After that, we were together whenever we could possibly arrange it. The first thing I did when the new term started was to present her with a small token of my affection. Well, it was a pretty large token, actually. It was a life-size stuffed animal – a reclining standard poodle covered in soft black velvet fluff. Terri loved it. She christened it "Ebony" and slept with it in her narrow dorm bunk every night.

Of course we couldn't be together *all* the time, but we did our best to make the most of whatever time we could find. Terri was in her final term at Ferris and so was I. She was carrying her usual full complement of classes along with her daily cosmetology lab, but,

Terri with "Ebony" in her dorm room

since I had attended classes nearly full time the previous summer, I only needed three more classes to graduate, which seemed like a pretty light load, academically speaking. But I was also still working my custodial and scrub crew jobs, from 5 to 9 weeknights and 8 to 5 on Saturdays. Sometimes it seemed as if our combined class schedules and my work hours were conspiring against us to keep us apart.

My three classes were all held in the Starr Building or the Science Building on the west side of Ferris, while Terri's were mostly in the Alumni and East Buildings on the extreme northeast corner of the sprawling campus. Nevertheless, whenever I had a free hour or two during the day, I would walk or jog the four or five blocks that separated us and be waiting outside her classroom or the cos lab when the bell rang to signal the end of the period. All that running back and forth across campus kept me lean and eager, and

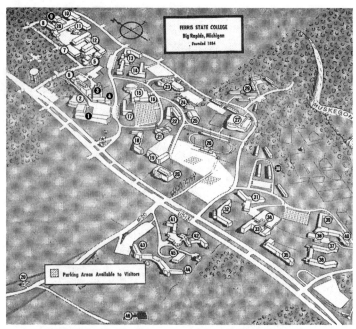

1967 FSC map. My classes were mostly in buildings 1, 3 and 4.
Terri's cosmetology classes and labs were in building 9.
The Dobsons lived in married student housing, number 30.

FACILITIES KEY

★ Main Entrance to Campus
1. Starr Educational Center
2. Starr Auditorium
3. Science Hall
4. Pearson Lecture Hall
5. Power and Maintenance Bldg.
6. Science Facilities Addition
7. Trade and Industrial Annex
8. West Building
9. Alumni Building
10. East Building
11. Temporary Trades Bldg.
12. Trade and Industrial Center
13. Masselink Commons
14. Carlisle Hall
15. Student Center
16. Green Room (Auditorium)
17. Helen Ferris Hall
18. Vandercook Hall
19. Hallisy Hall
20. Westview Campus Bldg.
21. Music Activities Center
22. Clark Hall
23. Swan Technical Arts Building

24. Johnson Hall
25. Student Health Center
26. Top Taggart Field
27. Health & Physical Ed. Bldg.
28. Library
29. Campus Heights Apts.
30. South Campus Heights Apts.
31. Pickell Hall
32. Taggart Hall
33. Ward Hall
34. South Campus Food Center
35. Miller Hall
36. Travis Hall
37. Merrill Hall
38. Knollcrest Food Center
39. Brophy Hall
40. McNerney Hall
41. Puterbaugh Hall
42. Henderson Hall
43. Glenn C. Bond Hall, North
44. Glenn C. Bond Hall, South
45. All-Purpose Building
    (Living-Learning Center)
46. New Residence Hall Complex

the smile on her face when she would emerge into the hallway and find me waiting never failed to do weird things to my heart's normal rhythm. Maybe it had something to do with the fact that I'd skipped lunch – or forgotten it completely in my urgent need to see her again – but I doubt it. There was a romantic ballad made popular that year by Ed Ames which probably better described this somewhat frightening physiological phenomenon. It was called "My Cup Runneth Over (with Love)."

There was a tiny restaurant situated just across Oak Street from the Alumni Building called The Coffee Cup. I say "tiny" because it had probably originally been just a small ranch-style house, and had never been meant to accommodate the milling crowds of hungry students who came pressing into its narrow confines during the breaks between classes. Inside the door was the short end of an L-shaped Formica-topped lunch counter with stools which ran the length of the establishment. There was a row of several narrow booths which ran along the west wall opposite the long end of the L. The Coffee Cup was always noisy and full, but it was the place everyone on that end of campus headed for whenever there was a free minute or two to fill. In retrospect, I think probably one of its greatest assets was its proximity to the cos lab just across the street.

Aerial view of the entire Ferris campus in 1952.
The arrow indicates The Coffee Cup.

The girls in the cos program were, for the most part, a very attractive and impeccably groomed and coiffed bunch of babes. They even managed to look good in their nurse-like white nylon uniforms which were required by the program. Since coloring hair was part of their curriculum, their heads were a rainbow of every conceivable shade, from blondes and reds to frosted brunettes and even blacks so dark as to be nearly purple.

Whenever this flock of colorful clucking hens was released from their "coop," there was always a number of hopeful and interested strutting cocks – er, roosters, maybe? – waiting outside, where they would all blend together and flow streaming across the street to The Cup. Terri and I became a regular part of this scene our last term at Ferris. She even introduced me to a couple of her principal instructors, Mr. Bill Sneden and Mrs. Vivien Wisner, who tried their best to keep some kind of watch over the beautiful, impressionable members of their brightly-plumaged flock. I'm not sure if she made the introductions because she was proud of me. Maybe she did it so they wouldn't think I was stalking her. Whatever her reasons, my heart did another one of those funny little cartwheels and my chest puffed up in pride when she called me her "boyfriend." Holy shit and *halleluia*! I was her *boyfriend*! I could have jumped for joy and clicked my heels, but it's nearly impossible to do that and still look cool, so I was cool – at least on the *out*side.

Bill Sneden and Vivien Wisner

Maybe the best thing about The Coffee Cup was that it was always so crowded between classes. There were never any seats by the time we got inside. People stood packed together in the narrow aisle between the booths and the counter, trying to get one of the waitresses' attention to order a bear claw or a Bismarck and coffee. I would stand pressed against Terri from behind, my arms protectively encircling her. I didn't want anyone else touching her. And to tell the truth I didn't really give a shit if we got a donut or pastry or anything else. I had all I needed right there in my arms. Well, maybe not all I needed, but it would have to do for those few blissful moments.

As the lengthening days of April grew warmer and milder and the last dirty remnants of the winter's snow disappeared, I grew to hate my evening janitor's job at the Science Building. I was acutely aware that Terri was just across the street in her room at Helen Ferris waiting for me, while I was stuck sweeping and emptying waste baskets. When I finished my work early and would pull a stool up to the counter in the janitor's room to try to study, I couldn't concentrate. I would get up and pace the hallway and wander out to the entrance doors and gaze longingly across the street at the Helen Ferris lobby, less than fifty yards away. I think I was subconsciously trying to "will" Terri down the stairs from her room, out the lobby doors and across the street into my arms. I can recall at least one occasion when it seemed to work.

Helen Ferris Hall, Terri's dorm

165

Ed Howe, the head custodian for the building and my boss, had apparently noticed my restlessness when I returned from my Florida trip. I hadn't said anything to him about Terri. What was happening between us seemed much too special and too private to share – especially with Ed, who had a wicked sense of humor and could be something of a randy old rake. He did love to ogle the girls who came and went in his small domain. One soft spring night, as I sat fidgeting at the counter in the janitor's room, scowling at the text for my Contemporary Dramatists course and trying to memorize the names of the plays of Albee, O'Neill and Pirandello, Ed came sidling in the door and grinned at me.

"Hey, Tim," he whispered conspiratorially, "There's a blonde bombshell down at the other end of the hall you've just *got* to see."

Sighing in exasperation, I grimaced and retorted, "*C'mon*, Ed! I ain't got *time*! I gotta learn all this crap for a *test* tomorrow!"

But Ed persisted, his smile widening. "I think you'd better come look, Timmy. She said she was lookin' for *you*."

That got my attention. I jumped off my stool and pushed past Ed and out into the hallway. And there, at the opposite end of the hall, was – and I kid you not, as ol' Jack Paar used to say – a *vision*.

It was my Terri, of course. But there was something so absolutely beautiful and so perfect about that moment, about the way the last rays of the evening sun poured pinkly through the window behind her, creating a kind of roseate halo around her hair and a magical play of light and shadow around her body. I was stunned by her beauty in that singular magical moment, and I can still call that picture up in my mind after all these year, like a three-dimensional softly filtered living snapshot.

There is a line, I think, in *Romeo and Juliet*, where a love struck Romeo espies Juliet from afar and exclaims in wonder. "It is the *sun*. It is my *love*." Well, actually, I've never been much of a Shakespeare scholar (although I have always loved R&J, especially Zeffirelli's film version), so I could be wrong, but it doesn't matter. If old Will never said it, then I'm saying it now. I have called that moment – that epiphany – back up in my mind as I write this. She *was* the sun. She was – *is* – my love.

I stood transfixed in the hallway, and the dumb pole axed look on my face must have been pretty unmistakable, because Ed's tone of voice changed, softened. For once he refrained from using his usual stock of lewd comments. Instead he gave me a small shove and, with a catch in his voice, he growled, "Go on and get outa here. I'll punch your time card out at nine."

I don't think I even thought to thank ol' Ed, as I bolted for my jacket and books, hot footed it down the hall, grabbed my girl and was gone.

There were so many things crammed into those first couple months of our courtship, so many memories being made, that I hardly know where to begin. To call it a "courtship" might be a bit pretentious. Perhaps "hot pursuit" would better describe what happened between us that spring. She was hot, and I was in pursuit. I was the hound and she was the hare. But that's a lousy metaphor. The truth is there was an extremely strong physical attraction between us, a nearly palpable "chemistry," if you will, from the first time we met, and it didn't diminish. Alas, however, I cannot turn this narrative into a sexual potboiler. For one thing, my "censor" will not allow it. For another, the actual "deed" never happened. To quote a recent two-term and impeached president, "I did not have sex with that woman."

Terri was a "good girl." Eight years of schooling at St. Anthony's in Belleville had left its indelible mark on her, just as my nine years of Catholic education had provided me with a lifetime supply of that most cursed of moral commodities – "Catholic guilt." From sixth through eighth grades there was hardly a day that went by that didn't include some admonishment from a nun or a priest regarding the inherent evils of "impure thoughts" and – God forbid – "impure touch." And all this during a time when we boys were just secretly discovering that our dicks could be used for even neater things than writing our names in the snow or winning pissing contests. And I'm pretty sure that girls that age were making similar discoveries of their own about their bodies around the same time. I've always wondered a bit about the propensity of prepubescent and teenage girls to sit in that particularly curious fashion with their legs crossed tightly and that top foot going up and down to beat the band, their faces creased in utter concentration. Was there something sexual going on there, or were they just trying to come up with the correct equation for that next Algebra problem?

In any case, the nuns had done a number on both of us during our formative years, so we both knew that sex without benefit of clergy, as they used to say, was unacceptable and wrong in the eyes of the Church. *My God, where did that come from? It's like I'm quoting from Church doctrine or the Baltimore Catechism!* You see what I mean? Marked for *life*!

So what am I trying to say here without going into any graphic detail? Perhaps just that pre-marital sex back in the sixties could still be fraught with frustration, especially if you were Catholic and had paid any attention at all to what the nuns told you. That didn't make it any less exciting, however. In fact, the taboo nature of all that front-seat and back-seat clutching and groping might have even ratcheted up the excitement level a few notches. After all, we *were* risking the eternal fires of hell – at least if those nuns had been telling us the truth we were. Even so, in the damp heat of the moment, it always seemed worth the risk. So kids, I know you probably don't want to hear this, but the fact of the matter is we were once something more than just your mom and dad – or, more recently (and *halleluia* for this), your Grammy and Grandpa. Yup. We were young once too, and fulla juice and hot to trot. And it was a glorious time in our lives too.

Now that you know that sex is a dangerous and touchy topic in this particular volume, what *can* I talk about?

I've already told you a little about our first "date" and how we *almost* went to the Casa Nova. Well, we finally did get there, just the two of us, a couple weeks after I got back from Florida. And that second time is one of our favorite memories. Well, actually it's more one of *Terri's* favorite memories. My courtship was, admittedly, a poor man's version. Money was always tight in the college years, so many of our early "dates" consisted of driving around or sitting parked in my car, but occasionally I would try to do something special. On this particular night we ended up in a dark booth at the Casa Nova. I ordered a draft and she ordered a Pepsi. While we were waiting for our drinks, I went over to the jukebox and punched in a few of my favorite songs, including "Somethin' Stupid," a recent number one hit by Frank Sinatra and his daughter Nancy. I picked that particular tune for a reason. I had just about worked up the courage by this time to formally declare my love to Terri, and the tag line in the song's chorus is, of course,

"And then I go and spoil it all, By sayin' somethin' stupid like 'I love you.'"

So anyway, as I slid back into the booth opposite Terri, our drinks were delivered. The lights were low, the bowling pins and pinsetters were clattering softly in the background. Frank and Nancy were singing their song. The time seemed right. So, gazing soulfully into her eyes, I reached slowly across the table to take her hand – and knocked over my beer.

SHIT! The beer puddled and flowed quickly off my side of the table, even though I quickly grabbed the glass and righted it, saving at least half of its contents. I had instinctively raised a few inches off the vinyl-covered bench when I grabbed for the glass, and when I sat back down it was directly into a cold puddle of beer. *FUCK!* I remained cool on the outside, however. I really wanted to follow through on this thing. Frank and Nancy were still crooning softly, "And then I go and spoil it all ..." But when I looked back over at Terri, the expression on her face was such a mixture of half-concealed mirth and real alarm at my embarrassment and discomfort, that I wasn't sure what to say. So I sat there, the beer soaking slowly into the seat of my pants, that perfect moment so obviously gone now. By the time we left the bar, my pants completely saturated with beer, we had both managed to see the humor in the situation, which was probably a good thing, because I know I sure must have looked pretty damn ridiculous as I duck-walked, spraddle-legged, across the parking lot, plucking fastidiously at the seat of my trousers, trying to be unobtrusive about extracting the wet material from the crack of my ass. Thus do we both remember one of our first "special" dates. It was "Somethin' Stupid" all right.

* * * * *

22

THE GCG'S OF ROOM 303
AND OTHER FERRIS BEAUTIES

When you finally meet that special someone, you also, necessarily, begin meeting a lot of other people too, people that are special to her, both family and friends. First I started meeting Terri's friends at Ferris.

Terri's roommate when we began dating was a petite brunette from Plymouth named Marsha Stahl. I should probably at least try to be a bit circumspect about how I describe Marsha, but what the hell. Marsha was *gor*geous, with a capital *Gee*! She had long lustrous dark hair she often adorned with colorful headbands and scarves. Her eyes were huge and soulful like the ones you see in those paintings of beautiful waif-like children. She was the kind of girl that just naturally caused whiplash in guys as they did double- and even triple-takes and stared when she walked by. But probably the most attractive thing about Marsha was that she seemed completely clueless and oblivious to her own beauty.

And that wasn't all she was clueless about either. According to Terri, she was also pretty much a total innocent when it came to matters of sex – another "good Catholic girl," naturally. I'm not sure if she stayed that way, because she was dating Larry Miller that term, a notorious Vet's Club Lothario and ladies' man (hey, there's one of those great redundancies, like déjà vu all over again). It seems very likely, however, that her GCG upbringing kept her on the straight and narrow. Sorry, Larry. Join the club.

As a matter of fact, now that I think about it, all of Terri's suite-mates were GCG's. Well, at least they were all raised Catholic. I've already mentioned Marilyn LeRash, who had introduced me to Terri, and was dating Pat O'Connor. She was another very pretty girl, but very probably also a practicing GCG, so Pat was in the same club with Larry and me, no question.

The fourth girl in the suite (two double rooms which shared a common bathroom in between) was Norma Wisniewski, a Polish Catholic like Terri, who was indisputably the most interesting of Terri's friends. Norma, at five ten, was a tall Amazonian bleached blonde with a very bawdy sense of humor and a great laugh, who wasn't afraid to call a spade a spade (or a hoe a hoe – or should that be a ho'?). I really *liked* Norma (and still do). Not too long before I met her, Norma had gone under the knife for an elective rhinoplasty. I never met Norma's real nose, but as far as I was concerned her new one was pretty much perfect, and she was really an impressive babe, with her imposing height, long shining locks, dark eyes, cynical sense of humor, and irrepressible potty-mouth. I won't include Norma in the GCG bunch. Back home in Bay City Norma often clerked in her uncle's drug store, where she daily dispensed such personal items as tampons, douche bags and condoms to the store's clientele, which may have accounted for her rather matter-of-fact savoir faire regarding certain sexual matters. I strongly suspect then that she may have served as the sexual sage and mentor for that clueless gaggle of near-innocents with whom she shared the suite. She was studying commercial art at Ferris. I saw some of her work and she was a natural and talented artist.

There's one more thing I have to share about Norma, just to illustrate her unique sense of humor. While I was researching this book, I asked Norma (and a lot of other folks) for pictures from their Ferris years. Norma was unable to find any photos, so she sent me instead this "Polish haiku" to use in lieu of a picture.

"It came to me in a mist, so to speak," she wrote. "It enveloped me with its sheer genius of form and fit ..."

Cauliflower
farts, in the
shower
Hooh! Rendous!

That's the Norma I remember. Bingo!

Terri's first roommate at Ferris had been a girl named Marilyn Wilcox, another cos major who came from East DeWitt, down by Lansing. As Terri recalls, Marilyn was a girl who liked to party, and chafed under the strict curfew rules of the dorm, so, after the first term was over, she found a room at ground level where she could crawl through a window if she got back after the lobby doors were locked. She shared that first floor room with another cos girl, Pat Rogers, from Evart, who I think also turned up at some of the Vet's Club parties that year.

*Marilyn Wilcox,
Terri's first FSC roommate*

In a room across the hall from the third floor suite Terri shared with her three Catholic roomies were two other strikingly attractive girls whom it was my good fortune to meet that term when they both started dating two other vets.

Rinda Person

Rinda Person was a farm girl of good Swedish stock from Allegan, a natural blonde with a lush figure and a kind of luminous beauty that was such that she gave off a kind of warm glow. Like a lot of genuine blondes, her cheeks were covered with a fine down which may have actually emphasized that inner glow. Rinda started dating John Nibbelink shortly after I met Terri. John, who was a very handsome guy, in a rugged, square-jawed fashion, had not had much luck with girls up until then. He did harbor an unspoken crush on Marsha, but she was already dating Larry Miller, who was John's roommate and one of his best friends at the time. John was much too loyal a friend and too honorable a guy to try to make time with Larry's girl, so one night at a party, depressed and deep in his cups, he pleaded with Marsha to "*please* find me a nice girl, Marsh!" He may have even been lying prone on the floor, falling down drunk, when he made this earnest and heartfelt plea. Within days, Marsha had found him Rinda, and John pretty much quit any serious kind of drinking from that moment on. He was a happy man, even though on their first date, a semi-formal dance the Vets threw at Miller Auditorium in Reed City, Rinda showed up on crutches. She had sprained her ankle, but John was perfectly content to forego dancing that night and simply bask in the reflection of Rinda's tawny golden glow.

Rinda's roommate was Linda Querback, a tiny girl with short brown hair and large mischievous dark eyes. There was a delicate kind of elegance about Linda whose slim figure belied a wiry toughness and a streak of tomboy-ishness. She seemed a perfect match for John Cook, who began dating her that term, because John was definitely the exception to the rule of the typical vet. Around campus he could usually be found in a shirt and tie, often with a sport coat or sweater. There was

Linda Querback

something a bit more sophisticated and cosmopolitan about Cook. Perhaps that explained his instant success on the campus political scene, both within the Vet's Club and later in the student government. I always figured John would make a natural diplomat or politician. In any case, he and Linda Q made a striking couple.

I just noticed that all the girls I've described thus far seem to be cute, gorgeous, beautiful and attractive. You're probably wondering, were *all* the girls at Ferris such babes? Well, it often seemed that way to me, especially my first year, when I was largely on the outside looking in, and didn't really *know* any of these girls. But I don't think my memories of Ferris being chock full of beautiful girls are necessarily far off the mark, particularly when I leaf through the *Ferriscope* yearbooks from those years and see and remember some of the girls I admired from afar, the ones whose

Terri and Marsha. Note the sign – the GCG motto.

PRIVATE KEEP OUT

Marilyn, Terri and Norma. Legs!

Roomies – Marilyn, Marsha and Terri

Clockwise from bottom: Marsha, Linda, Norma, Terri and Rinda in center

Popcorn night – Marsha, Marilyn and Norma, snackin' and snortin'

Linda and Rinda. Oh, those Allegan girls!

pictures were always plastered on posters all over campus around the time of Homecoming and other big social events.

After I started dating Terri, who was a newly pledged Delta Zeta, I actually met some of those girls – girls like Laurie Coburn, a DZ sister, and Linda Hale, a Homecoming Queen who lived, I believe, in Helen Ferris too. And there was Carla Holmgren, Terri's "big sister" in the sorority, whose exotically dark good looks belied her Scandinavian heritage. (Carla was also a Reed City girl, one I had noticed years before, in high school.) Other distant (to me) campus beauties of the era were Sue Gilbert, Rae Derrick, and Sue Hagel. Yup, there really were plenty of pretty girls around Ferris during my scant two years there. I doubt that any of these former beauty queens remember me, but I remember them – the unreachable "glamour queens" who provided the glitz to my college years.

I know, I'm digressing again, and probably in a most unacceptable manner too, daydreaming about girls from way back in the mid-twentieth century, many of whom are undoubtedly grandmothers by now. *Sigh* – the gorgeous Ferris girls of yesteryear. Where are they all now?

* * * * *

Homecoming Queen candidates are: (seated) Sue Hagel, Sue Gilbert, and Mary Burnett, (standing) Sharon Turner, Pat MacDona, Gayle Hardies, Jan Pontz, and Laurie Coburn.

Just a few of the many campus beauties at Ferris in the mid-sixties, every one a "10"

The candidates for 1966 Homecoming Queen are: (SEATED) Toni Hough, Mary Armstrong, Luana Wieland, (STANDING) Rae Marie Derrick, Debbie Husel, Linda Hale, Carolyn Henk, Rita Alter.

177

Miss Helen Wild
Advisor

Trudy Proctor
President

Mary Steiner
Corresponding Secretary

Mary Farnsworth
Recording Secretary

Carla Holmgren
Treasurer

Lynn Strong
Membership Chairman

Donna Slodowske

Donna Roberts

Laurie Colburn

Carol Thiele
Pledge Mistress

Barbara Kern

Donna J. Holmgren

Mary Gower

Patty Knapp

Susan E. Mozac

Marilyn Leroan

Joy Schwartz

Alice Platt

Judy Robinson

Judith Yck

Jean Verheule

Judy Schaner

Grace Fitch

Sandra Tillotson

Betty Jane Francis

Sandra Pray

Marsha Bailey

Barbara Pokone

Sandy Jones

Nancy Meles

Joyce Garrett

Carol A. Meyers

Jeannette Yunker

Jerri Zimmer

179

23

MEETING THE ZIMMERS – WANDA, CHET AND DICK, AND DISCOVERING TERRI'S DARK SECRET

Where the hell was I? Oh yeah, I was meeting Terri's friends. Now I need to talk about meeting her family.

I think I met her mom first, when she drove up to Big Rapids one weekend to attend the annual "hair show" that the cosmetology program presented each year – a kind of "coiffure recital" that gave the cos students a chance to show what they'd learned.Wanda Rose Zimmer (*nee* Bartuzel), a product of Detroit's Polish enclave of Hamtramck, was a tiny auburn-haired woman, just five foot one, but somehow she managed to seem larger that first time I met her. It may have been her low, raspy smoker's voice, but it was probably more the way she was so obviously and boldly sizing me up. It wasn't until sometime later that I heard the story Terri still loves to tell about why she "picked" me. When she had left home for college, she had told her mom that she was tired of feeling bigger than many of her girl friends – and some of the boys too – and pledged to find the biggest guy she could, one who would make her look small. Well, after searching for nearly two years, she had found me, so Wanda was undoubtedly doing a bit of mental measuring when she looked me over at that first meeting. Wanda was a beautician, which I suppose explained Terri's choice of educational program at Ferris, because there was a very close and special bond between mother and daughter. Wanda had waited through the birth of three sons before she finally got her girl, and she loved her only daughter with a mama-lion fierceness that would have given pause to any man who might have designs on her. Well, if anyone had dark designs in mind about Terri, I did, but for some reason Wanda liked me, and I enjoyed her company too during the few hours we all spent together at that first meeting, which could have easily been awkward, but wasn't.

In the weeks that followed I would meet other members of the Zimmer clan. In those days, Ferris was often referred to as a "suitcase college," because a large number of the students, especially the "downstate" ones, packed up and headed home for the weekends. There was a "ride board" on the wall in the Student Center where kids posted their names, telephone numbers and destinations, in hopes of either getting rides or – if they owned cars – riders to share fuel costs. Terri was one of those students who tried to get home on weekends whenever she could. After we started dating she stayed on campus during the weekends, but I could tell she missed her mom, so after a couple weeks I agreed to take off from work and drive her home.

On one of our first trips to Belleville, we stopped off to visit Tom and Charlotte Gordon, friends of mine. Tom and I had been in the army together in Germany and had kept in touch after he and Charlotte were married. At the time we visited them, they were renting a tiny house in Troy, and had just recently adopted a St. Bernard puppy. At several months old, however, Freckles was already a hundred pounds or more of mischief. While teething, he had left his mark on nearly every piece of furniture the Gordons owned, including the centerpiece of their small living room, an elegant oak finish home entertainment center that held a TV and stereo system. All the corners and edges of this once-lovely piece of furniture had been gnawed down to splintered raw wood. But Freckles was a lovable lug, constantly smiling his big dorky doggy smile and flinging drool in all directions whenever he shook himself, and always trying to climb into your lap whenever you sat down. Tom shut the dog in their back room while we went shopping at a nearby mall, having carefully spread newspapers all over the floor. When we returned a few hours later, the floor was awash in a large lake of puppy piddle. Poor Freckles hadn't been able to hold it, and was obviously quite ashamed of himself, so Tom couldn't really get mad at him. It was an odd and interesting visit, both as a peek into the marital bliss of the still-newlywed Gordons, and also into the joys of pet ownership. I was proud to show Terri off to Tom and Char though, and they enjoyed meeting her, and were gracious if somewhat dog-harried hosts.

That same weekend I met Terri's father for the first time. Chet Zimmer was a gruff but friendly-enough guy with a firm masculine handshake. He was a trim and fit-looking fifty-six, a former Golden Gloves boxer. At an even six feet he had to look up at me, but that didn't seem to bother him. He was a confident, self-made man who had completed only six years of school back in the steel-mill town of Wierton, West Virginia, where he'd grown up. The rest of his schooling was of the practical experience and hard knocks variety. His name had originally been Ziembowicz, but when he and his brothers had emigrated to the Detroit area in the thirties to find work in the auto plants, they were constantly and cruelly harassed and teased about their name and Polish heritage. They were forever battling and brawling to defend themselves over such ethnic slurs and insults as, "Zimbuvitch, sumbitch." So in the late thirties the Ziembowicz brothers went together to a Detroit courthouse and had their name legally changed to Zimmer – just in time for the war with Germany. Sometimes, you just can't win.

So Chet came up the hard way in life and was proud of it. When I first met him he was a scheduling supervisor at Ford's River Rouge steel plant. I often wonder if Wanda softened him up some before I met him, by telling him something to the effect that *Treva really likes this boy, so you'd better be nice to him*. But probably not. Chet was a very friendly and gregarious sort naturally, and was also impressed with the fact that I'd been in the army, and regaled me with a few stories about his own "service" time in the Civilian Conservation Corps during the Depression.

I know. I know. You're probably thinking, hey, wait a minute, back up. Who's "Treva"?

Sorry, Dear. It's time to reveal your "secret identity."

The first time I visited the Zimmer home, there was some immediate initial confusion, at least on my part, over Terri's name. It seemed her given Christian name (but *is* it a *Christian* name?)

was Treva – Treva Jean Zimmer. She was named after one of her mother's best friends, Treva Sobecki. Somewhere around the onset of puberty, young Treva Jean apparently decided her given name was a "stoopid" name. No one had ever *heard* of that name! So, by the time she made the transition from St. Anthony's Catholic school to Belleville High School, she had unilaterally declared herself no longer Treva, but Terri, a much more modern and infinitely more chic moniker than that awful ol' hokey name that her parents had chosen so carefully to honor her mother's friend.

Lots of kids re-invent themselves when they start high school, or at least try to. It's part of growing up and trying to distance yourself from your folks and be your own person. My oldest brother Richard, who was always "Rich" in our family, mysteriously morphed into "Dick Bazzett" when he got to high school. But he was always still Rich at home. Well, the same thing happened with Treva/Terri. There were of course the normal small glitches and confusions that always accompany a name change. Her parents and her brothers of course refused to acknowledge the change. At home she was still Treva, or Treve. As a matter of fact, she probably would have been shocked if any of them had called her anything else. (Actually, her brothers did have a few other much more uncomplimentary names they sometimes tormented her with, which we won't go into here.) Her classmates from St. Anthony's mostly ignored her name change too, which is understandable. And the people who did acknowledge her as Terri – her new high school friends – had to be continually reminded that it was "Terri with an 'i', *not* 'y'." And the fact that one of her high school boyfriends was named Terry didn't help matters either.

But *enough*! "Terri" has now been officially "outed" as Treva. It took me a couple of years to start calling her Treve, like the rest of her family, and during those two years or so I always felt faintly like an outsider whenever we visited Belleville. It's been hard for me to call her Terri in the narrative thus far, because she's been just Treve to me for over thirty-five years now. HOWEVER – I will accede to her wishes in continuing to call her Terri for the purposes of this story. To her, Treva is still a private family-only kind of name. Are you confused yet? Good, I thought so. Imagine what it was like for *me* then – even *after* we were married. (Note to the kids: Don't worry. Terri *aka* Treva is still just Mom or Grammy to you.)

Terri had three older brothers: Don, Bob and Dick. (Her dad was fond of telling people that if he had known he would have three boys in a row he'd have just named them "Tom, Dick and Harry.") Don and Bob were already married and gone when I met Terri. Both had graduated from Michigan State. Don had also completed Law School at Wayne State and was an attorney in Charlotte. Bob was an assistant park manager at a state park up near Traverse City.

Dick, the youngest of the boys (and thankfully spared from being "Harry"), was still living at home and working as a mechanic at a local service station and garage. He had already gained something of a reputation in southeast Michigan on the auto-racing circuit, and also dabbled in motorcycles. A few months younger than me, Dick Zimmer personified the strong silent type, and, with his dark good looks and ever-smoldering cigarette, was the epitome of indifferent "cool," a kind of cross between Robert Mitchum and James Dean. I was never sure if Dick consciously cultivated this image or if it just came naturally, but it obviously worked, because there was always a bevy of good-looking Belleville babes waiting in line to have Dick "change their oil," if you know what I mean. Dick and I never had much in common, which is not surprising, since I have always been mechanically challenged and klutzy with girls. But he was always pleasant enough to me, perhaps hoping I would be the one to finally remove his little sister from the household, thus freeing up more bathroom time for the rest of the family.

In any case, I was made to feel welcome in the Zimmer household from my very first visit, although their dinner times took a little getting used to. I had been raised in a house where Mom was always home and supper was usually served at 5:30 sharp every night, or shortly after Dad got home from work. Well, this wasn't the case at the Zimmers, where Chet often worked overtime hours at Ford, and Wanda sometimes didn't get through at Madeline's Beauty Shop until after six, and then went grocery shopping at the A&P, so it wasn't unusual to eat supper as late as 8 PM. But what *sumptuous* suppers came out of Wanda's kitchen! T-bone or Delmonico steaks with French fries and salads. As someone raised mostly on burgers and beans, those steaks were a rare and delicious treat for me, like restaurant meals with all the comforts of home, since we often ate on TV trays in the living room.

* * * * *

24

FAMILY STORIES
AND A CAUTIONARY TALE

I'm pretty sure that I met Terri's family – or most of it – before she met mine. Since my folks lived much closer to Ferris, a mere twelve miles up 131 in Reed City, it may seem odd to some that I didn't bring her right home to meet the parents. But I think most guys will probably remember how, when they first met that special girl that they thought just could be *the* one, they initially felt very territorial and overprotective about her. They didn't want any other males nosing around her for one thing. And when it comes to introducing this special girl to your family it can become very touchy, because sometimes families – i.e. *parents* – have their own favorite special little stories and anecdotes or small tidbits of biographical data that you'd rather not have your girl know, at least not at this early and still very delicate stage of your relationship.

For example, one of the "cute" stories my dad used to like to tell to company about my childhood was about the time when I was around three years old and I got over-excited or tickled too hard while playing with my older brothers one evening and had an "accident." I was so ashamed that I went and hid behind the door of the bedroom I shared with my brother Bob. (I should probably add here that since I was already nearly as big as Bob, who is only 16 months older than me, we also shared most of the clothes in our chest of drawers.) I didn't show up at the table when Mom called us all to supper, so she came looking for me and found me crouching behind the door.

A strong smell of ammonia must have given me away, because in a gently admonishing tone of voice, Mom asked, "Why, *Tim*, did you wet your pants?"

Retreating farther into the dark crevice behind the door, I hung my head. "No," I replied in a small voice.

"Now don't lie about it," Mom persisted. "I can smell it from here. You did *too* wet your pants!"

"I did not!" I insisted. "These are *Bob's* underpants!"

With each re-telling of this cutesy bit of family lore, Dad or Mom would chuckle fondly in remembrance. But, as you might well understand, when you're twenty-three years old and an army veteran, for cripes sake, you don't particularly want this kind of tale trotted out when you bring home your best girl for the first time, anymore than you'd want her to know, say, that you had still sucked your thumb on occasion when your were twelve years old.

Families can be wonderfully insensitive to such subtle nuances which could easily damage or even ruin a delicate, early-stage romance. My folks didn't sabotage my budding romance with Terri though. They waited a few more years to tell her some of these charming family tales. But I wanted to say here, just for the record, that I understand completely why our own son, Scott, was so slow and reluctant in bringing *his* future bride, Kathy, home to "meet the parents," and why, when he finally *did* bring her home, he kept her closeted and cloistered away from us and from his brother as much as possible. Probably a pretty smart move, Scott.

The day in early May when I brought Terri home with me for the first time my mom wasn't home. She was attending an overnight or weekend retreat, or *cursillo*, at St. Philip's School. As we came into town from the south, I could see a tall column of smoke rising into the sky from the hill where we lived, on West Church. During the previous week, Dad had contracted with someone to tear down my grandparents' old farm house next door to our place. The job had been completed and most of the debris had been hauled away. What was left had been pushed into the old cellar and Dad was burning it that day. A bulldozer was coming on Monday to cover over whatever was left.

When Terri and I drove up the driveway we saw Dad sitting in a lawn chair several feet back from the blaze, a garden hose at the ready on the ground nearby as a safety precaution. He got up and came over to greet us as we rolled to a stop in front of the garage. He hands were blackened with soot from tending the fire and his face was reddened from the heat. I introduced Terri to Dad and explained, in as casual a tone as I could muster, that I just wanted to show her around town and where I lived and stuff, and we weren't going to stay very long. Dad nodded agreeably, apologized for his dirty hands, and told us to make ourselves at home, his eyes wide and his mouth just a bit ajar as he took in Terri's flaxen blonde hair, friendly smile and lush young body. I think I know, at least *gen*erally, what he was thinking: *Holy* crap*! How did our Tim hook up with a babe like this*? I know this because the apple really *doesn't* fall far from the tree, and I'd been thinking the same thing myself ever since I'd first met Terri, but I had finally managed to close my mouth and maintain some small semblance of cool in the face of my great good fortune.

When we came into the house, my sixteen year-old sister, Mary, was sitting at the dining room table with a textbook and spiral notebook open in front of her. Arrayed in a neat row next to her notes were five Milkbone dog biscuits of varying colors. Our dog Runt was nowhere in sight, but as Mary turned to look at us, we were both startled to see her take a delicate bite of a sixth biscuit – a green one, I think. Probably a veggie flavor. I have no idea why Mary was nibbling kibble. She wasn't fat, so I don't think it was some sort of weird diet. And she wasn't a bow-wow sort of girl either. I mean I was her brother, and even *I* thought she was reasonably attractive. In any case, Terri still remembers this, Mary. You know what they say about first impressions.

This reminds me of a story. (Digression alert!) It concerns this elderly woman – I'll call her Mrs. Poopleheimer – who lived in a small town where everyone knew each other. For several weeks, the check-out clerk in the supermarket had been noticing that she was buying canned dog food every week, but he had never seen a dog in the Poopleheimer's yard.

Finally his curiosity got the best of him and he commented to her, "Gee, Edna, I didn't know you and George had a dog."

Looking perplexed, Mrs. Poopleheimer replied, "Why, we *don't* have a dog."

"Then why are you buying dog food every week?"

Brightening, Edna quickly explained, "Well, you know beef has become rather expensive lately, and I've found I can make meatloaf and casseroles from this dog food, and George just *loves* it."

Shocked, the grocery clerk responded, "Gosh, Edna, I don't think that's a very good idea. This stuff is formulated for dogs, and might not be very healthy for people."

Mrs. Poopleheimer pooh-poohed the clerk's warning and told him that was nonsense. Then a few weeks went by when Edna didn't show up at all for her regular shopping. Finally, one day she returned, dressed in black and looking quite bereft. The clerk commented that he hadn't seen her in quite a while, whereupon Mrs. P explained sadly that her George had passed away. The clerk was quick to offer his condolences, but then he couldn't resist noting that he *had* warned her about the possible hazards of feeding her husband dog food and how it could even possibly be toxic to humans.

Poor Edna looked confused for a moment, then exclaimed, "Oh, *no*. George *loved* that meatloaf. It didn't have anything to do with *that*. No, it was just a freak accident. One night after supper he was all happy and curled up on the couch, and he was just twisting himself around trying to lick his balls like he always did, and he fell off the couch and broke his neck."

So, Mary, if you ever still have cravings for dog treats, remember the cautionary tale of poor George Poopleheimer.

Terri also met my "little" brother, Chris, that day. At fourteen, Chris was already nearly as tall as I was, gangly and pimply and painfully shy (just as I had been at that age), but he managed to mumble a greeting when I introduced him. We didn't stay very long. I showed Terri around the house a bit, and she was quite impressed with its six bedrooms and three baths. The house, built in 1960, was still quite new and my folks were justly proud of it. With its innovative "radiant" heating system, it had been the first "all-electric" house in town. And after more than twenty years of marriage and six kids, they finally had a house spacious enough to spread out in a bit. Of course by 1967, Rich, Bill and Bob had already moved out for good, so the house seemed even bigger than when we'd first moved in.

By early May then, we had met each other's families and were both still infatuated with each other, perhaps at this stage in love with the "idea" of being in love. But I think it was more than that even then.

* * * * *

An abbreviated Bazzett family in 1966;
l-r: Chris (with Runt), Mom, Mary Jane and me. (Dad probably took the picture.)

25

PROPOSITIONS AND PROPOSALS

Probably at least some of you have watched the HBO series, *Sex and the City*, considered by all the TV pundits and entertainment experts to be very hip and on the cutting edge of current cultural trends, particularly when it comes to dating and the ongoing mysteries of the differences between men and women and how they think. We've never subscribed to HBO, but all the old episodes of *Sex and the City* are now in syndication on TBS. Terri has become addicted to this show, and I will blushingly admit to having sat through a few episodes myself. (Do women *really* talk like that among themselves?) Anyway, recently I watched an episode that has apparently become legend among today's twenty- and thirty-somethings, and even spawned a best-selling book last year. It was called *He's Just Not That Into You*. The premise of the show – and the book too – was basically that if a guy is truly interested in a woman, he's going to *be* there with her, all the time, and he's going to want to have sex all the time. Well, this may be a twenty-first century TV show, but that is definitely *not* a new idea. My story – this book – is, after all, about events that transpired nearly forty years ago, and I am here to tell you that even *waaay* back then, in the ol' twentieth century, I definitely wanted to *be* with Terri every minute of the day, and thought about her all the time when we were apart. I also definitely *wanted* to have sex with her all the time, to *know* her in the Biblical sense. Unfortunately for me, alas and alack, Terri was a well-indoctrinated GCG, as I have already noted, and those eternal fires of hell and the sad and disappointed face of Jesus still lurked somewhere in her subconscious and served very well to keep her panties firmly in place.

So my siege continued apace. I had to somehow up the stakes, so I cast blunderingly about for new arguments and strategies with which to further my case, because I really did want to beeeee with this girl in the worst way – worst in *every* sense of the word.

Here's the strategy I finally hit upon. Well, "hit upon" is probably a bit misleading, since it implies clear, logical, well-reasoned thinking, and I don't think I was even capable of that, what with my blood constantly rushing south and my brain turned to testosterone-impaired oatmeal. But it was the *sixties*, for cripes sake, supposedly an era of flower children and free love, of loosening morals and an if-it-feels-good-*do*-it ethic. In the books and movies of the time, college kids were always moving in together and setting up housekeeping. It all looked so easy. We could do that, *couldn't* we?

It was the middle of May, and Terri and I were both painfully aware that our final term at Ferris was drawing quickly to a close. She knew I was planning to transfer to Central Michigan in the fall. Her own plans following graduation were not that clear. Maybe she'd get work at Madeline's where her mom was, but she wasn't really sure. Since she had no definite plans after Ferris, I figured the time was right to make my "proposition."

I had taken Friday night and Saturday off from work so I could drive Terri home to Belleville for the weekend. That Saturday night we sat up late after her folks had gone to bed. Her brother Dick was out with friends for the evening. We were, for all practical purposes, alone. After one of our usual sessions of impassioned necking and heavy petting, we had finally come up for air, gasping with a mix of pleasure and frustration. We were sitting in the kitchen having a post-midnight snack of leftover pizza and Cokes when I first broached the subject of "our future." I told her haltingly how I didn't think I could stand going to Central all by myself; that I couldn't bear the thought of not seeing her every day the way we had been ever since I'd gotten back from Florida. Terri looked sad and miserable and her eyes began to fill with tears. That's *good*! I thought. So I *went* for it. I suggested that it didn't have to be that way; that she could come with me to Central; that we could get a place of our own there and stay together, and never be apart again. At least I *think* that's a pretty good approximation of what I said that night.

Terri's face immediately brightened, and she asked, her eyes still glistening with tears, "Are you asking me what I *think* you're asking?"

A little confused, I smiled hesitatingly and replied, "Well, er, sure. What do you think I'm *asking*?"

Throwing her arms around my neck, Terri gave me a quick kiss on the lips and exclaimed, "Oh, *yes*! *Yes*! Of *course* I'll marry you. I *love* you!" And she buried her face in my shoulder, her tears, now tears of *hap*piness, flowing freely and soaking the front of my shirt.

Now really confused and maybe even a bit panicked, I was probably thinking something like, *Hang on. Wait a minute, wh-, what did I ... But I didn't mean ... Aahh, what the hell ...* Because, as any dolt can see, had I chosen at this tender moment to try to backpedal and explain the subtle difference between a proposition and a proposal, I would have revealed myself to be nothing less than a total bastard, and I'm pretty sure I'm not one, so I kept my mouth shut, returned her joyful heartfelt embrace, and found myself murmuring wonderingly into her hair, "I love you too, Sweetheart." And at that moment I suddenly realized I was telling the truth. I. Loved. This. Woman.

The kitchen was lit only by a small nightlight plugged into the wall above the table. The radio on the counter was tuned to CKLW's top forty station in Windsor, the volume turned low. Tommy James and the Shondells were singing their latest hit, "I Think We're Alone Now." Terri and I had known each other exactly two months and we were engaged. Somehow, in my own inimitable bumbling fashion, I had just won the biggest prize of my life, and, although I was still perhaps more than a bit dazed and confused, I suddenly felt like the luckiest guy on the face of the earth. I was twenty-three years old. Terri was nineteen.

* * * * *

26

A GOOBER GETS ENGAGED

Twenty-three and nineteen. By today's standards, getting married at those ages would probably be considered most ill-advised, or maybe just criminally stupid. In 1967 though, we were probably pretty average, and not just in terms of age, but also in our blissful ignorance and our total unpreparedness for marriage. At the time I never thought of us as too young to be married. Why would I? Most of my married friends had started even younger. I didn't have to look any further than Keith and Dianne Eichenberg, who had been just twenty and eighteen when they married, and were, as far as I could tell, living the proverbial "happily ever after." And there were Donnie and Mary Ellen Dobson, Terry and Molly Karnitz and Bruce and Sherry Jensen. And my army buddies, Tom Gordon and Larry Sanders, were both married already. All of these people had married at very young ages and seemed to be quite happy and managing just fine.

I think I may have immediately begun marshaling all these arguments in my mind as soon as I awoke the next morning, figuring there would be some resistance to this marriage, certainly from Terri's parents, who had only just met me, after all, and maybe from mine too.

I needn't have worried. Wanda was all smiles when I came downstairs that morning and greeted me with a warm hug and a kiss and congratulated me. Apparently Terri had been unable to save her big news until morning. After I had gone to bed, my mind still reeling, she had awakened her mom and excitedly poured out her news of my "proposal," and the two of them had sat up talking about it long after I was asleep.

I guess Wanda had relayed the news to Chet, because he too congratulated me with a firm, manly handshake. Then, nodding meaningfully toward Terri, he said, "I hope you know what you're getting into. Treva can be quite a handful."

I responded soberly, gripping Chet's hand, nodding and looking him in the eye with my most responsible adult look. "Thank you, sir. Yes, sir." (My army training.) What I was thinking – what I couldn't help thinking – was, *I can't wait to get into her, to get my hands full of her*. When the sap is running high and strong in the springtime, lust springs eternal, even in the most serious of situations.

Before Terri and I packed up to return to Ferris that afternoon, we were part of a brief informal family conference held in the living room to talk about our "plans." *Plans? What plans?* Hell, I had just somehow managed to get myself *engaged*. I was still trying vainly to figure out how *that* had happened. When would I have had time to make any *plans*? But it seemed like everyone – even Terri – was looking to *me* to get this discussion started.

The first thing I managed to realize was that I needed to somehow get my mind off from Terri's breasts and bottom and onto a "plan."

"Umm," I began hesitatingly, "You mean like *when* we want to get married?"

All three heads nodded in unison, and Terri looked distinctly proud of my mental acuity. I figured I must be on the right track. This was encouraging. Now if I could just come up with an actual plan. My mind racing, I tried to remember how I'd gotten into this fix, what I might have said to Terri last night when I'd propositioned, er, I mean *proposed* to her. Oh yeah, it was coming back to me – September, and going to Central alone, or something like that. But not September. That was when fall term started and I'd already have to *be* there then, right?

"Umm, well, I was thinking, like maybe *August*?"

Both Wanda's and Chet's brows furrowed in unison, and they exchanged troubled meaningful looks. Wanda shook her head slowly, and Chet let out a long slow breath, and then said, "I don't know, Tim. That's awfully soon. And you kids have really just met.

I was thinking you probably should wait a little longer than that, so you can have time to get to know each other a little better. Maybe *next* summer would be better."

Wanda had been nodding right along with Chet until he mentioned next summer and saw how both Terri's and my faces fell, then she jumped right in to try to make repairs, just as Treve wailed in response, "*Daddy!*"

"Maybe a whole year isn't really necessary, Chet," she said, patting Terri's arm. "I think six months might be reasonable though. What would you kids think about that? I know *we* would feel better if you took at least that long to think things over, and it would probably take at least that long to organize the wedding and reception and all."

With Terri's pleading look trained on me, I did some panicky mental calculations about the six-month suggestion now on the table. There was a long uncomfortable silence while I tried desperately to remember what month it was. Finally it came to me – *May! It was still May, yeah, May. Lemme see* – mental finger counting …

"You mean like, umm, No*vem*ber?" I asked.

Wanda's brow smoothed, and she nodded brightly. Chet still had a stern look on his craggy face, probably already trying to mentally calculate how much all this was going to cost him, but he stayed silent.

I looked to Terri and asked, "Well, I don't know. What do you think, hon?" (And that may have been my very first "hon," as in "Honey." My *God*, I already sounded married.)

Her brow now slightly furrowed, Terri nodded slowly. "I guess November would be all right," she replied, none too enthusiastically. "If it's okay with you."

Now it was my turn to nod slowly, and if I looked at all reluctant or glum about this "longer" engagement, I don't think anyone noticed. It was settled. Wanda and Terri immediately got up to go consult the kitchen calendar and start looking at dates and making tentative plans. My input was no longer needed, a situation, and a "feeling," which would persist over the next six long months as the snowball that wedding plans are began to roll, growing larger and heavier with every revolution.

I was already learning new stuff. I didn't get my preferred August wedding. I would have to go to Central by myself after all come fall. But at least we wouldn't have to wait for a whole year. We had split the difference. Welcome to being half of a couple, Bazzett, and to a whole new world – a world called "compromise."

The next day was a Monday. I had gotten home very late the night before, having finally deposited Terri at the dorm doors, following a prolonged period of passionate petting and excited planning for the big event. Well, actually I was the petter and she was the planner. Every time we came up for air she would begin babbling excitedly about things like bridesmaids and flowers and churches and caterers, all of which is very distracting when a guy is just trying to feel as much flesh as is possible in a parked car right in front of the dorm. We were both pretty flushed with excitement (although probably for quite different reasons) by the time Terri finally slipped into the lobby under the distinctly disapproving glare of Mrs. Megowen, her housemother, who was waiting to lock the doors.

So I was still rubbing sleep out of my eyes when I came upstairs early the next morning to bolt some breakfast before heading back to campus for classes and work again. Mom was already in the kitchen packing lunches for me and Dad, who was still shaving. While I was fixing my Wheaties, Mom asked me how my weekend in Belleville had gone. The few remaining cobwebs of sleep quickly vanished at Mom's question, as I suddenly remembered the confusing welter of events of the last couple days. Oh yeah, I was engaged, and should probably tell Mom and Dad.

"Pretty good," I mumbled. "I sort of, I mean we kind of, umm, got engaged, Terri and me."

Mom put down the bread and the butter knife and turned to face me, her eyes wide. "You got *engaged*?"

Pouring milk over my cereal and feeling suddenly a bit panicky, I nodded my head. "Yup. We did."

Apparently at a loss for words, Mom, who hadn't even met Terri yet, finally managed to say, "Why, that's *won*derful! I had no idea things were that *serious*! Do you *love* her, then?"

I continued to nod stupidly, a moronic grin creeping across my face. "Yup. I do. Yup."

I can't remember if my mom hugged me at this point. I know it would certainly have been a natural thing to do at this kind of a momentous announcement, and she may well have, but we were not really a hugging family, so maybe she just hugged herself or something. In any case, there was certainly no mistaking the excitement in her voice and her face. She was absolutely beaming as she congratulated me warmly. I was immediately relieved; I could even feel myself relaxing from a tension I hadn't even acknowledged until that moment.

Mom followed me over to the table where I sat down to eat my cereal. "Did you give her a ring then?" she asked brightly.

The tension came tangoing back in, and I sat suddenly erect in my chair, dripping cereal-and-milk-laden spoon suspended in front of my open mouth. *Ring? Of course, ring, you moron! When you get engaged, you give the girl a ring! Everybody knows that!*

The Simpsons weren't around yet in 1967, but I'm pretty sure it wasn't Homer Simpson who first came up with his trademark expression, *DOH!* Nope, it was me. *I* did, right there at the breakfast table that morning. *In*side I was saying *DOH!* On the *out*side though, I just said, "No. I mean, not yet. But I will, as soon as I can save enough money."

Mom nodded thoughtfully, her brow furrowed, thinking.

I hurriedly gobbled down my cereal and went back downstairs to my basement bedroom to gather my books and papers and brush my teeth. By the time I got back upstairs to leave, Mom had retreated to her back bedroom to get dressed, but there on the dining room table beside my brown bag lunch were five wrinkled twenty-dollar bills with a short note in Mom's neat precise handwriting. It read simply: "A girl should have a ring. Love, Mom & Dad."

That was my mom, the first woman I had ever loved and whose love for me I had never questioned, graciously and selflessly handing me over to this "other woman" whom I had chosen. It was certainly a leap of faith for Mom, since, as I said, she had never met this girl, but I guess she must have trusted me to pick a winner.

Of course Dad must have approved too, and he had met Terri, and may have even been guilty of a little subtle ogling of the goods. And they both knew that she was Catholic, an extremely important point in those days. A Catholic boy should marry a Catholic girl.

Therefore, beautiful blonde babe (Dad), plus good Catholic girl (Mom), apparently equaled a parental stamp of approval. Thank God! And thank you too, Mom and Dad.

Because I can't honestly remember if I ever did properly thank them – or if I ever paid the money back either. Probably not. My head and my heart were too full of myself and my brand-new fiancée that May morning, so I grabbed up my lunch, took the money and ran. I couldn't wait to get my stupid self back to Big Rapids, find my girl, and head for the nearest jewelry store to buy her a rock, and make this engagement *official*!

A ring! *Damn straight, Mom. A girl should have a ring!*

* * * * *

27

BUYING THE RING
AND TELLING THE WORLD

That afternoon I got a short and fast education in economics and engagement rings. I was waiting for Terri at her dorm when she came back from classes. As soon as she came up the walk, I took her arm and said, "Come on. We're going shopping."

Looking a bit startled, she asked, "What do you mean? What for?"

"For a ring," I said. "You should have a ring."

"A ring?"

"An engagement ring," I clarified.

Terri's face was a study in uncertainty, excitement, confusion and trepidation as I helped her into the car and threw her books in the back seat. I got behind the wheel, backed out of the parking slot and headed up the street between Masselink and the Automotive Center, then turned left up Ives, heading for town. Obviously, buying "the ring" was somehow scarier than the actual acceptance of a marriage proposal. A ring made it more real. The deal would be "set in stone," so to speak, once she had a ring on her finger. She hadn't even had forty-eight hours yet to get used to the idea of being engaged. As I was nosing the VW into a parking spot in front of Whalen's bar on Michigan then, she began to protest mildly, perhaps only just beginning to realize that her life was about to change forever, and that events were spinning rapidly out of her control. What about the plans she and Marsha had made to go to

Mackinac Island for the summer and get waitressing jobs and have *fun*, just as they had the previous summer when they had gone to Florida together for two weeks where they had stayed with Terri's Aunt Stella in Sarasota and baked on the beach and checked out all the guys? On a very subconscious level she was probably thinking, *What about my youth? What about all the things I'd planned to do? What about meeeeee?*

On the surface, however, all she could manage was a mild, "Honey, you don't have to get me a ring yet. We can wait a while."

But I was unswayed. My billfold bulging with Mom's money, I was a man with a mission. A girl should have a ring.

Of course I knew nothing about diamonds or engagement rings or jewelry in general. Nada. Zilch. Absolutely clueless. So the first store we went into, Rogers Jewelry, was a classic case of sticker shock, at least for me. We told the saleswoman we were shopping for an engagement ring. She congratulated us warmly, and obligingly pulled out a velvet-lined tray of rings for our perusal and stood politely by as Terri looked the selection over, making all the appropriate girl-noises and oooh's and aaah's. Terri removed a couple rings from their slots and tried them on. The saleslady explained the various finishes and cuts and carat values. Finally I couldn't keep my mouth shut any longer and began inquiring after the prices of each ring. Well, the one Treve was admiring at the moment turned out to be priced at something like $595. *Holy Crap*! I almost dropped my teeth. My first *car* had only cost $600! My mouth must have fallen open in horror, because Terri glanced back at me with a worried look. So I began asking then about prices on some of the smaller more modest-looking rings until we'd worked our way down to the least expensive of the lot, which was still $150. My education was continuing apace.

After what I considered a decent interval of looking over a few more rings, I took Terri's arm and told the saleslady we'd think about it and might be back, then steered Terri back out onto the sidewalk on Maple Avenue. As we turned the corner back onto Michigan I explained, I suspect rather shamefacedly, that I only had a little over a hundred dollars and couldn't really afford any of those rings we'd been looking at.

Terri was a trooper. She patted my arm consolingly and said it didn't matter, and that she'd really meant it when she said she didn't need to have a ring right now. Perhaps she viewed this revelation of my relative poverty as a temporary reprieve from making this frighteningly permanent commitment. But I don't think so. I didn't know her that well yet at the time, but I have since learned that my girl is one of the most kind-hearted and compassionate people you will every meet. She was genuinely concerned at my disappointment and embarrassment.

As we walked south on Michigan in the bright May sunshine, I saw two stores up ahead. On our side of the street was Woolworth's, a place where I'd eaten lunch a number of times and sometimes thumbed through their records in the music department. I thought briefly and longingly of their costume jewelry counter where I knew you could get a perfectly nice-looking ring for ten or fifteen bucks. Then I quickly put these cheapskate and most ungallant thoughts from my mind. We crossed the street at the corner of Michigan and Elm and went into the darkened, tastefully decorated interior of Emil's Jewelry.

This time, armed with the new knowledge of my meager financial means, Terri went directly to the ring display with the most modest-looking pieces, where we immediately found three rings in the hundred dollar range. After briefly pondering this small selection, she chose one with a gold Florentine finish and a miniscule diamond, which I usually characterize as an "umpteenth" of a carat, but she insists is probably at least an eighth of a carat.

Today's readers might wonder why I didn't just go ahead and get her a decent-sized rock and finance it. But buying things on credit was not nearly as common a practice in 1967 as it is today. It would have been possible, but the truth is, I was always horrified at the thought of buying things I couldn't pay for up front, and I was already making payments to my dad on the Volkswagen, so I simply couldn't con*ceive* of making payments on something else at the same time. After all, you couldn't *drive* a diamond ring, or *live* in it. It was just *jewelry*, for cripes sake! I may have been a romantic, but by God I was a *practical* romantic. Yes, a girl should have a ring, but a ring shouldn't equate to a millstone of debt around a guy's neck.

The ring that Terri selected was a perfect fit right out of the case. I wanted her to put it on and start wearing it right then, but she dissuaded me. She had a plan. That coming Saturday was the Delta

EMIL'S JEWELRY

Corner of Michigan and Elm

An ad for Emil's Jewelry from 1970. I probably still couldn't have afforded that ring.

Zeta spring dance, and she wanted to officially announce her engagement and unveil the ring at that function and take advantage of the small pomp and ceremony that such an occasion entailed within the sorority. I reluctantly agreed to her plan, even though I really wanted that ring on her finger right then. It may not have been a big impressive rock, but it represented to me that somewhat selfish symbol of "ownership" that guys associate with engagement rings. *See that ring? It means that this girl is already spoken for. She is mine!* It was – *is* – a custom only slightly more evolved than the branding of cattle.

So with the ring safely ensconced in a small deep blue velvet box and tucked into Terri's purse, we emerged from Emil's, engaged. The smile on my girl's face and her arm tucked tightly under mine as we made our way back up the street made me feel like a millionaire, empty pockets and wallet notwithstanding. Bolstered by the arrogance and confidence that only the very young possess, the warm sunshine and soft spring breeze that afternoon all seemed to belong to us and to us alone. We had no idea what the future held for us, and we didn't care. We were in love.

I am so thankful for a couple of now-precious photographs taken by my mom later that week, because I could never begin to adequately describe how beautiful my Terri was that Saturday night when I picked her up at her dorm for the DZ ball. She was wearing a white, high-necked long formal with a pale-blue sash and long white dress gloves that extended up past her elbows, and also served to conceal the secret of our engagement until the appropriate moment later in the evening. Her skin was already a delicate honey-brown hue, the result of several afternoons of sun-bathing on the concrete apron or the lawn behind the dorm with her roommates. Her new tan blended and contrasted perfectly with her carefully

Terri and me the night of the DZ Spring Dance, where Terri announced our engagement. Ain't she just flat-out gorgeous?!

teased flaxen-blonde bouffant hairdo, a frosted pink lipstick and her deep brown eyes. I was literally stunned when I saw her that night coming down the stairs and into the lobby of Helen Ferris Hall. I felt like such a totally unworthy goober in my three year-old suit and too-short tie, as I helped her with the wrist corsage I had brought for the occasion, a spray of tiny pink tea roses tied with a pale blue ribbon.

After tucking this vision in white – *my girl*, by God! – carefully into the front seat of the Bug, I steered north up 131 to Reed City, where I proudly displayed her to my parents. Never had I been more acutely aware of just what an incredibly lucky slob I was. Looking at those pictures again today, and then at the woman this girl has become, I still feel the same. I am one lucky guy. Thank you, Lord. Life is a crapshoot and I just keep on winning.

That night at the DZ dance our engagement became official in the eyes of the campus Greek community. In a darkened ballroom the sisters all gathered in a colorful circle and a candle was lit and passed from hand to hand around the circle. If a girl was newly lavaliered, pinned or engaged, when the candle reached her she blew it out. This revelation was followed by much squealing, jumping up and down, and happy tears and hugs from all the girls present. Terri had her special Greek moment and displayed her miniscule new diamond to all her sisters, and then we were allowed to lead off the first dance. The deejay asked what we'd like to hear. Since "I Think We're Alone Now," which had become "our song," is a fast tempo tune and wouldn't have been considered romantic enough for this occasion, we picked, rather randomly I now think, a Gerry & the Pacemakers song called "Don't Let the Sun Catch You Crying" for our first dance. If I had had more time to think about it, or if I could do it over again, I would pick "The Way You Look Tonight," because on that very special night Terri was indeed "lovely," and in my heart that will "never, never change."

* * * * *

28

SHOWING OFF MY GIRL

We attended one other classy dress-up affair that spring when the Vet's Club threw an elaborate dinner dance bash in Reed City at Miller Auditorium, probably one of the most elegant venues for miles around. Since the Vets were the largest student organization on campus at the time, their spring dance was well-attended and a rousing success, with well over two hundred people there that night. I think my friend, Gary Perdew, was largely responsible for organizing the event, and he did himself and our group proud. Terri and I both had plenty of friends there that night. Larry Miller brought Marsha Stahl. Pat O'Connor and Marilyn LeRash were there, as were Wayne Shook and Dianne Miller, a petite and vivacious girl he had recently begun dating. A smiling John Nibbelink was there with Rinda, radiantly blonde and beautiful, crutches and all. A live band was playing and the hall's trademark lighted crystal ball turned slowly above the crowded dance floor, creating a magical surreal setting. I had my best girl in my arms for most of the evening and all was right with the world.

Now that I was finally part of a couple, I proudly paraded my newly found "other half" around to meet my married friends. We had dinner one night with Keith and Dianne at their apartment in Reed City. Dianne went all out and made a delicious meal and spent the evening drawing Terri out and finding out all about her, smiling and clucking contentedly in that special way that still-new wives

Keith and Dianne, taken Christmas '65

have. Keith, after checking out the goods, gave me a discrete thumbs-up while the women were in the kitchen.

On another evening Terri and I went to a party at the Karnitzes' place on Ives. Terry and Molly had just purchased a new Jeopardy board game. Bruce and Sherry Jensen were there, and I think Marsh Draper and his wife came too, so Terri got to meet quite a few of my scrub crew buddies that night as we all munched salty snacks and guzzled beer and pop while trying to impress each other with our encyclopedic knowledge of trivial facts.

On another afternoon shortly before the end of the term, Don and Mary Ellen Dobson invited us over to their place in married student housing up in Campus Heights. Don grilled hot dogs to go with Mary's salad. We couldn't help noticing that their big front picture window was missing, temporarily replaced by a large sheet of plywood. When I asked about it, they both laughed, and Mary, blushing and smirking, said, "That's Donnie's fault. I'll let him tell you about it."

Still chuckling, Don explained that Mary had developed the rather annoying nosey habit of peeking out through the blinds at their neighbors' comings and goings. Don was always telling her to stop it, and to mind her own business, which advice Mary chose to ignore. So one evening when he saw her standing near the front window, holding a can of pop in one hand and parting the blind slats slightly with the other and peering out into the yard, he crept up behind her and gave her a small shove in the small of her back and said, "Whyn'cha get a *good* look?"

Mary had already been slightly bent at the waist and when Don pushed her, she completely lost her balance and threw both hands out in front of her up against the blinds and the window. The whole plate glass pane cracked ominously, then shattered and Mary continued to fall forward over the low sill and suddenly found herself on her hands and knees outside on the sidewalk with broken glass and ruined Venetian blind slats and cords strewn all around her while Don looked on in horror.

Miraculously, Mary was completely unharmed, probably because the blinds had protected her from getting cut on the broken shards of glass.

"Hence the plywood," Don concluded, still laughing. "We're lucky they didn't send social services over to investigate me for spousal abuse."

"Well, maybe they *should*," Mary interjected archly, her chin out; but then she burst out laughing herself. And so Terri met two more of my closest friends, and we both learned a little more about the possible hazards of married life.

I even took Terri to meet a few of my teachers that spring, I was so proud of her. We visited the Wolfingers at their home on a hill west of 131 overlooking Ferris, where Mrs. Wolfinger – Dorothy – made a proper fuss, clucking approvingly over Terri and her ring, and then showed her proudly all through their custom-made home with all of its counters and cabinets built lower to the ground to accommodate her diminutive stature. She even pulled out the drawers built into their master bathroom, explaining sensibly how she'd always wanted to have her underwear in the bathroom, rather than having to go get it out of the bedroom after showering or bathing. Not that we really wanted a peek at my former English teacher's undies, but that was just Dorothy's enthusiasm for all the wonders of her new "nest." Dr. Wolfinger – whom Dorothy referred to repeatedly and lovingly as simply "my Bill" – took me downstairs and showed me through his private library, which filled almost the entire basement with its floor to ceiling shelves. As a budding bibliophile, I was extremely envious of Dr. Wolfinger's enormous and eclectic collection.

We also visited Margaret Croft and her husband, Arthur, a Ferris economics professor, at their home down near the river east of Ferris. Mrs. Croft and Mrs. Wolfinger had been my two favorite teachers in high school. After mixing with all the young couples, visiting these two long-married older couples served perhaps to balance our impressions of what marriage is all about. The Wolfingers and Crofts were living examples of what Robert Browning meant in his famous lines:

> *"Grow old along with me.*
> *The best is yet to be.*
> *The last of life*
> *For which the first was made ..."*

I have always loved those lines. I heard them first in Dr. Wolfinger's class on Browning. I understand them a lot better now than I did then though.

* * * * *

29

GRASSERS AND "RULES OF ENGAGEMENT"

Grassers. Remember "grassers"? Any former Ferris pinhead worth his salt *must* remember grassers. They were an integral part of the rites of spring around campus in the sixties. I don't know if that specific term has survived into the new century, but I'm absolutely certain that the custom or practice that the term represents is still very much alive, and not just at FSU, but on every college campus throughout these here New-nited States an' Texas. All you need for a successful grasser is a blanket, a six-pack, a soft spring day, and your best girl. I don't know if "grasser" was a term peculiar to Ferris, or if it was a universal word, but I do know it was once pretty much part of the working vocabulary of every guy and girl on the Big Rapids campus once spring had sprung.

Sometimes these grassers were loosely organized group events which fraternities or clubs would put together by buying a keg or two of beer and finding an empty field or a grassy clearing in the woods outside of town, or perhaps a patch of beach along Chippewa or School Section Lake. Whatever the location, all the participants would get together, maybe build a campfire, and then proceed to all get roaring drunk, to break down all those pesky inhibitions, and then hope for the best, romantically speaking.

I never attended a group grasser, although I'm sure the Vet's Club undoubtedly was instrumental in putting together at least a couple of them that spring. I *was* guilty, however, of staging a couple of impromptu private grassers during those last few weeks of our final term – just Terri and me. Both our grassers were during a time when we probably should have been studying for final exams, but what are you gonna do when the mercury rises to sixty-plus degrees in late May or early June and gentle breezes are blowing softly and drying the new green grass too long hidden under the sodden winter snow? All the conditions were right. It would have been absolutely un-American, most un-Bulldog-ish and pinheadedly criminal to spend such a day closeted indoors with books and notes, cramming for finals. So I called Terri, who didn't need much convincing, and we were on our way. I stopped in at Grunst Bros. and purchased a six-pack of Stroh's (the "fire brewed beer") for myself and something a bit sweeter for Terri, who didn't like the taste of beer. A pint of Sloe Gin, a deep pink-colored liqueur, looked promising, so I got her that and we headed north out of town, windows rolled down and WLS on the radio blasting out Jerry Keller's seasonal anthem with its eminently appropriate chorus –

"Here comes summer
School is out, oh happy day.
Here comes summer
Gonna grab my girl and run away ..."

In Paris we turned onto 21 Mile Road and drove west until a two-track trail presented itself, meandering south into a stand of scrub growth pine. I turned the Volkswagen down this path, bumping slowly along over rocks and roots, the weeds and brush in the high center of the track scraping the undercarriage of the car. About a quarter of a mile in we emerged into a grassy glade dominated by a huge old elm, which had somehow managed to survive the blight which had killed so many of its compatriots. Only about half of the tree seemed to be budding with new leaves, however, so it was probably in its final years. I saw its survival as a sign. This old tree was hanging on just for us. So I parked the car on the edge of the clearing. Leaving the car radio on, I spread my much-traveled but little-used old army blanket on the grass under the tree. We made ourselves comfortable, me with my beer and Terri daintily sipping a mix of Sloe Gin and 7-Up from a plastic cup, my college boy version of a Sloe Gin Fizz. I leaned my back up against the broad trunk of the tree and Terri settled her back against my chest, sitting between my upraised knees. I chugged half a beer, bent my head and breathed in the fragrance of her hair, sighing happily, completely contented. *This* was what I wanted. This was what I'd been searching for ever since I had first started school at Ferris. Tiny blue wildflowers, the kind I had always called "'violets of dawn," stirred gently in the tangled grass as a warm breeze blew gently through the glade. Birds sang. The radio played softly. We sat spooned snugly together beneath the tree, feeling smugly sure that we were the first ones to ever feel this way and to know this kind of contentment.

This, our first grasser, was a complete success. Of course there's a little more to a successful grasser than all the above-mentioned sugar-coated romance stuff. That was for you ladies. All the guys know that things have to get a little heavier and groatier than that, or else it's just a wasted six-pack. As the drinks continue to go down, the participating couple tends to get more and more horizontal and a game of ever-escalating sexual stakes begins. Petting is, after all, a practice that's been around for generations, and we all know it isn't about patting your partner on the head or scratching behind her ears.

It's a well-know fact, I think, that the rules change a bit once the girl has a ring on her finger and wedding plans are in progress. I don't know what the rules are in today's society, which seems to be much more permissive in every way, and especially in sexual matters. But back then there was an unspoken understanding that anything "above the waist" was fair game once that ring was on. For a whole generation of guys who cut their sexual teeth, so to speak, on the mammary-fixated glossy pages of *Playboy*, this was no small victory. It was a major step forward. Any other changes in the rules of engagement were strictly a matter of private negotiations, which were almost always ongoing from one date to the next. And that's really all I'd better say here on the matter of premarital sex in 1967.

But I'm not quite done with grassers, because it was our second (and last) grasser that was the most memorable for Terri and me. It was another one of those perfect spring days with all the right conditions. We made our stop at Grunst Bros. for the required refreshments. They were out of Sloe Gin that day, so I picked out another colorful sweet treat for my still underage sweetheart – a lime-flavored vodka that was a bright green which nearly matched the luminous shade of the new leaves on the old elm in our clearing west of Paris. There was no particular feeling of urgency to our pastoral tryst that day. Having spread our blanket in our special spot, we settled ourselves comfortably under the tree and sipped our drinks and talked dreamily of the future. Terri tried to interest me in the wedding plans that were already proceeding back in Belleville, and I listened politely, nodding and smiling as I languidly nuzzled her neck and hair and continued to refill her plastic cup. The colorful liqueur seemed to be loosening her up. She seemed so happy and animated that afternoon. Our mood seemed to match the top forty tunes that drifted lazily over to us from the car radio, things like John Sebastian and the Spoonful crooning, *"What a day for a daydream ..."*

The afternoon was progressing perfectly. The green vodka and the glistening green of the new grass and foliage were combining to work their magic as we slid gradually down the trunk of the tree and onto the blanket, alternating tastes of our drinks with tastes of each other. Buttons and button holes bowed gracefully and parted company. Silken rosette-covered clasps seemed to spring effortlessly open, and those famous "fawns, twins of gazelles" were just about to come out and play when, suddenly, we heard a car door slam.

Fuck! We both sat up hurriedly, Terri frantically re-snapping and buttoning herself back together while I got to my feet, angrily tucking my shirt back into my jeans. About fifty feet away, on the other side of my VW, I spied an old rust-streaked Ford pickup, and, striding purposefully in our direction was a large middle-aged red-haired woman. She wore a faded print housedress, and men's ankle-high work shoes. A blue babushka was tied carelessly around her hair.

When she saw first my head and Terri's come bobbing into sight over the roof of our car, she removed the cigarette that was hanging from her lips and pointed at us, shouting, "You kids ain't got no bid-ness bein' out-cheer! This here's private proppity, an' y'all are trespassin'! What the hell you think yer doin' out-cheer anyway?"

Red-faced, embarrassed and more than a little angry myself, I muttered something about not knowing this was private property, and was about to say something pretty nasty in return, when it came to me that I'd better shut my mouth. After all, my car was parked right here on what was apparently her land, license plates in plain sight. So, still simmering, I muttered an apology. Terri was still cowering behind me fastening up her last buttons and blushing furiously. We quickly gathered up our blanket, pillows and empty bottles and stuffed everything into the back seat of the Bug, all under the hostile, smoke-slitted stare of this fat farm wife who had so rudely ruined our idyllic afternoon.

She was still standing there watching us, fat freckled arms folded across her massive bosom and brogan-shod feet spread wide, as we drove out of the clearing and back down the trail. My anger and embarrassment made me drive a little faster than I should have, the car bouncing and jouncing over the rocks and roots jutting from the rough track as we made our way back to the blacktop road that led back into Paris. Hunched over the wheel, still cursing softly to myself, I failed to notice the effect the jolting ride was having on poor Terri until it was too late. I heard a soft moan from her side of the car and turned just in time to see her grab the door with both hands and then stick her head out the open window and vomit copiously all down the side of my car.

Fuck! My car! My new car!

I know, I *know*! Not a very loving or charitable reaction when the love of your life is feeling so sick and miserable. But *Geeze-o-Pete! My car!* I know women will never understand this, but you guys do, right? Because there's this guy-thing bond between a man and his vehicle, especially when it's his first-ever *new* vehicle.

Recovering quickly from my horror, I did my best to be sympathetic and sensitive, digging my nearly clean handkerchief out of my back pocket and offering it to Terri as she sagged back into her seat, moaning miserably as tears and snot streamed down her face in tandem from her eyes and nose.

"Oooooohh!" she groaned, wiping her cheeks and chin. "I feel *aww*-ful."

Then (*God-DAMN-it!*) she leaned back out the window and upchucked all over my car *again*!

Cringing inwardly as I subconsciously considered the probable combined effects of alcohol and stomach acid on what had been the pristine multi-coated paint finish of my beloved blue Bug, I nevertheless patted Terri consolingly on her back and shoulders as we made the turn south onto 131 and headed back towards Big Rapids. I didn't feel so good myself anymore.

Just a small postscript: the stain on the VW's passenger-side door stayed on – a permanent and ever-present reminder of our youthful passion and folly. I think Terri was relieved when we finally sold the car six years and two kids later.

Grassers.

* * * * *

Terri and me, washing the Bug – pre-puke stain

30

GRADUATION AND
"BEING RILEY" AT KEL-REED

The final few weeks of that last quarter flew by in a kind of blur. Almost before we knew it finals were finished and graduation was upon us. Neither one of us actually participated in the graduation ceremony, although for different reasons.

My reason was a simple and practical one. I was still working on the scrub crew and was offered the opportunity to get in eight hours of work that Saturday, putting up and then taking down folding chairs for the event. Looking back now, I realize I probably should have done the cap and gown bit, but at the time the money seemed more important than tradition. Perhaps I was already feeling the impending responsibility that marriage would surely bring. I probably made all of ten or twelve bucks for the day's work, which sounds like a piddling sum today, but didn't then.

Terri didn't get in on graduation because she found out at the last minute that she had failed one course, Intro to Business, and so was a few credits short of the required number to graduate. I will claim at least partial responsibility for that, since I was constantly pestering her those last few weeks, and obviously infringing on her study time. Her failure to pass the course and graduate was the *bad* news. The *good* news – at least as far as we were concerned – was that instead of going home to Belleville she would be staying at Ferris for the summer to re-take the class. I'm sure Terri's folks weren't any too pleased, but *we* sure were. Maybe sometimes

> *The President, Board of Directors and Members*
> *of the Ferris State College Alumni Association*
> *cordially invite you to attend*
> *an open house*
> *in honor of the Spring Graduating Class*
> *in the President's Room of the*
> *Student Center Building*
> *from seven-thirty to nine in the evening*
> *Wednesday, May twenty-fourth*
> *Nineteen hundred sixty-seven*

failure is good. We'd be together for most of the summer, at least nearly as much as we had been for the past two months.

The summer of 1967 is often referred to in the newer history books as "the summer of love." It was the summer when thousands of disenchanted and disenfranchised young people poured into the once-staid Haight-Ashbury district of San Francisco in hopes of finding – or perhaps *founding* – a new society. Unfortunately there were more potheads than planners in this uncentered amorphous movement. Too many dopers and dreamers and too few real visionaries. Drug dealers and other ruthless opportunists quickly moved in and took their deadly tolls on the too-trusting flower children and hippies who had spawned the movement.

Our own summer of love was quite different. Unlike the hippies, who espoused ignoring and upsetting the establishment and all its rules and sacred institutions, Terri and I continued to play by the rules and were rushing headlong towards that most sacred of societal institutions – marriage. We didn't drop out. We stayed in. If anything, I settled even deeper into the established rhythms of the working world that summer when I took a job at a local factory.

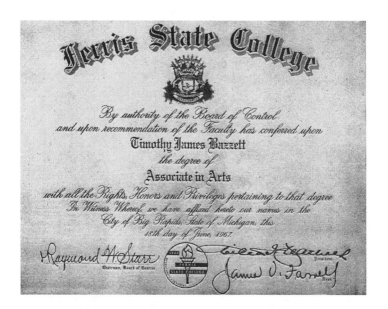

Kel-Reed was still a fairly new industry in Reed City in 1967, but to my still-young eyes it seemed to have just always been there. The building itself had gone up in 1950 and was home to the Goodrich Welding Equipment Company until that business relocated to Hudsonville. In 1953 Kel-Reed was born, as a screw machine plant and parts supplier to the Keller Tool Company in Grand Haven. Two years later Kel-Reed was purchased by the Gardner-Denver Company. By the summer I came to work there, Kel-Reed had gone beyond simply machining and supplying parts. They were actually providing finished products for direct sale to Gardner-Denver. The plant was turning out chiefly electric and pneumatic "wire-wrap" tools for the electronics industry. From a small town perspective, Kel-Reed was a major player in the local economy and was definitely in a period of major growth that summer. From its humble beginnings in 1953, when it started out with just thirteen employees, by 1967 the plant was running three shifts and had over two hundred people on the payroll.

I will be the first to admit that I didn't know diddly-squat about what went on at that factory when I went to work there in June of '67, and I didn't know a hell of a lot more when I left at the end of August. The only other businesses I had ever worked for were the

Kel-Reed, circa 1956

A&P grocery during my senior year of high school, and before that for my dad at the Kent Elevator. I won't count the U.S. Army, since their way of doing business was always a kind of lock-step clusterfuck as far as I could tell.

If it had been up to me, I would have been happy to have just kept my job on the Ferris scrub crew that summer where I was comfortable with the work and would have been closer to Terri while she was re-taking her class. She would have plenty of free time with only the one class to worry about. Unfortunately, I had already graduated. Well, no, wait a minute. It wasn't unfortunate that I'd *grad*uated. *That* was a good thing. What I mean was that my graduation precluded me from staying on the scrub crew, since those kinds of jobs were reserved for students – a kind of unofficial financial aid, or maybe student jobs were in reality a kind of work-study program. I was never really entirely clear on that. I had always just been glad to have the job and make some money.

Anyway, at the urging of my father, I had put in a job application at the Kel-Reed in late May, just before I graduated, and about a week later I had been called in to start work.

I hesitate to admit that I was scared shitless about the prospect of going to work at Kel-Reed that June, but the fact of the matter was I was pretty damn nervous and unsure of myself. I had always thought of factories as places where people's parents worked, not someone like *me*, for cripes sake. I don't think I was quite ready to become part of the world of working stiffs. It seemed to be too big a step, and too suddenly, into the grown-up world. I know I was

218

twenty-three years old and shouldn't have felt that way, but you can't always control the way you feel. As Popeye used to say, "I yam wot I yam."

I needn't have worried so much about the job or about fitting in. The people at the plant couldn't have been friendlier. And I began seeing familiar faces from the very first day. There was Dave Yost, older brother to Steve, Tom and Bill. I had gone to school with the Yost kids since St. Philip's and had seen Tom occasionally at Ferris for the past couple of years. Some time that first week I also saw John Roberts, a former high school classmate who had just started work there when he came home from the service the previous fall. Donna Filley, one of my first dates at RCHS, was there too, all grown up and a working woman now. And there was Norv Scharkey, who'd gone to school with my brother Rich. The folks at Kel-Reed weren't mysterious strangers after all. They were kids my brothers and I had grown up with and people I'd seen around town all my life.

As unskilled labor (most *definitely* unskilled), I was assigned to work in the Assembly Department. I had always envisioned assembly lines as having moving belts carrying complicated pieces of unfinished machinery quickly along past a line of workers who each added or assembled another part to the product. I figured I would have to add on a part or two and worried that I wouldn't be able to keep up with the movement of the belt and would foul everything up. You know, kind of like that famous episode of *I Love Lucy* where Lucy and Ethel got jobs in the candy factory and the belt kept going faster and faster. Fortunately for me, there were no conveyor belts on the Kel-Reed assembly line. We sat on metal stools at long tables which held boxes of small parts that needed to be added to nearly finished products.

I know that Kel-Reed was probably making a fairly wide variety of power tools that summer, but to be perfectly honest, I can only remember one with any degree of clarity. In my short experience it was the power drill from hell, and could be the reason I still don't own any power hand tools. To be fair though, it was probably a fine power drill, or had the potential to be, as long as they kept *me* out of its assembly process. My task was – *should* have been – a fairly simple one. I had two or maybe three small parts to assemble, a couple plastic pieces and a tiny spring that all went into the drill's nosepiece. Manual dexterity, small motor coordination and handling tiny things have never been my strong suits, so this assembly process was *not* a simple thing for me. I was painfully slow at it, and, as often as not, just when I thought I'd gotten it right and would place the assembled pieces carefully into the completed tray, some joker would stroll by and *pound* the table, causing my "finished assembly" to fly back apart into its separate components again and send me back to square one. It was exceedingly frustrating to me, but what these table-pounders were actually pointing out to the "new guy," albeit none too subtly, was that I had *not* gotten it right.

Luckily for me, there were a couple of women working near me in the department who took pity on me and kind of took me under their wings and tutored me in the subtleties of assembly. One was Donna Borck, who had been working at the plant for several years already. She worked most of the time in Shipping and Receiving, but was also expert at assembly and helped out there whenever she was needed. As she walked me through the proper and most efficient way to put things together, she told me about how she'd been scared to death about coming to work there after her third son had started school, which made me feel a bit better about my own nervousness. Her calm demeanor and kindness were a great help to me, and under her tutelage I started to get the hang of things a little better, although I know I never gained anywhere near the expertise she possessed.

Another woman who helped me get through that summer was Gladys Peterson. She sat at the same assembly table with me, and, like Donna, she took pity on me and my pitifully inept assembly skills. At first I was a bit shy with Gladys, even though I had known her most of my life. She had always been "Mrs. Peterson" to me, the mother of Cheryl and Randy, and part of the grown-up world. The Petersons lived in a small rancher at the foot of my grandparents' driveway on West Church. I had delivered fresh eggs from our chickens to their house since I was ten years old, and my little brother, Chris, and Randy Peterson had been playmates all their lives.

I think perhaps Gladys had had a soft spot in her heart for me ever since the day when I was eleven years old and had arrived sobbing at her door carrying the still-warm body of Bootsy, the

The assembly department –
Theron Bergey (with crutches), Donna Borck (at back table)

"The power drill from hell"

l-r: Gary Komerska, Donna Borck, Gladys Peterson, Bert Faber

Petersons' dog, who had just been killed by a car down on Chestnut in front of the Gulf station. I had gotten off the St. Philip's school bus there and discovered the dog crumpled against the curb, black blood pooled around its gaping mouth. Bootsy, a small black dog with two white front feet, had been one of those likable little mutts that roamed the neighborhood freely (like many dogs did back in the fifties) and was a friend to all the kids in a several block radius. With Mrs. Peterson's permission, I had buried Bootsy, wrapped in an old burlap sack, next to our garage, and marked the site with a large stone which I dragged over onto the grave and painted the dog's name on.

Maybe Gladys was remembering that kid when she befriended me at the plant and made me feel welcome, despite my obvious ineptitude at putting together tiny parts with springs. And she may have even been the one who tactfully suggested there were other jobs I could probably do around the place, also unskilled labor. So one day when Ken Lofgren, one of the foremen, came through our area looking for someone who could be spared to cut the grass and do yard work, Gladys looked meaningfully in my direction and raised an eyebrow. I was off my stool in an instant, nodding like a fool.

"I can do yard work, Ken," I volunteered. "Just show me where the mower and tools are."

And thus began my main job that summer as yard-boy, sweeper-upper, and all-around general go-fer. Thank you, Gladys, for sparing me from all those tiny springs and sprockets.

I did continue to work in the Assembly Department from time to time, but I gave up all hope of every becoming particularly proficient at the job. I resigned myself to being "the slow kid." I would finish one assembly in the time it took someone like Donna or Gladys to complete three or four.

You know how when you buy a toy or a bike or a piece of furniture that's marked "some assembly required" and it comes with printed instructions and little plastic bags containing so many each of nuts, bolts, washers and screws? And then you're real careful and follow the instructions to the letter, but when you're all finished and the assembly is complete, you find there's one nut or screw or bolt left over and you have this nagging suspicion you must have skipped a step or missed something and you go back over the instructions and then scrutinize your finished product scrupulously but you can't find anything wrong. There's just this extra part left over. Well, in the Kel-Reed work force I often felt like that superfluous screw or the odd bolt or neglected nut – the washer that wasn't needed. I was "the little engine that couldn't."

I couldn't even play cards. You might not think of card-playing as a necessary skill in a manufacturing plant, but if you wanted to fit in at Kel-Reed, it was. Every time the break buzzer sounded for that ten-minute break a klatch of avid card-players would converge at either end of the assembly table. Hands would already be dealt before everyone had even sat down, and the pace of the game was fast and furious. They played Euchre at Kel-Reed, and their style of play was a study in economy of time and motion. I remember Norv Scharkey was always in the game, and could eat a whole bologna sandwich and play two or three lightning hands of cards in those ten minutes. I never did learn to play Euchre. I'm pretty sure that if I had tried I would have been way too slow at the game and an awful annoyance to the hard-core card sharps like Scharkey or Jim Cooper. Nope, those card games remained just as much a mystery to me as most of the other workings at Kel-Reed. I was an outsider – an extra part – and I stayed one.

l-r: Les Knapp, Bobby Esch, Cy Kingsbury, Ken Lofgren, Woody Lake

"Up front" – the machine shop at Kel-Reed

I'm not sure if Kel-Reed had an official policy of hiring "summer help" back then. I'm pretty sure, however, that everyone knew that's what I was, from Donna and Gladys and the other folks in Assembly, all the way up to Cy Kingsbury, the plant superintendent.

But I was happy to have a job, even if my main contribution turned out to be nothing more than keeping the grass mowed, the shrubs trimmed, the trash picked up and the floors swept. I could do that. Sometimes as I merged with the flow of day-shift workers every morning and made my way through the doors to the time clock where I would dutifully punch in, I couldn't help feeling like Chester A. Riley, carrying my metal lunch bucket in to work at "the plant." Often at lunch time I would even find a cold meatloaf sandwich in my bucket, just like the ones Honey-Bee had always fixed for Gillis, Riley's pal and next-door neighbor. I was living one of my favorite childhood sitcoms, so much so that often I would look through the faces, half-expecting to see Waldo, or Otto Schmidlamp, other buddies of Riley.

I was making some much-needed money though, and putting some aside for my fall tuition, rent and other expenses that the next school year would surely bring. I was also acutely aware that I was working and saving for two now, because the wedding plans were gathering steam back in Belleville.

* * * * *

31

DAIRY QUEENS,
DRIVE-INS AND POPCORN

While I didn't really dislike my job at Kel-Reed, sometimes the days would seem to drag on endlessly as I watched the clock and waited impatiently for quitting time. When that proverbial five o'clock whistle blew I was out of there like a flash. I would hurry home to shower and change, grab a bite of something to eat on the run, and then fly down 131 to Ferris, where Terri would be waiting for me at the dorm. She was usually watching for me from the lobby, and would come running out when she saw my blue Bug pull in. She would slide in on the passenger side and we would reach hungrily for each other and my *real* day would begin. Because that summer wasn't just the summer of love for the hippies in Haight-Ashbury. It was *our* summer of love too. We were together every evening and found something to do every weekend – with family, with friends, or just by ourselves.

Since we never had much money and were both conscious of the need to save what little I was making, our "dates" were pretty frugal for the most part. Some evenings we would drive over to the Dairy Queen on State Street and get a cone or a malt and sit in the small wooded park near the creek down below the DQ, where we would share our sweet concoctions and listen to the car radio, and would intersperse our smooching with licking the melted ice cream from each other's chins. Or we might split a frosted mug of root beer at the A&W, then treat ourselves to a couple of fifteen-cent hamburgers at the Satellite just across the street from campus. On weekends we would sometimes splurge and buy a whole pizza at Pizza King.

Of course it wasn't all violins and roses (or burgers and root beer either). I continued to constantly test the limits and the unspoken sexual ground rules of our engagement. And Terri continued to gently remind me of those limits and to softly but firmly enforce the rules. The sexual tension was always there and could be extremely frustrating, but I was committed now and kept coming back for more.

One of the things that came to bother me those summer nights was my car. I did love my new Bug (puke-stained passenger door and all), but there's just no way to get very seriously horizontal in the front seat of a VW, and the back seat's not much better, and I knew anyway that had I suggested we adjourn to the rear, my motion would have been vetoed. Nope. I think it was Elvis who once so succinctly put it: "There's no room to rumba in a foreign sports car."

One weekend, then, I arranged to borrow Dad's car, a huge four-door Pontiac that seemed like a luxury yacht in comparison to my little blue dinghy. This was still a time before they were putting bucket seats in everything, so the Pontiac's long front bench seat seemed to stretch away to infinity. Seat belts were still optional then, so another advantage of the bench seat was your girl could tuck herself right snug up against you while you drove, which I'll admit could be a distraction, but it sure was a pleasant one.

So what did I do with that big car and its long inviting front seat? Remember drive-in movies? Yup. I took my girl to the drive-in. I know it's lame, and I can't really explain why I did it. I know now that I probably should have just headed off to one of our secluded spots on a back road outside of town and laid siege to the ramparts of GCG virtue. But no; we went to the drive-in. I think it must have been some recessive adolescent gene in action, the one that compels a boy, when he gets to use Dad's car, to take his girl directly to the drive-in movies, that legendary passion pit of high school fantasies, that place where girls supposedly suddenly become "easy," fling caution to the wind, and just "go all the way." Or maybe I took Terri there because of my notable *lack* of success at the drive-in during my high school years. Hell, I think I only took

A 1970 ad for the Big Rapids Drive-In

a girl to the drive-in a couple of times when I was a teenager and never got much beyond the kissing stage, and maybe copping a feel of a bare shoulder.

Anyway, here's what happened. I got interested in the movie. (*DOH!*) Yup, I did. It was kind of a modern-day western called

228

Nevada Smith, a spin-off story from the tremendously successful book and film, *The Carpetbaggers*. I had read the book by Harold Robbins while I was in the army, and had later seen the subsequent film version, in which the Smith character had been played by Alan Ladd, in one of his last big roles. In the newer film Smith was played by Steve McQueen. I've always been a sucker for a good movie, particularly a western. I was brought up on B-westerns, and consider myself one of original "front-row kids." And I had admired and envied Steve McQueen ever since he had "done the right thing" with an exquisitely yummy young Natalie Wood in *Love with the Proper Stranger*.

So there we were, snuggled comfortably in that great big bed on wheels, and what did we do? We ate popcorn and candy and ice cream and watched the movie like a couple of excited little kids. A night to remember.

Movies and popcorn were actually pretty routine for us during our summer of love, mostly at my house in Reed City, where I would pop the corn, usually quite a lot, since it wasn't just for Terri and me, but also for Mary and Chris, and sometimes also for our live-in high school exchange student from Uruguay, Carlos Cal, if he happened to be at home that night. On those nights we would all gather in the living room in front of the TV, happily munching away and watching whatever was on Saturday Night at the Movies. Mom and Dad were around too, but would usually tactfully absent themselves and withdraw to another room. On nights like these Terri got a pretty accurate peek at my family life and perhaps just a small preview of what "our" nights would be like someday. She must have liked what she saw then, because I still make her popcorn on Saturday or Sunday nights and she still likes it.

* * * * *

32

GRANDMA BAZZETT

That July Terri got to meet the rest of my family when my Grandma Bazzett passed away and the larger extended family gathered for her funeral.

When Grandpa had died in September of 1965, Grandma had never gone back to their big empty house next door to ours after his funeral. I'm not entirely sure why, but she moved into the guest room in our house and never slept in her own house again. Her physical and mental condition began to deteriorate rapidly after Grandpa died. As is often the case with older people who have been a long time married, she just couldn't seem to adjust to being alone. She would nap in her chair in the living room during the day and began to prowl the house at night. My mom still remembers waking suddenly in the wee hours of the morning to find Grandma standing over the bed and peering down at her and Dad, a confused expression on her face. Or sometimes Dad would get up at night to go to the bathroom and would look out into the living room and see Grandma sitting in a chair with her hat and coat on, "waiting to go to Mass" – at 2 AM on a Tuesday. She began "seeing things" that weren't there. Sitting in the rocker by the dining room window, she might point out at the empty lawn and prattle on about "Ellis's chickens" which she could see out there "pecking in the dust." This strange unsettling behavior worried Mom and Dad enough that they finally took Grandma to see Dr. Paul Kilmer, who examined her and questioned her and duly noted her vague and absent manner.

But what Dr. Paul noticed even more during the visit was how drawn and exhausted Mom looked. He guessed that Grandma had probably suffered a small stroke, or possibly even several, and had her admitted to the hospital for some tests. Then he explained to Mom and Dad that Grandma would probably never be able to care for herself again, and would probably grow worse. He advised Dad quite bluntly to try to find Grandma a place in a nursing home as soon as possible, because the job of looking after her would just be too much for Mom and would end up making *her* sick. Taking the doctor's advice to heart, Mom and Dad reluctantly moved Grandma to Lakeview Manor, a nursing home in Cadillac, where Dad visited her faithfully every weekend, even after she became unable to recognize him. Mom usually went along on these visits, and sometimes Mary, Chris or I would go too. Grandma lived at Lakeview Manor for nearly a year and a half before she died, slipping gradually away into the ever-thickening fog of confusion and blankness that is dementia.

So that July, the same scorching month that saw Detroit, Newark, San Francisco and other major cities across the nation explode into the worst race riots in U.S. history, with dozens killed and thousands arrested, the Bazzetts and the Ellises gathered in Reed City to pay their last respects to Mary (Ellis) Bazzett, whom Grandpa had always called "Mamie." Dad's brothers – Don, Ken and Bernard – were all there with their families. (Uncle Vern had died of cancer the previous year.) My oldest brother, Rich, came home from his work-related travels, from Spain or Greece. Bill came home from his job in the twin cities area of Minnesota, and Bob brought his small family from Roselle, near Chicago. It was, I'm sure, a bittersweet occasion for Dad, both of his parents now gone, but all of his kids back home again for the first time in several years.

It was during this sad-but-happy occasion then that Terri was officially introduced into our family, and she sat in on our discussions as we remembered our Grandma, whom she had never met. We all reminisced about how happy Grandma had been when she and Grandpa had moved in next door to us back in 1953 when Chris was a new baby, and how she would come "hoo-hoo"-ing in our back door, often bearing her fresh-baked oatmeal-raisin cookies. Bill remembered how she let her parakeet fly free around the inside of the house, and how she would leave the tap in the

Our whole family reunited for Grandma B's funeral, July 1967 –
l-r: Bill, Chris, Rich, Dad, Mom, Bob, Mary, Terri and me.

kitchen sink running a thin stream of water, so the bird could walk under it for a "shower."

Bob reminded us once again of how the kitchen floor in Grandma's house slanted, causing the stove to tilt slightly, so every time Grandma baked a cake in the oven, it would rise unevenly in the pan, with one end thicker than the other. Grandma would "fix" this problem by simply layering her cooked frosting more thickly on the shallow end of the cake. That frosting set up like fudge once it cooled, and we would often lift it off, eat the cake first and then the solid piece of frosting as "dessert."

I remembered the ornately carved oak bookcase with its glass doors which stood in Grandma's unheated dining room. The shelves held her small but precious "library," which she allowed us to borrow from, introducing us all to bygone authors like Booth Tarkington (*Penrod, Penrod and Sam, Seventeen*), Zane Grey (*Riders of the Purple Sage, Valley of Wild Horses*), and James Whitcomb Riley, the "Hoosier poet."

We told Uncle Bernard about how much Grandma loved that first television set that he had bought her, before we even had one for ourselves. It was a huge dark wooden cabinet with a small round screen in the middle which displayed a very snowy picture. We kids would often sneak over to Grandma's in the evening after supper to sit with her and try to see through the snowy reception shows like *Inner Sanctum*, with its creepy "creaking door" introduction, or *The Jack Benny Show* or Milton Berle's *Texaco Star Theater*. Ironically, as the years passed and TV reception improved, Grandma's eyesight failed, but she would just move her chair closer to the television, so close that sometimes her nose was nearly touching the screen. She always faithfully watched *The Lawrence Welk Show*, with her favorite vocalist, Joe Feeney, who, she often declared, "sang just like an angel."

It was in the sometimes boisterous atmosphere of this memory-fest then that Terri first met my older brothers, who were all, I think, just a bit amazed that their little brother, who had always been something of a klutz when it came to the opposite sex, had managed to land this luscious-looking blonde. It was probably

Grandma Bazzett, her farmhouse behind her,
bringing us cookies. "Hoo-hoo!"

233

all perhaps a bit overwhelming to Terri, but I couldn't have been prouder of her. And I was pretty pleased with myself too. Not many guys get to land that "trophy wife" the first time around.

There was only one small (but still remembered) glitch that occurred during those two days of first meetings and introductions. That happened when Rich had just arrived home. Terri and I were sitting on the padded storage bench in the dining room petting Runt, who had been Rich's dog, but when Rich had left home nearly six years before, had become "the family dog." Too many little special treats and table scraps since Rich's departure had made Runt rather rotund, which Rich apparently noticed right away when he came in the back door and greeted her with, "Well, hi there, Bubble-Gut!"

Terri looked up, startled at this tall stranger who seemed to be passing judgment on her figure.

"He means Runt," I quickly assured her, and we all laughed, Terri a bit uncertainly, and Rich blushing deeply, as I made the proper introductions. We all always remembered that first-meeting faux pas though, and it would inevitably come up on each of those rare occasions whenever we would see Rich again.

* * * * *

In Memory Of
MARY E. BAZZETT
October 17, 1886   July 8, 1967

Services Held at
St. Phillips Church
Reed City, Michigan
10:00 A. M.   July 11, 1967

Officiating
Father Victor Gallagher

Interment
Woodland Cemetery

Casket Bearers
Ronald Bazzett   Richard Bazzett
Robert Bazzett   Christopher Bazzett
William Bazzett   Timothy Bazzett

Arrangements By
J. W. Livingston Funeral Home
Reed City, Michigan

33

THE OTHER ZIMMERS –
BOB AND DON

I met the rest of Terri's family before the summer was out too. One weekend we drove north, up past Traverse City to the Sleeping Bear Dunes, where her brother Bob was an assistant park manager at D.H. Day Park. He and his wife, Mary Ann, lived in a mobile home near the campground. Bob was a hearty, bluff outdoorsy type (of *course* "outdoorsy" – he was a *park ranger*!) who reminded me, alternately, of his father (Chet) or *McCloud*, the TV sheriff played by Dennis Weaver. He had the same kind of dark thick moustache and prominent hatchet-shaped nose. Since I'm not naturally very "outdoorsy," we didn't have much in common, but we got along fine, even though Terri had told me a few family horror stories of her own, about how mercilessly Bob had teased and tormented her as a child. In one of these stories, Bob had supposedly locked her in a closet, lit one of his dad's cigarettes and blew smoke under the door and shouted that the house was on fire, and then sit and snicker while she would pound on the door and scream in terror. In another scenario, whenever they disagreed over which TV show to watch, Bob would simply switch the TV to the channel he wanted to watch, then remove the knob and pocket it while Terri hollered in outraged protest. When Terri had told me these stories, I had expressed all the appropriate emotions of sympathy and horror, but had actually thought Bob's particular tortures to be quite inventive and imaginative. In any case, Bob and Mary Ann made us feel quite welcome that weekend. Bob showed me around the park and Terri spent some time holding and *ooh*-ing and *aah*-ing over their new baby, Kimmie.

A little later that summer we traveled south to Charlotte to meet her brother Don, his wife Sandra, and their one year-old daughter, Gwen. They were renting an old farmhouse outside of town off Chester Road at the time and Sandra was hugely pregnant again with their next child. Don had been an attorney for a few years by then. His practice was flourishing and he had just been appointed assistant prosecutor for Eaton County under prosecutor Willard Mikesell. He and Sandra had known each other since high school, but had only been married a few years and seemed to be making up for lost time, squeezing out babies as fast as they could. Their son, Donnie, was born that September, and their second daughter, Jennifer, joined them in early 1969, making their family complete.

I always found Terri's brother Don to be a very interesting and complex guy, although not easy to get close to. A lawyer by training, Don was interested in just about everything. He was a gourmet and connoisseur of fine food and wines and loved music, especially old-time country and bluegrass, although his considerable record collection also included a wide selection of old standards, and some jazz and classical music. He taught himself to play the banjo and encouraged Sandra to take up the "fiddle," and in later years they often initiated informal old-time music get-togethers at their home or at those of their fellow enthusiasts. Don was also very interested in conservation and nature projects. Some years later he would purchase eighty acres (later even more) of woods along the Thornapple River north of Charlotte where he had a house built that was totally heated by wood-fired stoves and a centrally located fireplace. He worked closely with his architect in designing the house, which was later featured in *Architectural Digest* and other such journals for its innovative design. He became a member and for a time, I think, the president of the Michigan Tree Farmers Association. While living in the woods, he bought a portable sawmill and set it up on the riverbank and learned to mill his own lumber from the various hardwoods and pines he culled carefully from his forest. Then he built an elaborate and meticulously equipped wood-working shop over his garage and taught himself joinery, cabinetry and wood-carving. He read voraciously in his spare time, mostly how-to books, but he was also knowledgeable about the classics and philosophy, although he rarely flaunted that side of himself. He always seemed quietly proud of his woods, his lumber and wood-working skills, his music and his family, although not necessarily in that order. Don died of cancer in December of 1998, just two weeks shy of his fifty-ninth birthday – much too early. I will always remember him as one of the few true Renaissance men of the twentieth century – a lawyer, scholar, conservationist, sawyer, carpenter, craftsman and musician. I'm sure I wasn't aware of *all* of his interests; they were simply too far-reaching and eclectic.

And did I mention chef? Because the weekend I first met Don and his family he did much of the cooking honors both at the stove and at the outdoor grill. Terri's parents were there, and so were her two quirky widowed aunts. Aunt Stella was visiting from Florida and Aunt Martha, or "Mart," had driven over from Monroe. It was, as I remember it, quite a festive family occasion, and everyone there made me feel welcome.

By summer's end then, Terri and I had both met most of each other's respective families and apparently received tacit stamps of approval. The wedding was still on for November.

* * * * *

34

SUMMER FUN IN THE SUN

In addition to these obligatory and mostly enjoyable visits to family, we also managed to squeeze in a couple of weekends of fun with friends. We went swimming several times, as I was always happy for any occasion that showed off more of Terri's lusciously rounded sun-browned body.

She tanned very deeply that summer and we both remember one Saturday afternoon when we dropped in at the Rohes' cabin out on Indian Lake. Since Dad had sold our cabin there in 1965, we had to depend on the hospitality of our former lakeside neighbors when we wanted to go swimming, but that was never a problem, since Barbara Rohe had always been like a second mom to me. On that Saturday when we arrived at the lake, young Al and his wife Joanne were there too with their three little girls. When Terri and I came down the hill from behind the cabin to the lakeshore, one of the girls, tiny tow-headed Amy, stared up at Terri in her white two-piece bathing suit – which even further accentuated her already deep tan – and asked with big-eyed innocence, "Are you white?"

Yup. She was white all right, Amy. I could personally attest to that, because every now and then – if I was good – I'd get a peek at some of that tender white flesh that never saw the sun. Even now it makes my jaws tight just thinking about it.

There were at least two other swimming parties I can remember from that summer. One was at John Nibbelink's cabin on Horsehead Lake, the same place where he'd hosted the ice-skating

Terri and me – dig that tan!

party the previous winter. It was a smaller gathering this time though, or at least I think it was, since I can only remember three or four couples from the summer swim party. John had brought Rinda, of course. And her roommate, Linda, came with John Cook, who had become quite the BMOC, or "big man on campus," by then, what with his involvement in both Vet's Club matters and student government. There must have been other couples there, but I can't remember who they were, probably because by then I was so wrapped up in Terri that I didn't notice much of anything else. (Or maybe it's just because I'm old now, and suffer from chronic CRS – that's "can't remember shit".)

What I *can* remember from that outing are clear blue skies and bright sunshine and being surrounded by beautiful, clean-limbed brown-skinned girls in two-piece bathing suits – although of course I really only noticed my *own* beautiful girl. John's folks had a raft on pontoons out in the deep water off their beach front that we dove from and basked upon that day. There were a couple of canoes we took turns with, paddling around cavorting in them, often tipping them over, then righting them and attempting to paddle them some more, even though they were half-filled with water. There were rubber rafts and inner tubes to play in too. And we played in the water like little kids all day, probably not giving much thought to the fact that carefree days like this would be few and far between as we grew older.

There was a speed boat with water skis which most of us tried our luck on, even though some of the girls had never been up on water skis before. The high point of the afternoon, at least for the guys (and I mean that in the nicest possible way), was probably when Cook's date, Linda, lost the top half of her suit during her take-off on the skis. She had already tried unsuccessfully several times to get up and away on the skis, and this time she had finally made it up and was *skiing*, by golly, and was so excited that for a few seconds she didn't even realize she was skiing topless. Of course everybody in the boat and on the raft noticed (and I'll bet everyone who was there still remembers it too). But good things in life never last long, and when Linda suddenly became aware of the wind and water spray hitting her bare chest, she immediately dropped the tow bar and crossed both arms over her breasts and sank slowly into the rippling wake of the boat, emitting a small high-pitched squeal of embarrassment. Completely mortified, she kept her arms crossed and continued to tread water while John Nibbelink brought the boat slowly back around, stopping to fish her top out of the water with a paddle. He then chugged slowly back up to Linda, who kept spinning around in the water trying to keep her back to the boat and all of its grinning occupants. John Cook, ever the chivalrous gentleman, tactfully averted his eyes as he gingerly proffered the dripping bathing suit top towards her, still on the end of the paddle. Reaching behind her, still leaking small *eeks* of mortification, Linda snatched the traitorous garment and got it back on in short order and the show was over – but the *telling* goes on.

To tell the truth, Linda, none of us really could have seen much, it all happened so fast. But you know how guys are, especially at that impressionable age. And there's that recessive Neanderthal gene that I mentioned earlier that always kicks in to obliterate any rational or polite thought anytime tits are around, especially bare ones. Well, probably that's "nuff said," as Hugh Morrow is so fond of saying when he ends his column in *The Pioneer*. Or suffice it to say, as old-time newspapers used to report, "a good time was had by all."

Fun in the sun – summer 1967

Rinda Person and John Nibbelink.

Linda Querback
and John Cook.

Terri and me.

The other swim party Terri and I were a part of that summer was at Higgins Lake, up just south of Grayling. We rode up with Rinda and John Nibbelink, who brought his canoe on top of his car. John Cook's folks had a summer mobile home on the shore of Higgins Lake. I think there were only four couples there that day. The water in Higgins Lake was a lot colder than it had been at Horsehead, but we did swim and canoe and ski anyway, and then gathered back at the trailer to get warm and fill up on burgers and hot dogs. Sadly, there were no impromptu hoochy-coochy shows on the water that afternoon. Probably what I remember most about that outing was the quality cuddling time Terri and I enjoyed in the back seat during the ride back to Ferris that night.

One of the reasons Terri enjoyed her summer so much was that her roommate, Norma, was there to share it with her. The two of them spent hours working on their tans that summer while I was hard at work "at the plant." Usually they would lie out on the concrete apron or the grass behind the dorm, but sometimes they would catch a ride with some other girls down to the damn at Rogers Heights, a favorite sun-bathing spot for Ferris co-eds.

On August 15 Norma turned twenty-one, and she and Terri and a few other friends all gathered at the bar in the Casa Nova to celebrate. When I finished work at Kel-Reed that day I drove down and met this festive group. They had all been treating Norma to drinks for nearly an hour already by the time I got there, so she was bleary-eyed and extremely happy when I joined the group.

Terri and I both also remember that occasion as the day she went "back to brunette." She had colored her hair while I was at work, and the change was so startling and abrupt that the first time I scanned the table of revelers I didn't even recognize her, much to the amusement of Norma and the other people there. Terri had been worried that I would be upset, and I probably was, at least initially, but I quickly got used to it. It was only the first of "minny minny" times that she would change or experiment with her hair in our life together.

Besides being Norma's birthday, August 15 is also, as any good Catholic knows – or *used* to know – a "holy day of obligation," the feast of The Assumption. So, being good Catholic boys and girls, after drinking the early afternoon away (those of us who were old enough), we adjourned to the Ferris chapel to attend five o'clock Mass. Unfortunately by this time, having been plied with powerful drinks like White Russians and Harvey Wallbangers all afternoon, Norma could barely stand up, let alone negotiate the repetitious stand-sit-kneel routine of Mass. About fifteen minutes into the service, Norma's butt slumped back against the seat and she began to sway slightly. Terri and I attempted to prop her up from either side, but she then began to take on a distinctly unhealthy green-ish pallor, and finally emitted a low moan of misery that turned heads all around us. Not a good sign, so Terri and I and Lee, a pharmacy major Norma had recently begun dating, hoisted her up and escorted her as quietly as possible out the back door. It was a damn good thing we did too, because as soon as we got her outside, Norma doubled over and barfed unceremoniously all over the sidewalk and Lee's shoes.

Without any discussion, we all somehow agreed that we had probably fulfilled our holy day obligation. Terri and I helped pour Norma into Lee's car, then we got into mine and scrammed, feeling a little guilty, but mostly wondering what the faithful would think upon emerging from Mass and encountering that rank pool of puke right on God's doorstep. What would God say? *Normie, your sins are forgiven. Go and sin no more ... oh, and Normie? ... Happy birthday, Sweetie.*

Terri and me, dressed up for my five-year HS reunion, summer '67

And so our summer of love passed blissfully by and all too soon it was over. At the end of August, the summer term completed, I helped Terri move her stuff out of the dorm and pack it all into her dad's Ford and kissed her good-bye before she headed back home to Belleville.

A few days later I punched out for the last time at Kel-Reed, having said my farewells to Donna, Gladys, Norv, and the others back in Assembly. I even stopped in at

243

the front office and thanked Cy Kingsbury for giving me the job for the summer. He wished me the best and I was gone.

Six months after I left Kel-Reed, the old sign came down and the plant officially became The Gardner-Denver Company, Reed City Plant. The operation continued to expand and grow for a few more years and changed names and ownership a couple more times. By the mid-eighties, however, things began to slow down. The economy went south, in more ways than one, and down-sizing took its inevitable toll in Reed City just as it did all over the country. In November of 1986 production shut down at Cooper Group Wire Wrap (the plant's final name), and by the following February the final few employees closed the doors for good. For hundreds of former employees, it was the end of an era in Reed City.

* * * * *

35

FINDING A HOME
IN MOUNT PLEASANT

The end of August marked the end of our time at Ferris, but Terri and I had already begun to lay the groundwork for the next phase of our life. Earlier that month I had made a quick day trip east across M-20 to Mount Pleasant to find out about the housing situation for married students at Central. At the CMU Housing Office I learned that there was a waiting list for the on-campus married housing complex, and that I wouldn't be able to even get on the list until after we were married, which was logical, but still frustrating to me nevertheless. I wanted so badly for our transition to Central and to married life to go smoothly. The responsibilities of marriage were already beginning to weigh heavily on my young shoulders, even months before the fact.

I picked up maps of the campus and of Mount Pleasant and started going through the ads for off-campus apartments, both from the bulletin board at the Housing Office and from the local newspaper. I made a list of several likely places. Armed with my list and maps, I set off to look for a new home for me and my bride. Turning north from the parking lot outside Warner Hall, I drove up the street towards the small commercial strip that marked the northern boundary of the campus and housed several businesses, including a beauty shop and the SBX (Student Book Exchange). I turned east on Bellows and had only gone about a block when I spied an apartment-for-rent sign in the yard of a house across the street from Barnard Hall.

Wow! I thought. *This would sure be convenient.* Pulling over quickly, I scanned down my list, but found no telephone number that matched the one on the sign. I copied down the number from the sign and becoming more excited by the minute, I parked the car in front of Barnard and got out and walked across the street for a closer look.

The house, which stood on a corner lot, was an old Victorian with a rounded, windowed turret, or cupola, jutting off the second story in front. That tower intrigued me, and as I stood on the sidewalk gazing up at it, an old rust-pitted Rambler station wagon came puttering slowly down Fancher from the north and turned into the driveway behind the house. I walked around back just as the driver was getting out of the car. He had long blonde hair pulled back and tied with a rubber band in a scruffy pony tail and was wearing faded cutoff jeans, a holey yellow tee-shirt and sandals, and didn't look any older than me. I introduced myself and told him I was looking for an apartment and had seen the sign and liked the look of the cupola on the front of the house. The guy, who introduced himself simply as Randy, laughed. Rubbing his stubbly jaw, he acknowledged that yeah, he'd always thought that the tower was cool too. Then he explained that the apartment that would be up for rental was his own, and it was in the back of the house. Unfortunately it didn't come with anything as fancy as a turret. My excitement dwindled a bit at hearing this, but only for a moment, because then, looking me up and down quickly and apparently deciding I was harmless, Randy asked if I'd like to see the place, as long as I was here.

My heart leapt again, and I said, "Sure. I mean if it's not too much trouble."

Randy shook his head. "Nah, it's no trouble, man. Lemme just make sure my girl friend's decent before you come up."

As he opened the screen door on the tiny back porch and went in, he explained briefly to me that the old house had been cut up into four apartments, two upstairs and two down, and he had the back upstairs one. Inside the door to the right, a narrow stairway, the worn wooden steps painted a dull brown, led upwards toward sunlight which streamed through a tall unadorned window at the top.

431 East Bellows in Mount Pleasant, front and rear views –
our first home together

"Jeannie?" Randy called up the stairs as we climbed, "Are you dressed?"

A girl's face appeared over the stair railing on our left, a curtain of long straight light brown hair keeping her features in shadow. "Yeah. Why?" she replied, then, seeing me, "Oh, hi."

"Jeannie, this is Tim. He's looking for a place for fall. I told him we were moving out at the end of the month."

We were at the top of the stairs now, standing on a narrow sun-drenched landing. Jeannie proved to be a tall, slim very striking-looking brunette whose hair fell halfway down her back. She was wearing a pair of very short blue shorts with a pink tank top. She was barefoot and also very obviously bra-less, which I tried valiantly not to notice, but *Holy crap*! as ol' Frank Romano would say. A guy just can't help noticing things like that. It was one of those *Wayne's World* "ka-ching" moments.

The girl gave me a curious look, then lowered her lashes prettily and gave me another shy, "Hi." Then she turned and walked back through a very small galley-like kitchen area, spluttering embarrassedly, "Oh, *Randy*, it's such a *mess* in here!"

Randy rolled his eyes at me and said, "He don't care, Hon. He just wants to see the layout of the place. Right, Tim?"

I nodded agreeably as I followed them through the galley, trying to take everything in and get my mind back to the business at hand and off this strange girl's gazongas. Those bodacious bobbling boobies. Those hellacious honkers. Those tasty 'tater tits. Those …

For Christ's sake, Bazzett, shame on you! You're here to find a place to live, dammit, a home for you and your bride! Gitcher mind outa the gutter! Thou shalt not covet and all that shit, ya know? In this fashion I finally internally admonished myself and tried to concentrate on inspecting the real estate as I came into the front room.

There was a small antiquated metal fan sitting on the dinette table positioned in front of a tall open window just inside the door from the kitchen. The fan rattled and whirred noisily as it tried rather pathetically to move the stiflingly hot air around the room.

"Oh yeah," Randy said. "I didn't tell you, but it gets hotter 'n hell up here in the summertime. The only way you can get any sleep at all is to sleep naked."

Jeannie nervously and self-consciously crossed her arms over her chest when Randy said this, and I tried my best to banish that "sleeping naked" image from my mind. I even tried imagining Terri sleeping naked here, but still felt guilty. After all, we weren't married yet.

The front room was dominated by a double bed pushed up against the far wall where a narrow rectangular screened window let in the shrill sound of singing cicadas from outside. The ceiling sloped down to just above the window. There was a battered old-fashioned-style wooden pedestal desk with three side drawers wedged against the wall at the foot of the bed, a chair from the dinette set pushed in under it. The desk top was piled with books and papers and the rumpled landscape of the unmade bed was strewn with odd pieces of clothing, a set of dingy-looking patterned sheets showing beneath the clutter. A large gray cat stretched on the bed near the window regarded the three of us solemnly with inscrutable yellow eyes. On the near side of the bed was a brown metal gas heater, obviously turned off for the summer, since its top was covered with more clothes and a crooked stack of tattered paperbacks perched precariously on the corner nearest the bed pillows.

"This is actually the living room," Randy explained, sweeping his arm in a wide gesture, "but we put the bed in here because it's warmer next to the stove in the winter, and in the summer you can catch a little cross ventilation between the two windows. " He reached across the bed and rubbed the cat's head. "An' ol' Zero here likes to lie in the window, don'cha, Sport?" The cat recoiled from his touch, gathered itself and leapt off the bed and ran into the adjoining room.

"Dumb fuck," Randy muttered. "That's why we call him Zero. Dumbest fuckin' cat ya ever saw."

"He is *not*!" exclaimed Jeannie. "He just knows you don't really like him." And she followed the cat into the next room.

Randy shrugged. "*Her* cat," he explained unnecessarily. Then he gestured across the room to a low door near the stove. "There's the bathroom." Through the door I could see a metal, rust-pocked shower stall, a sink and a toilet.

Then I followed him into the other room where Jeannie sat on a small worn love seat holding the cat in her lap, stroking its ears and cooing soothingly to it. This room was even smaller than the front room and was crowded with too much furniture. Besides the love seat, there was a vanity with a large round mirror and a padded stool, a chest of drawers, a small bookcase filled to overflowing, and a doubtful-looking overstuffed chair also covered with clothes and books.

"This is supposed to be the bedroom," Randy said. "That's why it looks so crowded."

I nodded and backed out of the room. That was it. I'd seen the whole place. I asked Randy about the rent. He said they'd been paying $65 a month for the summer, but the landlord had said the rent would probably go back up for the new school year, so he wasn't sure what it would be.

My mind reeled at this information. Most of the ads in the paper and on the bulletin board had been asking at least a hundred dollars and some of them much more. I couldn't believe my good fortune. What a *savings* that could be! Our budget would, after all, be pretty pitiful. It never occurred to me that someone else – like Terri, for instance – might see this place as a cramped, fetid rat hole, and find it totally unacceptable. I was thinking mostly in terms of dollars saved – and maybe, just a little too, of the two of us naked and sweating together on that bed on a hot night.

I used Randy and Jeannie's phone to call downtown to the realtor who managed the property and arranged to meet him to sign a lease agreement. The rent would be $75 a month – *still* a steal, I thought. I thanked the young couple, then drove into town and signed the papers and left a deposit. Our first apartment – our first *home!* – was a done deal. And I'd handled it all by myself. Maybe I really *was* becoming an adult.

Before leaving town I made arrangements with Randy and Jeannie to bring Terri back the following week so she could see the apartment too. They were agreeable to this, and Jeannie even promised to have the place cleaned up a little better by then. As I headed back west that afternoon my mind was boiling with plans, not the least of which was I needed to get Terri into one of those tank tops. Maybe an orange one; it'd look great with her tan. I could already imagine peeling it off her, like peeling an orange. A juicy one. Yeah, that was a *great* plan!

A week later I returned with Terri in tow and ushered her proudly into my frugal find. Jeannie had been true to her word and picked the place up and cleaned, and Randy had even moved a couple pieces of the old furniture from the bedroom out into the garage, so it didn't look quite so cramped and crowded.

I have to hand it to Terri. She wasn't put off by the near-claustrophobic dimensions of the place, but seemed genuinely as delighted with it as I was. In the tiny kitchen she examined the single appliance unit that housed all-in-one a small four-burner stove and oven and a sink and refrigerator, and exclaimed over its space-saving ingenuity. She peered out the kitchen window over the stove and ran her fingers over the small shelves on the opposite wall intended for use as a miniscule pantry. Randy explained to her that all the furniture went with the apartment except for the dinette set, which they had bought second hand. I offered him ten bucks if he would leave it and he accepted on the spot. Pocketing my ten, he told us there were some other old pieces of furniture stored in the garage that we could use too, if we wanted it. Terri looked approvingly about at the other two rooms and bathroom. Then she stood looking speculatively at the bed wedged between the wall and the gas heater. She glanced back into the other room again and said, "I think I'd rather have the bed back in the bedroom so we can use this room for a living room."

"No problem," I replied quickly. "I can do that as soon as I move in. Whaddaya think otherwise, Hon?"

Taking one last sweeping look around, she turned to me and squeezed my arm. "It's perfect," she said, smiling up at me.

Until then I hadn't even realized that I'd practically been holding my breath the whole time Terri had been inspecting the place. Letting out an involuntary sigh of relief, I decided all over again at that moment, *I love this woman.*

* * * * *

251

36

A BED MADE UP WITH LOVE

I moved into the apartment at Bellows and Fancher on September 7, a week before fall semester registration. I'm not sure why then, but probably because my lease began on September 1, and I must have figured if I'm paying for it, I might as well live in it. I was able to pack pretty much everything I needed into my VW – clothing, books, records, my small record player and transistor radio. I also packed my electric coil corn popper, the same one I had bought in an Ayer hardware store in December of 1962, soon after I had arrived at Fort Devens. Being able to pop my own corn again after the nightmare of two months of basic training had somehow helped to alleviate the dull ache of homesickness back then. I was probably hoping it would do the same for me this time, as I struck out on my own again, but this time without even the rough camaraderie that communal barracks life had provided.

Mom and Dad helped me with my move, loading up their own car with things they figured I would need to set up housekeeping – a small collection of pots and pans, dishes, glasses, cups, silverware and a few other kitchen utensils. They also provided me with sheets and blankets and an old white chenille bedspread that I remembered had once covered their own bed when I was small. They brought a few old lamps and light bulbs, throw rugs and a carpet sweeper, broom and dust pan and numerous other household necessities I never would have thought of myself. Mom also raided her own pantry and packed bags of canned goods, along with a dozen eggs and a loaf of bread. In short, she was making sure I wouldn't go hungry during my first week or two in Mount Pleasant.

Upon our arrival at the apartment, Mom even took the time to help me sweep and clean, even though Randy and Jeannie had left the place in pretty good shape. Dad helped me re-arrange things; we moved the bed from the front room back into the bedroom and switched the few other furnishings from one room to the other too. In the course of doing this, we discovered that the bed was missing one leg. It had one of those old-fashioned box springs with wooden legs screwed into the four corners. One corner was supported by three stacked bricks. It would be only the first of several surprises that bed held in store for us. I just shrugged and carried the bricks into the bedroom and re-inserted them back under the corner at the foot of the bed.

The last thing Mom did before leaving that day was to make up the bed with clean sheets and a blanket and that white bedspread, smoothing it lovingly with her hands as she tucked it up under and over the pillows. Taking a last look around, she and Dad both declared the apartment to be very nice. "Cozy" was the word they used, I think, and it was an apt description of the place, probably because of the way it seemed to be tucked up under the eaves of the house and the way its sloping ceilings made it seem even smaller than it actually was.

When Mom hugged me good-bye outside at the car, she was smiling, but there were tears in her eyes. She had already realized something it would take me a few more days to figure out, which was that I wouldn't ever really be coming home again. In less than three months I would be married, and this place would be my home, one I would share with my bride, and when Terri and I came back to Reed City, it would only be to visit. Looking back now, I can see how that final act of hers – making up that battered second-hand bed and smoothing out that threadbare old spread that had covered her and Dad for so many nights and years – was more significant than I could ever have understood at the time. I know I'm a little late, Mom, but thank you for that small gift – not just for the bedspread, but for all the love that went along with it and kept us warm and safe for those early years. The bedspread is long gone, of course, but the love remains. Since that day we have watched our own kids grow up, fall in love and move away, and we've made up a few of those beds ourselves. Now we understand.

* * * * *

37

BACH-ING IT ON BELLOWS – CMU

While it's true that I was pretty lonely during those final few months of my bachelorhood, I wasn't entirely friendless. My friends from Ferris, Don and Mary Ellen Dobson, had moved to CMU about a week before I got there. They were living in Shepherd, a tiny town several miles south of Mount Pleasant, where Don had found a job at Walt Dean's Auto Repair, and they had moved into a small upstairs apartment in Walt's sister's house nearby.

When I had first met the Dobsons in the fall of '65 they had been newlyweds. When we re-connected at Central in the fall of '67 they were "newly-parents." After Don graduated from Ferris, they had gone home to Maine for the summer where Don found work as a house painter. Their son, Dougie, was born in August.

Fatherhood hadn't changed Don much. He still had the same slap-happy goofy approach to life he'd always had, and little Dougie was like a new toy to him, as he proudly showed the baby off to me. He was also extremely pleased with the "new and improved economy-sized headlamps" now sported by his nursing wife, and wasn't shy about pointing them out to me either, much to Mary's – and *my* – embarrassment. But that was just Donnie. Life is short. Enjoy every moment of it while it's happening.

A couple days after I moved into my new spaces, Donnie came over to help me re-furnish it. I had found an old piece of a sectional sofa in the garage that was a little longer and in slightly better shape than the worn-out sagging love seat that Randy and Jeannie had been using, so we carried the love seat down the stairs and out into the garage. Then we brought the "newer" (and I use the term *very* loosely) piece out into the driveway for a better look. It was upholstered in a pale green faded brocade material and had an arm at one end, which I figured I could put up against the wall where the ceiling sloped down to the window. Then the armless end would adjoin my one end table and lamp. We noticed that the piece was coated with dust, so I whacked it a couple times lightly with the flat of my hand, which raised a small puff of dust. A couple more whacks produced still more dust clouds. *Hmmm* … Perhaps a more thorough cleaning was called for here, so, after poking around a bit in the corners of the garage, Don and I found an old cracked softball bat which had been repaired with tape and a nearly tine-less broom rake, which we brought outside. Leaning the long seat cushion from the sofa up against the back porch steps, I proceeded to lay into it mightily with the rake. Dense billowing clouds of the dust of ages rose from the cushion. Meanwhile Don began flailing the back cushion of the sofa with the bat, producing similar results. We kept at it, but it seemed like the more we pounded, the darker and thicker the dust became. After a few minutes of this we both stood panting, sweating and laughing, amazed at the amount of filth this single piece of furniture seemed to hold.

Shaking my head, I pondered the situation, and then asked, "Whaddaya think, Don? Can this sofa be saved?"

Don laughed and said, "You sound like the goddamn *Ladies' Home Journal* – 'Can this marriage be saved?'" Then he picked up the couch seat cushion off the steps, tucked it back into place and sat down on it right there in the driveway. Bouncing his butt gently up and down, he moved from one end to the other. "At least there ain't no springs pokin' you in the ass," he said. "I say fuck it. It's good enough. Let's take it inside and you can cover it up with somethin'."

And so we did. I had an ancient Indian blanket Mom had given me that was so thin in some places you could nearly see through it. I folded it in half and used it as a throw to cover up "that filthy fuckin' piece of shit," as Don and I came to affectionately call the former cast-off couch.

Don actually became quite fond of that ratty old sofa as the fall term progressed. He had an early class three mornings a week, followed by an hour or two before his next one, so he would often let himself into the apartment while I was still sleeping (I gave him a key), drop his books on the table and sack out on the couch, his feet on the end table, and would be snoring contentedly when I got up a little later to fix some breakfast. Those two o'clock feedings at his own place were obviously screwing up his sleep patterns.

About a week after I got settled in, I took the ACT's and registered for a full load of classes, fifteen semester hours. It wasn't a bad schedule, especially considering what a free-for-all competitive clusterfuck registration was back in those pre-computer days, with crowded shoving lines of harried students queuing up at long tables set up in the field house to consult with equally tense and frustrated teachers filling in as "academic advisors." Mondays, Wednesdays and Fridays I would be busy all day long, but Tuesdays I would have no classes and only one on Thursday. I had managed to get three English courses (Advanced Composition, Creative Writing, and College Grammar), a sociology course (Juvenile Delinquency), and a speech course. At least I was through with math and science courses, which was a tremendous relief to me.

But the most important part of my finally getting registered and having a confirmed class schedule, at least to me, was that now I could find work too. As far back as August, during my house-hunting jaunt, I had stopped in at the university work-study office and inquired about getting a job with the custodial crew like the one I'd had at Ferris. At that time I'd been told that I couldn't really be hired until I was formally registered and knew what my class schedule would be. So on the same day I registered I also stopped in at the cafeteria food commons that served Barnard, Ronan and Sloan Halls and applied for a job. After checking over my paperwork and application forms and noting that I had worked for nearly two years at Ferris, the woman in charge of Food Services asked me how soon I could start. I told her I could start right then, but she told me to report the next night instead. I found out I could work from five to eight on weeknights, and then could work every other weekend if I wanted to. I was so pleased I damn near jumped up and clicked my heels.

Why was I so excited about washing dishes and sweeping and mopping floors? It was the money, pure and simple. By today's standards, of course, the amounts were truly piddling sums, since it was a minimum wage job. But I think the minimum wage had only recently "jumped" to $1.25 an hour, and even a minute increase like that was cause for rejoicing for a cash-strapped student. The truth of the matter, however, was that I was pretty near flat broke at that point and was desperate to generate some income. My GI Bill money was temporarily in limbo during my transition from Ferris to Central, and I wasn't sure when that would start again. It was still a hundred bucks a month, which seemed like a small fortune to me, particularly in my present financial circumstances.

I started work the next day, but it would be a while before I got my first pay check and got the GI Bill paperwork all straightened out, so I ended up having to borrow a couple hundred bucks from Dad to pay my next month's rent and sundry other expenses.

There's no way I would remember all this after all these years, but here is an excerpt from a letter I wrote to Terri about that time. It's postmarked September 16, 1967.

"... You know, the last time I was home for the day (last Sunday) something hit me that I hadn't really thought much about before. I've left home for good now. At present this apartment is my home and will be until we move out, because I'm never going home to stay again. I mean I'm not crying about it or anything like that, but I've realized that an essential period in my life has passed. I'm my own man from now on. It's kind of scary when you stop to think about it. I suppose everyone thinks about this at one time or another though, especially when they're getting ready to get married. It was different when I was in the army, because I always thought about going home again, but not this time. After November 24th there's no going home anymore. Wherever we settle – that's home. I suppose you've already thought of these things, but you know me, I'm kind of slow.

Well, now after all this talk about being my own man I'll

tell you something else that doesn't jive with it very well. I've only got about $5 left and I haven't bought any books yet and all my bills and rent are coming due before long and my first pay check here won't be for 3 or 4 weeks and my GI Bill won't start until at least November the Vet's clerk told me, so – I'm gonna have to borrow about $200 from my dad. I sure am independent, huh? Oh well ... Thank goodness for generous, loving parents, I guess."

Thank goodness indeed.

In her return letter, Terri enclosed a five-dollar bill, she felt so sorry for me. I was so embarrassed about getting money from my girl that I refused to spend it. Instead – and I informed her of this action – I put it with a couple more dollars and opened a savings account at the Isabella State Bank downtown. The account held $9.36 and I called it "the baby fund."

* * * * *

38

WEDDING PLANS
AND FAMILY PLANNING

You might wonder at this point (since I neglected to tell you –
DOH!) what Terri was doing while I was pining away for her at
Central. Well, she was home in Belleville where her mother had
gotten her a job as "shampoo girl" at Madeline's Beauty Shop.
Since she wasn't yet officially licensed as a beautician, she couldn't
do much else, so she kept busy doing shampoos, cleaning combs,
sweeping and doing general go-fer work around the shop. And of
course she and her mom were also very busy with the on-going
wedding plans, about all of which I remained blessedly oblivious,
other than finally providing, under some duress, a guest list from
my side of the family, which Mom helped me put together one
Sunday.

I had tried to get Joe Capozzi, my best friend and roommate for
most of my three-year hitch in the army, to be my Best Man, but he
was engaged himself by then back home in New York, and wasn't
able to come, so I tapped my favorite older brother, Bill, for that
honor. I'm not really sure how typical I was as a prospective
bridegroom, but the truth was I didn't really give a shit who the
Best Man or Maid of Honor were, or how many people should be
in the wedding party, or whether we should have liquor at the
reception, or what color dresses the bridesmaids wore. All that crap
was just so much *yadda-yadda-yadda* and *blah-blah-blah* to me. I
just wanted to get it over with – to be *married*.

TIMOTHY JAMES BAZZETT

Because I was pretty miserable for much of that waiting time, from September through November. I was living for every other weekend, when I would finish work at 8 PM on Friday night and jump in my car and fly low all the way to Belleville where Terri would be waiting for me. But even on those much-anticipated and precious weekends it seemed there was never enough private time for us. The world seemed to intrude at every turn, and suddenly it would be Sunday night and I'd have to head back north again – alone.

Being together only every other weekend was a compromise to the reality of our financial situation. I had to earn the money just to make ends meet, but every payday I also made myself put at least a dollar or two in the bank, into that "baby fund."

We were young and dumb and in love, so we did dream about babies, and talked about them too. I wanted one right away, but Terri, who was nearly four years younger than me, wasn't quite so sure. I think perhaps my enthusiasm on the subject may have frightened her a bit, but she was game; I'll give her that. Since I came from a family of six kids and had enjoyed a reasonably happy childhood, either five or six seemed like a good number to me. But it you're female, and only nineteen or twenty years old yourself, maybe those numbers wouldn't sound so good. *Now* I can understand that, but at the time I was, as I said, young and dumb.

Let's talk a bit about birth control, okay? Because Terri and I, we talked about it, even before we were married. We both knew that "in the eyes of the Church" (or sometimes – even *more* guilty-making – "Holy Mother Church") any form of artificial birth control was a sin, and a "*mortal*" one at that.

In Maryland we once had an aged Redemptorist priest who liked to tell anecdotes about Calvin Coolidge, a president who was very stingy with words, and so had become known as "Silent Cal." One of Father Litz's favorite stories was the one where Coolidge went to Sunday services, and when he came home his wife asked him, "What did the preacher talk about today, Cal?"

"Sin," the president responded.

"And what did he have to say about it?"

"He's ag'in it." Coolidge replied.

Well, like ol' Silent Cal, when it came to the "sin" of birth control, I was ag'in it. And so too, at least in principle, I think, was Terri. Like I said, we were both young and dumb – and in love – which I suppose made things even more complicated, because here we were, two good Catholic kids on the verge of marriage, and we both wanted to do the right thing. I mean marriage itself was pretty scary without bringing this volatile and potentially divisive issue of birth control into the mix.

About the only thing I knew about birth control was using rubbers, or "pulling out," and neither option was ever considered a particularly pleasant one, at least if you were a guy, I mean. On a scale of one to ten, my experience with either method was probably, oh, maybe a one and a half to two, and Terri's was, umm, well – zero.

And hey, I'm not even gonna try to talk about the "rhythm method," which was really little more than a bad joke perpetrated against conscientious Catholics. It was, however, along with abstinence, the only method condoned by the Church and approved by the Pope. But as the more cavalier Italian Catholics of the time were purportedly fond of telling the Holy Father, *"Aay, Papa. You no playa da game, you no make-a da rules, eh?"*

But it was a new era – the sixties – and a new factor had entered the birth control equation by this time, and they called it "the Pill."

About two months before our wedding date, Terri went to her gynecologist for a routine pre-marriage physical. In the course of taking down her medical history, the doctor determined that Terri's periods occurred at rather irregular intervals, so, of course, he wrote her a prescription for six months of the pill, in order to "regulate her periods."

The fact of the matter is this was a pretty standard practice at the time. The prescription was a kind of "gift of time" from doctor to patient. I mean we're all adults here, right? And we all know that it's hard enough for two people to adjust to each other's habits, quirks, and idiosyncrasies in those early, sometimes difficult first days of a marriage. If you suddenly throw a third brand-new person – a *baby* – into the mix, it can make things a lot more complicated, if not downright impossible.

I can say *now* "we all know." But *then*? Hell, I didn't know shit from Shinola back then about marriage or babies, and neither did Terri. So when she told me about the results of her physical the next day over the phone, and particularly about her new prescription, I jumped right on past the *good* news that she was healthy and sound, and fastened right on to what I thought of (in my youthful brainwashed ignorance) as the *bad* news about those god-awful forbidden pills. I can almost see again my clueless and smooth young brow and how it must have wrinkled in righteous concern over this insidious incipient *sin* of "the pill." It was probably a Saturday and I had just returned from my weekly trek to confession, where I had once again mumbled through the curtained grill my tired guilty litany of sins, especially that one ubiquitous sin that all young men are constantly tortured by – the one that feels so good when you're doing it, but makes you feel so bad and ashamed afterwards, at least if you've been brought up as a GCB. Washed clean once again and feeling pretty good about myself, and then came this phone conversation with my girl, whom I missed so terribly, and it's about birth control, which I know in my heart the Church says is a mortal sin, and yet – God help me – just talking about it probably gave me a long-distance hard-on. The sixties GCB equivalent of phone sex.

My confused and strenuous objections to Terri's new prescription then, however morally well-intentioned they might have been, were obviously upsetting to her. She had no doubt been rather relieved when her doctor had explained to her the necessity of the pill for the aforementioned "regulatory" reasons. It had made sense to her. She was, after all, barely twenty years old, and although she wanted babies in an abstract sense, the reality of motherhood was still a pretty scary proposition to someone who had, just a few scant years before, still been playing with her Barbies and Betsy-Wetsy.

If I remember correctly, after listening to me bluster on for a few minutes about how "wrong" taking the pill would be, Terri began to cry over the phone, which stopped my stupid pseudo-theological proselytizing dead in its tracks. I couldn't bear to hear her cry, so I back-pedaled quickly from my rigid stance on the matter and promised her that I would talk to a priest about it. She wasn't at all sure about how much good that would do, but at least she stopped crying. I was quickly learning that this marriage business was a whole lot more complicated that it had appeared to be. Hanging up the phone, I wondered unhappily when did the "happily-ever-after" part start, anyway.

Of course, Terri and I were not the only engaged or newly married Catholic couple struggling with this troubling issue of birth control – although it probably seemed that way to us. There was a school of thought among young Catholics in that era, however, that believed birth control could be integrated into your marriage without guilt, and even without sin. It was simply a matter of shopping around until you found "the right priest." Because the Catholic clergy in the United States was radically divided on this one particular issue, despite what Rome or the Holy Father said (and still *does*). It was a time of new freedoms and winds of change were in the air in the American Church. There was even open rebellion against certain rigid inflexible tenets laid down by Rome, particularly among the younger priests, who preached – and *believed* – that God was *not* the righteous, vengeful god of the Old Testament. No. Their message was "God is Love," and "God understands," and "God forgives."

1958 seminary photo of Roger Dunnigan, my CMU campus pastor in 1967

We got lucky. I didn't even have to shop. The parish priest at the CMU Catholic chapel of St. Mary's was an old friend of mine from my St. Joe's Seminary days in Grand Rapids. Roger Dunnigan had been an upperclassman there when I was a high school freshman. He was still pretty new to the priesthood in 1967 and seemed genuinely delighted to see me when I showed up at the campus rectory looking for some guidance and advice. He seemed more like a good friend than a priest, and he immediately put me at ease and made me feel better.

TIMOTHY JAMES BAZZETT

It is difficult for me to describe, in retrospect, the anxiety and concern I was feeling at the time, so I won't try. Instead I will include here a passage from another letter I wrote to Terri after my meeting with "Father Roger." My young, innocent, cocksure, moralistic and chauvinistic self shows painfully through, but here it is (postmarked October 10, 1967).

"... Yesterday I talked to Roger Dunnigan (Father) like I said I was going to and lo and behold, your stupid fiancé found out a lot of things firsthand which you had told me before but I couldn't quite bring myself to accept and I still don't completely, but I have seen the light anyway. I explained the whole situation to him and asked him what the Church thought about it. He kind of spread his hands and said, "Nothing." He says it's perfectly all right and then he went on to explain himself. He says there is no sin in taking the pill as long as you have a justifiable reason for it. I went on to ask him if one could use the pill, then, to space or regulate a family, and this too is acceptable. He explained that there can be no sin in this as long as it is done out of love. He also speculated that the pill might not work in the way it's supposed to, to regulate your period, because this doesn't always work. Now, with all this in mind, and armed with the knowledge that it is permissible to use the pill when necessary – I'll give you my renewed views on it. I think you should continue to take them for as long as they're prescribed – 6 months, I think you said. This will give us some time to get on our feet financially. (He also said it was permissible to use them when it's a matter of economical sense.) But now I'd like to tell you what I would like to do and I hope you don't think I'm unreasonable because you know how much I love you, despite all my funny little quirks. After your prescription runs out (after this 6 months) I don't want you to renew it, because (and I suppose you knew this all along) I want to start a family. And if we do have a baby right away then you can start taking the pill again for a time so we won't get all bogged down like Bob and Maureen or Don and Sandy. This won't be for long though, because I hope after I

265

graduate that we can come to depend less and less on this method. Now that we do have a clearer picture of things and the necessary information, there's one more thing we have to do, Honey – that's to pray to God that He will bless us with children that we can love and who will love us back and to hope that we can be as good parents as our parents were for us ...."

I can't resist adding here my own postscript to this letter, which requires a short explanation. In our talks about having kids someday, we also talked about possible names for our kids, and Terri always said the same thing. She wanted to have at least two boys and a girl, and she had already picked out her first boy's name. He would be called Jeffrey Thomas. So as a gesture of peace and good will, at the end of this somewhat stilted, arrogant and angst-ridden letter, I added:

"I'm looking forward to meeting Jeffrey Thomas someday – I hope it won't be too long. I love you."

(I finally had the extreme pleasure of meeting Jeffrey Thomas on May 3, 1969.)

Flash forward twenty-four years – Jeffrey Thomas Bazzett at the corner of Bellows and Fancher in November 1991. The house had been razed, but behind him is Barnard Hall.

266

Talk about contrasts and priest shopping! I have to tell you now about the priest we visited in Belleville one weekend for what amounted to the totality of our pre-marriage counseling.

Father Welsh was the assistant pastor at St. Anthony's parish where Terri had grown up and attended eight grades of Catholic school. He was probably not much older than Roger Dunnigan, perhaps even the same age, but he seemed light years behind Roger in his attitude – or comfort level – in talking about things like sex and birth control, which needed to be discussed in these pre-Cana sessions. Terri and I had both read some booklet or pamphlet we'd been given and Father Welsh asked if we had any questions. We didn't, so then he reminded us of our obligations regarding having any children that should "issue from our union" properly baptized in the Church and raised as Catholics. We readily assured him that we understood this.

Then, obviously uncomfortable, and seemingly unable to look either of us in the eye, Father Welsh looked down at this desk and nervously shuffled some papers and said, "And you do both understand, of course, the Church's position on, ummm ..." Here he faltered and dropped his chin down into his shirt front and mumbled, very softly, "umm ... *brdptrol?*"

Both of us leaned forward, trying to catch his words. *Huh? Bird patrol?*

"Excuse me, Father. What did you say?" I asked.

Blushing deeply to the very roots of his hair, poor Father Welsh repeated, "Do you both know where the Church stands on the, er, matter of, um, (*phlegmy throat-clearing noises here*)-trol?"

Both Terri and I must have still looked pretty blank, so finally the priest managed to spit it out. "Birth control. Do you understand the Church's position on it?" Father's face was beet red by now. He seemed to be scrutinizing a section of his study wall directly behind us and just above our heads.

"Oh, *BIRTH* control," I replied. "Yes, Father. I've already discussed it with our parish priest at Central."

"Well, that's good," he sighed in relief. "Well, then, if you haven't any further questions, umm ..."

And that concluded our official pre-marital instructions in the Church. Not only were we lucky in love. We had also gotten pretty damn lucky in our priest shopping too.

I would like to point out here that I am *not* trying to poke fun at the Church. I'm poking gentle fun at people, and I realized many years ago that priests are people too, just like us. Their job encompasses the best and the worst of the human lot. By the best, I mean I think a priest holds an enviable position, one much nearer to God. He has God's ear. He enjoys God's love. By the worst, I mean I think that, from a human standpoint, it can be one of the loneliest jobs on earth.

* * * * *

39

PEST CONTROL, PIZZAS AND MY BROTHER BILL

But enough of my half-baked shanty-Irish theology. How did I manage to stave off my own loneliness in those months before the wedding? Well, I kept busy. I worked in the food commons every night after classes, and it was all I could do to keep up with all the reading and writing that my teachers kept piling on as the semester progressed. And there were small unpleasant glitches in my humdrum semi-monastic life that also relieved the tedium from time to time.

Here's one I remember well. During the very first week after I took up occupancy in my apartment, I began to notice an angry rash around my ankles, an *itchy* rash. I would wake up mornings and start scratching. It wasn't awful, but it was bothersome. I medicated it with the only thing I had on hand that I thought might help: a half bottle of Solarcaine left over from my Florida trip. It seemed to work and gave me some relief, but after about a week of this, the rash and the itching weren't going away, and I had scratched my ankles raw in a couple of places, so finally I took myself to the student health clinic on campus. The doctor who examined my raw itchy ankles hemmed and hawed a bit, then asked me if I had a dog, or maybe a cat.

Perplexed, I said, "No. Why?"

Stroking his chin and peering once more at my ravaged ankles, he murmured, "Because those look suspiciously like insect bites, and I wonder if you might have some fleas around."

A light bulb lit up in my brain and illuminated a scene from just a few weeks past. It was a scene of a large gray cat called Zero stretched across the foot of a bed – the same bed that was now my nightly resting place.

Shit! That goddamn fucking cat had left me a parting gift!

I quickly explained to the doctor about the previous tenants and the cat. He nodded sympathetically, smiling wryly, then gave me a small tube of medicated cream to relieve my itching and recommended I find myself an exterminator. "Probably got some sand fleas in the mattress," he speculated.

I thanked him, pulled on my socks and shoes and headed back home, nearly running in my haste to find out if it were true. Bursting into my bedroom, I looked at the rumpled bed. Nothing. Hmm … Turning on the ceiling light, I looked more closely. I picked up my two pillows and looked under them. Still nothing. Carefully I lifted up the edge of the top sheet and then yanked it and the spread down to the foot of the bed. Nope – except for a few black specks on the bottom sheet down near the foot – nothing. But as I reached down to brush these flecks away, they *hopped*!

Eureka! I mean, *DAMMIT!* I had *FLEAS!* The doctor had been right! I yanked the sheet further down. A few more specks. I leaned in closer and swept a hand slowly across the sheet. More hopping – and disappearing. *Sneaky bastard vermin!*

Of course I couldn't afford a pest control service to exterminate these tacky unwanted tenants, so I drove over to the Yankee store and bought two or three aerosol cans of bug bomb, which included fleas in the fine print on the cans, and that Friday night I closed all the windows up tight, stripped the bed, and then methodically and liberally sprayed the whole mattress and box springs. Then I sprayed all the windowsills and all along the baseboards and any other visible cracks and crevices in both the bedroom and the living room. Once the whole place had been generously dosed with the insecticide, I locked it up and went to Belleville. I waited until early Monday morning to return, and then opened up all the windows before I went to class. That night I took all my bedding to the laundromat on Mission Avenue and washed it. It was after midnight by the time I'd cleaned up the apartment and re-made the bed and fallen into an exhausted sleep. But the next morning my ankles didn't itch, and I was never bothered by fleas again. My amateur extermination efforts had been a success.

There were other more pleasant distractions too that fall. My brother Bill came to visit one weekend. He was working in Minnesota but had come home to Reed City for a long weekend and drove over to Mount Pleasant on Saturday to spend the night.

Of my four brothers, Bill had always been the easiest to get along with. Maybe it was because we seemed to be interested in many of the same things – books, music, movies, perhaps a little solitude now and then. I remember particularly one of our last summers at home together when I was still in high school and Bill was home from Michigan Tech, and we were both working for Dad at the elevator. Mom was living out at the cottage on Indian Lake for the summer, along with our two younger siblings, Mary and Chris, and I think Bob was working at Bonsall's Drugs by then. Bill and I always looked forward to Saturday afternoons and Sundays when the mill closed and Dad would go to the lake. We would then have the house in town to ourselves. We had a kind of unofficial division of labor agreement for those two lazy days. Bill would cook and I would clean up. Bill's specialty was homemade pizza. He would buy a tube of pizza dough downtown at Erler's grocery or the IGA, and sometimes some tomato sauce too, but everything else had to come out of whatever was on hand in the refrigerator or cupboard at home. We tried things on pizza like dill and sweet pickles, mustard, olives, and onions. We often didn't have any Italian or mozzarella cheese, so Bill would just lay on a few slices of American or Velveeta. For meat he would slice up a couple hot dogs or maybe some Vienna sausage or bologna. And we both grew rather fond of tuna pizza that summer too. Dessert was almost always ice cream. We Bazzett boys were always avid ice cream lovers and could never seem to get enough of it.

I remember one Saturday afternoon when we'd polished off our hybrid Velveeta-tuna-olive-and-onion pizza and were still feeling pretty hungry, so we decided to do the unthinkable – something we would never be allowed to do if Mom and Dad were home. We opened up a new half gallon of vanilla ice cream, peeled down all four sides of the box, and split it between us. I sliced the block of ice cream in half with a large carving knife, and then we each put our half into a large serving bowl and covered it with chocolate syrup and whipped cream, finally topping the gluttonous concoctions off with half a dozen Maraschino cherries. And then we ate it – *all* of it! *Braaaa-roouup!* I would not recommend this dessert dish on a regular basis. Once really was enough.

When Bill came to visit me that fall we ordered a pizza from Giovanni's, a sub and pizza takeout place housed in an A-frame out on Mission. And we did have ice cream for dessert, but moderate portions. We sat up late that night, talking and listening to music. Bill had brought along a new album, the Bee Gees' first American LP, which contained their first hit, "New York Mining Disaster, 1941" – an unfortunate title that no one could remember, but most people do remember the plaintive refrain –

"Have you seen my wife, Mister Jones?
Do you know what it's like on the outside?"

Anyway, it was a great song and a good album too. We played it over and over that night as we talked of life and my impending marriage, and reminisced quietly about various other songs and shared pizzas past. When we ran out of things to talk about, we simply sat in companionable sibling silence, something that had always been easy for us.

Bill slept on that awful half couch that night, with his feet hanging over the end table, but he didn't complain. It was never in Bill to complain about anything. The next day when he left he told me to keep the Bee Gees album, claiming he didn't really like it that much, which I knew wasn't true. He just wanted to give me a gift without any fuss or embarrassing thank yous. But I thanked him anyway.

That quiet weekend with Bill, always a self-effacing and gentle man – my Best Man – was my "bachelor party," and I can't really imagine a better one. It was enough.

* * * * *

There's one thing left to do
Before my story's through
I've got to take you for my wife
So the story of my life
Can start and end
With you.

MISS ZIMMER

Ferris Students Engaged

Mr. and Mrs. Chester J. Zimmer, of Martinsville road, Belleville, announce the engagement of their daughter, Treva Jean, to Timothy James Bazzett, son of Mr. and Mrs. Ellis Bazzett, of Reed City.

Miss Zimmer is attending Ferris State College and will graduate in September with an Associate of Applied Arts degree. She is an active member and historian of Delta Zeta National Sorority.

Her fiance will graduate in June from Ferris with an Associate of Applied Arts degree and will attend Central Michigan University in the fall.

No definite date has been set for the wedding.

Mr. and Mrs. Chester J. Zimmer
request the honour of your presence
at the marriage of their daughter
Treva Jean
to
Mr. Timothy James Bazzett
Friday, the twenty-fourth of November
at half after seven o'clock
Saint Anthonys Church
Belleville, Michigan

Reception
immediately following ceremony
Rogalli's Banquet Room
on Haggerty off I-94

Engagement announcement
from Belleville newspaper and
wedding invitation

40

"DOES YOU TAKE THIS WOMAN? ..." – MARRIED AT LAST

So September and October passed and then it was November and suddenly Thanksgiving weekend loomed before me. Our wedding date was set for the Friday after Thanksgiving, an unfortunate coincidence that has made it virtually impossible to remember the actual date these last thirty-eight years. I always quite naturally think of our anniversary as the Friday after Thanksgiving, so why can't we just celebrate it then each year? But *nooooooo*! That's not *good* enough, she says, and "How can you not remember your own anniversary?" Well, I think I just explained that, didn't I? In any case, I can usually come within a week or so of the correct date. You'd think that would be close enough, but for some reason wedding dates require a particular preciseness that does not come naturally to the male animal.

I spent the Tuesday before Thanksgiving thoroughly cleaning the apartment and also took all my bedding and towels and throw rugs to the laundromat that day and washed everything. I wanted all to be clean and perfect when I returned with my bride the following week. The next day, Wednesday, I could barely stand to sit through my classes, and I'm not sure why I did, since a lot of students had chosen to skip and head home a day early. My attendance probably had something to do with my only recently acquired acute awareness that by God I had *paid* for those classes and I was entitled to every *minute* of them. This feeling was, of course, an offshoot of my valiant attempts – also recent – to be a responsible adult. In any case, I managed to stick through all of my classes and also informed each of my instructors that I wouldn't be there the following Monday because I was getting married on Friday.

As I look back over these last few lines in which I'm trying to describe "the last days," it sounds like I was very methodical, very calm and collected in making all my final preparations, but the truth was, suddenly I was scared shitless. Well, actually not, because the mounting excitement that week literally turned my bowels to water. I couldn't seem to eat much, and everything I did eat came splattering back out in short order. So was I scared shitless or into "mucho shittingness"? I know that sounds awkward, but normal words fail me here as I attempt to describe the rising tide of near panic that began to engulf me that last week before the wedding. I mean it wasn't that I'd changed my mind about Terri or about marriage or anything like that. I knew I loved her, or at least I was pretty sure, given my limited experience in such matters. No, I think the thing that really scared me was the knowledge that soon I would be responsible for the care and feeding of another whole human being. It was a lot more serious than getting a puppy or a kitten.

Remember how your folks admonished you, "Now you have to realize, Son, that if you take this puppy home, it will be your responsibility to feed her and make sure she always has fresh water and take her out when she needs to go, and if she makes a mess you're the one who's gonna clean it up."

And you would answer, "I *know*, Mom, and I will, I will. I rilly rilly rilly *want* this puppy though, so can I have her? Please, please, *please*?"

Well, that was kinda the way I wanted Terri. I wanted this girl with that same kind of desperately innocent childish wanting, and I wouldn't care if she *did* make a mess from time to time. I'd clean it up, honest, if could just puh-*leez* take her home with me.

I'm still not sure if I'm getting this right, but it's the best I can do, because I was just such a boiling welter of mixed feelings and conflicting emotions. I was a fucking basket case, and I'm not at all sure how I managed to get through that final week.

One final point. Many of you, particularly female "yous" (*ewes?*), might find offensive my assumption that I would be completely responsible for Terri once I married her. After all, everyone knows that women are perfectly capable of taking care of themselves, right? Well, everyone did *not* know this in 1967. Or at least *I* didn't know it, and I'm not sure Terri knew it either. We were perhaps the last generation to feel that way, but I think we did both feel that it was a husband's responsibility to take care of his wife. By today's standards and values (or perhaps *lack* of them), this may sound narrowly condescending and chauvinistic, but it didn't then. That's just the way it was. Hence my creeping sense of panic.

On Wednesday night I threw some clothes in my car and headed north up 27 to Clare, and then west on 10, speeding through Farwell and into the sunset toward Reed City and my last Thanksgiving as a free and unfettered man.

I have absolutely no clear memories of the next two days, only free-floating dream-like fragments of events. Isolated random moments and comments come back to me on occasion, but I have never been able to accurately piece together any of those really significant words and actions that serve to unite two people in holy matrimony. Here are some of the things I *can* vaguely remember.

On the drive back to Reed City on Wednesday a Saginaw radio station deejay spun an oldie that I couldn't get out of my head all the way home. It was an obscure tune called "Big Bopper's Wedding," by J.P. Richardson, the Big Bopper himself. The tag line from the song that stuck in my head? That's right. You guessed it.

"Does you take this woman
To be yo' aw-ful wedded wife?"

Yeah, I know. It's not exactly a line you want looping repeatedly through your brain when you're about to get married. Of course the Big Bopper had been dead for nearly ten years by then; had gone down on the same plane that took Buddy Holly's life, and I *knew* that, but it didn't help. The line kept repeating persistently: *aw*-ful, *aw*-ful, *aw*-ful! I'm tellin' you. It was *awful*! Why couldn't that damn deejay have played Lloyd Price's "I'm Gonna Get Married," or the Dixie Cups' "Chapel of Love," or even ol' Buddy's own "Peggy Sue Got Married"? Nope. Instead I got the Bopper and his "*aw*-ful wedded wife" line. Some days it just doesn't pay to turn on the radio.

The next day was Thanksgiving. I'm sure Mom must have cooked a turkey and all that other good stuff that goes with it, but I can't remember any of it. The only memory I have from that day is going to the movies with Bill downtown at the Reed Theater, and I'm not even positive if we actually did *that*. And if we did, was it an afternoon holiday matinee, or did we go in the evening? And was the film we saw *really* a James Bond thing called *Thunderball*, or is all of that just a false dream?

The next day, Friday – our wedding day – is even more hazy and fragmented. I can't even remember how I got from Reed City to Belleville, but Terri says I drove down early that morning with Bill – a three- to four-hour drive I just don't remember.

Everything from here on in is mostly what other people remember, because I think I must have been in a walking semi-functioning state of pre-marital shock for my whole wedding day.

My family retinue – which would have included Dad, Mom, Bill, Mary, Chris, and Bob and Maureen, who had driven up from Chicago – all checked in at rooms reserved at the Belleville Howard Johnson's. There was a rehearsal at the church sometime that morning, and then the wedding party all gathered at the HoJo restaurant for a luncheon.

Hang on a second while I go find our wedding book to see who was in our wedding … Okay, got it. Lemme see here now … I was the groom. Terri was the bride – my "*aw*-ful wedded wife." Bill was Best Man. The Maid of Honor was Marilyn LeRash, who, with Pat O'Connor, had introduced us waaay back on St. Patrick's Day. The groomsmen were Patrick, of course; and Dick Zimmer, Terri's brother; and Tom Gordon, my army buddy and roommate from Germany. Well, Tom wasn't actually from *Ger*many. He was from Ferndale, or Hazel Park – or was it Troy? – and he brought along his own still new and lovely bride, Charlotte. The bridesmaids were Barb Schlund, one of Terri's best friends since grade school at St. Anthony's; Marsha Stahl, her Ferris roommate; and my sister, Mary Jane.

So there was the rehearsal luncheon and then there were five or six hours to fill until the wedding itself, which was – lemme check the book again – at 7:30 that night. One more blank block of hours which other folks have filled in for me over the ensuing years. According to my mom, I spent at least part of that time

Wedding party – l-r: Marsha Stahl, Barb Schlund, Mary Bazzett, Marilyn LeRash,
Terri and Tim, Bill Bazzett, Pat O'Connor, Dick Zimmer, Tom Gordon.

Bride and groom with their parents –
l-r: Chet and Wanda Zimmer, Terri and Tim, Daisy and Ellis Bazzett

shopping – for some important items I hadn't thought of myself. One of those items was a pair of pajamas. I don't think I'd worn pajamas since I was eleven or twelve years old. I usually just slept in my underwear, as did all my brothers. Apparently *some*one – *Mom? Terri?* – suggested I should have pajamas for my wedding night though. So I guess I went to Moss Bros. Men's Store sometime that afternoon and purchased a pair of pale blue pajamas. I know what color they were because they were the only pajamas I had for quite a few years. I very seldom wore them, but they were there, tucked in the back of a drawer or on a closet shelf.

The other thing I shopped for that afternoon was a "gift for the bride." I think it must have been a re-run of that "a-girl-should-have-a-ring" moment, and it was no doubt once again one of those gentle nudges from a tactful mother to her still-clueless son. So I made a stop at a jewelry store in town and selected a gold clasp bracelet with a Florentine finish that matched Terri's rings. I only know this because every now and then she'll dig that relic out of her jewelry box and wear it and remind me of where it came from and the occasion, and tell me how thoughtful it had been of me to get it for her. And I always nod agreeably, as though I can remember it all like it was only yesterday, when in reality I have absolutely no memory of ever buying that piece of jewelry.

I like to think that I'm not the only guy in the world who felt so nervous about getting married that he suffered from this selective amnesia. Terri and I know a couple, Joe and Janice Ross, both from Belleville, who also got married at St. Anthony's, and they like to tell the story of how Joe – who is a really big guy, bigger than me certainly, at about six foot nine – actually fainted dead away right on the altar halfway through the nuptial Mass. Now *that* is a real case of nerves. While it may be true that I have no recollections of my wedding, at least I apparently managed to stay upright throughout the ceremony, and must have managed to mutter the "I do" or "I will" or whichever response was being used back then, because, well, because here we are – married.

And so we were married; and when we emerged from the church that evening it was just beginning to snow – big fat flakes drifting lazily down. And this I *do* remember: I put out my tongue in the gathering darkness and tasted the pure clean essence of that first snow of the season. Aaah, sweet! And then I thanked God with everything that was in me for finally answering my prayers and sending me someone to love; for sending this girl – this *woman* – to share my life with me.

* * * * *

AT ST. ANTHONY'S

Treva Zimmer, Tim Bazzett United In Evening Ceremony

In a candlelight service November 24, in St. Anthony's Catholic Church, Treva Jean Zimmer became the bride of Timothy James Bazzett. The nuptial mass at seven thirty in the evening was read by Fr. Richard C. Welsh, before an altar graced with bouquets of green and white chrysanthemums.

Faith Schweiss, soloist for the double ring ceremony, was accompanied at the organ by Mrs. Walter Krawulski.

Treva, the daughter of Mr. and Mrs. Chester J. Zimmer, of 16428 Martinsville road, Belleville, was escorted to the sanctuary by her father. She appeared in a toe-touching creation of peau de soie distinguished by a high-rise bodice with a boat neckline, bracelet-length bishop sleeves, and lace appliques studded with seed pearls. The lace motif was repeated in borders at the sleeves and hemline and again as back interest for the paneled train which drifted from below the shoulders.

Seed pearls and tear drop crystals frosted the petaled headpiece which secured the bride's bouffant veil and she held cascading white orchids, miniature pom pons and greens.

Marilyn K. Lerash, a sorority sister from Detroit, was asked to be maid of honor. The bridegroom, son of Mr. and Mrs. Ellis Bazzett, of 355 W. Church street, Reed City, chose his brohter, Bill, of Minneapolis, Minnesota, to be best man.

* * *

DRESSED INDENTICALLY to the maid of honor, the trio of bridesmaids were Marsha Gale Stahl, of Plymouth, the bride's college roommate; Barbara H. Schlund, of Belleville, a close friend since elementary school days' and Mary Jane Bazzett, of Reed City, the bridegroom's sister.

White lace was used to form the bodices of their gowns which were fashioned with long, chiffon sleeves and skirts of moss green chiffon over taffeta. Each of the four attendants carried cascade bouquets of green and white mums accented by floor-length streamers.

The corps of ushers included Tom Gordon, of Hazel Park; Dick Zimmer, the bride's brother; and Pat O'Connor, of Jackson.

Rogalle's banquet room was reserved for the reception which followed. The 150 guests were greeted by Mrs. Zimmer in a mint green coat-dress ensemble of silk and wool with beading for contrast. Her shoes and handbag were in matching green and her corsage was of cymbidium orchids. The bridegroom's mother, Mrs. Bazzett, received in a honey-colored knit costume to which she added brown accessories and cymbidium orchids.

Now making their home at 431 E. Bellows, Mt. Pleasant, the bridegroom is currently attending Central Michigan University there as an English major. He spent two years at Ferris State where he earned an Associates of Art degree and served for three years with the U. S. Army. He is employed parttime on campus.

The new Mrs. Bazzett also attended Ferris as a cosmetology student and was a member of Delta Zeta sorority.

MR. AND MRS. TIMOTHY J. BAZZETT

Since I remember almost nothing about the wedding, here are some details from the Belleville newspaper. Is she beautiful, or what?!

POSTSCRIPT

How do I end this story – the story of our love? I can't, not really, because it's not over yet, and I hope it never is. I still wake up every morning and go to sleep every night with that same prayer of thanksgiving on my lips and in my heart. I still love this woman who has walked through life with me. I love her with a fierceness that often frightens me, and words fail me when I try to describe just how I feel about her.

I felt much the same way when our love was still fresh and new, and neither one of us had any idea what the future held in store for us. The night we got engaged I wrote Terri a letter trying my best to express the way I felt about her. It's written in pencil. It's naïve and it's unabashedly maudlin and sappy. I know I've cracked wise and poked fun at the whole idea of "young love" throughout this narrative, but I can't read that letter these days without tears filling my eyes. I know I will never be able to read the letter out loud in a public setting. Hell, I can't even read it to Terri without choking up, my voice stilled and my heart too full – all those memories. But I will share it with you here, although not without some trepidation, knowing I'm leaving myself wide open to a possible bashing from feminists and probably some scorn and ridicule from the more "macho" sector. But what the hell – I'm gonna share it anyway. So many things have happened to us since that long ago night. We've been through so much together. I have so many more stories I could tell. For now though perhaps it's enough that every year I still taste that first new snow – and that she's still here beside me. Thank you, Lord.

May 17, 1967

To my pretty little brown-eyed girl,

It's 12:00 but I can't sleep – my mind and heart are too full of you. I just wanted to tell you that when I'm with you I can never seem to say what I want to. I suppose it's because of some silly feeling that you won't take me seriously and you might laugh if off or something – I don't know. But I do want you to know how I feel.

I love you. This is what is uppermost in my mind constantly these days. I want so much to take care of you and make you happy – and all the time I'm so afraid I'll fail you somehow. I don't want to and I hope I never will. And if things are kind of rough for us at times (and no doubt they will be), I want you always to keep in mind how much I love you. We can have a wonderful life together, this I know for sure, and together we can make it over the rough spots if we never lose faith in each other. My folks keep telling me how hard it will be and I know they're right, and I also know you're more than a little scared about the whole idea, and I understand – but I can't wait any longer, Terri. I need you right now and it's awfully hard for me to be practical where you're concerned. I love you so much that it's become almost an ache deep within me. But I also love you enough that I can wait for you. It'll be difficult, but I want so much to do right by you. I love you, I love you ... Even saying I love you over and over again seems so pitifully inadequate, but there just aren't any other words to express how I feel. Perhaps I don't mean that either, because when you say those three short words to me, I'm happy beyond all words. I feel that I must be the luckiest man alive to have someone as wonderful as you say "I love you" to me. My cup truly runneth over.

Well, I still haven't said everything I want to say to you, but it's only because my mind is dominated by the singular thought, "I love you." So I'll leave you with that. I hope I never let you down.

I love you – always,

Tim

– The Beginning! –

* * * * *

AFTERWORD

Music has always played an important part in my life. There are multiple musical references in all three of my books, but this time I thought I'd write up some "liner notes," just in case any of my readers who are more computer savvy than me want to create their own double CD soundtrack for this "mind movie" of an important part of my life. If you choose to do this, don't forget to pay for the tunes you download. No publishing piracy, please, as you enjoy your own "Pinhead Soundtrack."

Pinhead Soundtrack

1 "The Story of My Life"
Marty Robbins
I loved this song (along with Marty's "A White Sport Coat") when I was thirteen years old just because it was a great tune. Now that I'm actually writing the story of my own life, it means even more to me. I was really surprised to learn that it was written by David and Bacharach.

2 "Lookin' for Love"
Johnny Lee
And once we reach a certain age we're all lookin'. A big hit from the Urban Cowboy soundtrack some years back. Remember John Travolta in a Stetson riding that mechanical bull at Gilley's?

3 "Black Betty"
Ram Jam

Not really my cup of tea or even from my era, but my boys had the 45 and used to play this rockin' noisy sucker to death, so since I called my first car by the same name, here it is.

4 "Hang On Sloopy"
The McCoys

Another one-hit wonder group, The McCoys were riding high with this one during my Ferris years. Heard it a jillion times in The Pug, at Dome Room dances and on the radio. One of Terri's favorite dance tunes.

5 "Norwegian Wood"
The Beatles

An odd but pleasingly melodic acoustic number from the boys' Rubber Soul album. The Beatles were so hot in the early sixties that virtually every tune they recorded, even weird album tracks, got air play.

6 "Kind of a Drag"
The Buckinghams

This group charted several Top 40 hits in the sixties, and then disappeared. Lots of horns a la Chicago. Their close harmony version of Cannonball Adderly's jazz composition, "Mercy, Mercy, Mercy", was also a big hit for them, as was "Susan" – my daughter's name.

7 "(Hey, You) Get Offa My Cloud"
The Rolling Stones

A follow-up and sound-alike to "Satisfaction", this was a great dance tune, popular at the Friday night mixers in the Dome Room.

8 "Jenny Take a Ride"
Mitch Ryder & the Detroit Wheels

A hybrid mix of two old R&B songs, this was a monster hit for this motor city group. I loved dancing to this whole album and took it with me to Nibbelink's skating party and everybody rocked out to it!

9 "I'm a Girl Watcher"
The O'Kaysions

The title is self-explanatory. Aren't we all?

10 "Numbers"
Bobby Bare
Bare was one of those country crossover artists like Marty Robbins. Earlier he had great songs like "Detroit City" and "500 Miles" that I listened to in the army and got homesick. This is a devilishly funny tune. Bare also recorded a really delightful children's album about "Singin' in the Kitchen."

11 "What a Wonderful World"
Sam Cooke
I've always loved Sam Cooke and his cha-cha rhythms. I decided to include this song because I still "don't know much about algebra." (Sorry, Mr. K.)

12 "Satisfaction"
The Rolling Stones
Probably one of the Stones' most recognizable signature songs. Since I was still basically a good Catholic boy dating a good Catholic girl, I couldn't get much satisfaction either.

13 "Drinkin' Wine Spodee-Odee"
Jerry Lee Lewis
Although the "Killer" calls it a wine drink, there was a little bit of just about everything in Gary's barrel. Dangerous shit, man. Imbibe at your own risk.

14 "Let's Hang On"
The Four Seasons
One of the biggest hits Frankie and the boys ever waxed, this bass-heavy tune on The Pug's jukebox used to rattle the windows there daily.

15 "The Happening"
Diana Ross & the Supremes
I first heard these Detroit gals on the jukebox at the Deuce in Germany. Immediately bought their first album, which remains one of my all-time favorites. This tune was just one of an incredibly long string of hits for the Supremes, but for me it will always be linked with our 1967 spring break in Lauderdale.

16 "Where the Boys Are"
Connie Francis

The girl with the "teardrop voice," Connie's songs reverberated through my youth from the time I bought her first album at DeWitt's Radio & TV in Reed City. With great songs like "My Happiness", "Who's Sorry Now?", and "Lipstick on Your Collar", she was key to the soundtrack of teen-dom during the fifties and sixties.

17 "Here Comes Summer"
Jerry Keller

I think this may have been Keller's only hit, but you can still hear it on the radio every summer, a seasonal classic, like Mungo Jerry's "In the Summertime" or Brian Hyland's "See You in September".

18 "Daydream"
The Lovin' Spoonful

Another one of those idyllic summertime songs, from the Spoonful's first album, with its monster hit, "Do You Believe in Magic?".

19 I Think We're Alone Now"
Tommy James & the Shondells

This is still "our song," although we both feel a bit foolish dancing to it now at our age. James was from Niles, Michigan, and, with his many hits like "Mirage" and "Mony Mony", by God, this cat rocked!

20 "Perhaps Love"
John Denver and Placido Domingo

If you've never heard this song, then you're in for a treat. Denver and Domingo seemed an unlikely pairing, but their duet is just flat beautiful.

21 "This Kiss"
Faith Hill

When you hear this song from the lovely Mrs. McGraw you can't help remembering that first kiss you shared with your own special someone – "It's that pivotal moment."

22 "Somethin' Stupid"
Frank and Nancy Sinatra
Unfortunately, I'll probably always associate this with sitting in a puddle of cold beer, not a favorite memory, but Terri still loves to tell the story. And it is still a very pretty song about the frustrations of being in love by this famous father-daughter duo.

23 "Don't Let the Sun Catch You Crying"
Gerry & the Pacemakers
This Gerry Marsden tune was popular during my year in Germany. I must have admired it, because I penned a tune of my own called "Please Love Me Again", which I performed with The Panics, and its melody sounded suspiciously like Marsden's.

24 "The Way You Look Tonight"
The Lettermen
This song goes way back and has been recorded hundreds (perhaps thousands) of times, but The Lettermen's version is my absolute favorite, from an album I bought in high school. I can't tell you how many times Terri and I have danced in the kitchen to this tune.

25 "New York Mining Disaster, 1941"
The Bee Gees
Although it's a pretty grim topic for a pop tune, it's not alone. Remember "Timothy" by The Buoys?

26 "Big Bopper's Wedding"
The Big Bopper
A 45 from my early adolescence. I was a secret Bopper fan. Loved his "Chantilly Lace". I cried when he and Buddy and Ritchie died – "the day the music died."

27 "Chapel of Love"
The Dixie Cups
Ferris State's St. Paul's will always be the chapel of love for Terri and me. If you've never been there, make a visit. It's still pretty much the same. Maybe you'll find someone there too.

28 "I'm Gonna Get Married"
Lloyd Price
Mister "Personality", Price was one of the great R&B performers of the fifties who, like Chuck Berry and Jackie Wilson, crossed that racial chasm and into the Top 40 pop charts.

29 "Brown-Eyed Girl"
Van Morrison
Morrison, who seems to pride himself on being an avant garde kind of musician, has tried unsuccessfully to distance himself from his early pop hits like this one, but it has become a permanent favorite to everyone who is lucky enough to have found his own brown-eyed girl.

30 "Remember When"
Alan Jackson
I wanted a round number for this list, and since I did a lot of remembering and shed more than a few tears while writing Pinhead, Jackson's poignant paean seemed the perfect choice for a filler. And it offers another great opportunity to gather up the love of your life and waltz her around between the stovetop and the kitchen sink – and remember when.

* * * * *

Thank you for taking the time to share my memories.

Tim Bazzett
July 2005
Reed City, Michigan

ACKNOWLEDGEMENTS

Once again, I am extremely grateful to my son, Scott Bazzett, the genius behind Rathole Books, who takes my manuscript and a package of pictures, clippings and documents and magically turns them all into an actual book. I would be hard-pressed to find a more talented or conscientious book designer/publisher.

Thanks too are in order to my mother, Daisy Bazzett, still my staunchest supporter and also a persistently nit-picking and unpaid proof-reader.

I offer additional thanks to the following people who helped me with my research or just talked with me on the phone or in-person about these long-ago days: Carol Yost Andres, Pete Baar, John C. Bazzett, Donna Borck, Rob and Linda (Querback) Chisholm, Linda Cook, Jim Crees, Kim Day, Don and Mary Ellen Dobson, Keith and Dianne Eichenberg, Marsha (Stahl) Ellis, the FLITE staff, Rudy Grahek, Hugh Griffith, Rick and Bonna Hult, Terry Karnitz, Patty Knapp, Irene Knauf, Robert Kosanovich, Gordon Lindland, John Nibbelink, Patrick and Sharon O'Connor, Gary Perdew, Gladys Peterson, the Reed City Public Library staff, Kenneth Roggow, Norval Scharkey, Tim Taylor, Steve Westhoff, Norma Wisniewski, Robert Zimmer, and Sandra Robson Zimmer.

I know I've probably forgotten someone, so thank you to everyone who has helped me out and supported me in the past year or two, particularly all of you who have read and recommended my books.

Finally, thank you, Ferris State, for a sound foundation in my pursuit of higher education – and for all the beautiful girls, especially the one who chose me.

* * * * *

ABOUT THE AUTHOR

Timothy James Bazzett was born in Charlotte, Michigan, in 1944. He is retired from the Department of Defense and lives in Michigan with his wife and two dogs. *Pinhead* is his third volume of memoirs.

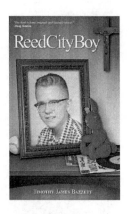

ReedCityBoy

Part 1

To order send check or money order for $14.95 made payable to TJ Bazzett to:

PO Box 282
Reed City, MI 49677-0282

(Michigan residents add 6% sales tax)

For more information, visit us online at:
www.rathole.com/ReedCityBoy

SoldierBoy

Part 2

To order send check or money order for $16.00 made payable to TJ Bazzett to:

PO Box 282
Reed City, MI 49677-0282

(Michigan residents add 6% sales tax)

For more information, visit us online at:
www.rathole.com/SoldierBoy

Pinhead

Part 3

To order send check or money order for $16.00 made payable to TJ Bazzett to:

PO Box 282
Reed City, MI 49677-0282

(Michigan residents add 6% sales tax)

For more information, visit us online at:
www.rathole.com/Pinhead

PRAISE FOR TIM BAZZETT'S BOOKS

Reed City Boy
(Rathole Books, 2004)

"For anyone who has ever thought about living in a small town –
where most people, it's true, do know your name – Tim Bazzett has
written the perfect book. For those who grew up in small towns, in
places like Reed City (where I was born), this tale is a reminder of
those lost spring afternoons when the redwing blackbirds called
down by the river, and the smell of the creosote bridge was in the
air, with your whole life ahead of you.   This book is funny,
poignant, and blazingly honest."

Doug Stanton, author of *NY Times* bestseller, *In Harm's Way*

"A good, honest and straighforward portrait ... A touching story."

Ronald Jager, author of *Eighty Acres: Elegy for a Family
Farm*, a modern classic of country memoirs

"The best autobiography I have read in years ... Paints a picture
with a fine artist's brush ... *Reed City Boy* has universal appeal
[and} could easily become a best-seller."

Dr. Maury Dean, Pop Musicologist and author of *Rock and
Roll Gold Rush*

"Bazzett manages to capture the magic and mystery as well as all
the quirks and foibles of growing up in Small Town U.S.A. ... This
is a fun book! Well worth the read."

Jim Crees, *Pioneer News Network*

"Bazzett shares his memories of growing up in Reed City,
attending Catholic boarding school in Grand Rapids in the 1950s
and working at the local A&P grocery store."

Lansing State Journal

"A real piece of American history ... Very well done: honest and frank and very Midwestern (and from me that's praise)."

Samuel Hynes, Professor Emeritus of Literature at Princeton University and author of *The Growing Seasons* and *Flights of Passage*.

"'Don't tell Mom, OK?' In *Reed City Boy* Tim Bazzett tells all, making his parents proud and leaving his readers anxiously awaiting his next book, which we certainly hope will not be his last."

Amy J. Van Ooyen, author of *Transplants*, and Michigan's U.P. Writer of the Year

"As anyone who has gone to Ferris knows, just north of Paris is not the city of Rouen, but Reed City. In *Reed City Boy*, Bazzett pays tribute to the town that shaped him ... And as for his style of sledding? 'I was hospitalized for weeks and couldn't walk for months,' Bazzett confesses. An even worse fate than Jean Shepherd's famously ill-fated Christmas gift of a Red Ryder BB gun!"

Marc Sheehan, *Crimson & Gold*/FSU

"Thank you for *Reed City Boy* ... (a) delightful book. It is a fine addition to my library."

Hon. Jennifer M. Granholm, Governor of Michigan

Soldier Boy: At Play in the ASA
(Rathole Books, 2005)

"I will highly recommend this book to any and every old ASA buddy I can track down, as well as to anyone who simply wants to know how a boy turns into a man. If you served, you will live it all over again. If you didn't, here's what it was like. A great read!"

> LTC Chuck Squires, US Army (ret.), former Defense Attache, US Embassy Bishkek, Kirgyzstan - and former ASA ditty-bopper

"I read *Soldier Boy* with great enjoyment. Never mind that it doesn't have a war in it - it has a very likeable and convincing soldier ... A gift for detail and keeping the narrative moving. Well done."

> Samuel Hynes, author of the classic WWII memoir, *Flights of Passage*

"Bazzett, who wrote the completely charming *Reed City Boy*, has an insouciant approach to his own life, [which] he makes his way through with wit and humor and more than a bit of brazenness ... His look at his army days is unvarnished. He remembers everything ..."

> Elizabeth Kane Buzzelli, *Traverse City Record-Eagle*

"Tim Bazzett's book should be a required read for any ASA veteran ... A touching and honest memoir that will make you veterans smile ... Reading this book will make most of you say, 'Holy Cow! I'd forgotten that and now it triggers my memory bank of old buddies' ... Forts Leonard Wood, Devens and Meade, then Turkey and Germany. It's all there in a whimsical style, with chicken crap and Mickey Mouse events scattered throughout the book."

> Elder R.C. Green, 1SG, US Army (ret.), and editor of the ASA Turkey veterans' newsletter, *Days of Our Lives*

"I'm still laughing my ass off ... classic!"

Capt William Sims, USAF (ret.), author of *Somalia Diary*

"*Soldier Boy* brought back memories of my own service as a young enlisted soldier in the early 1960s ... A world full of adventure and camaraderie only those who have served far from home in the military understand ... If you want a good read, this is a book well worth your time. I enjoyed it."

Col Henry W. Neill, Jr., US Army (ret.)

"A truly affectionate snapshot of a genuinely more innocent and gentle time ... A very funny service narrative that many with armed forces experience will automatically identify with. I am passing the book on to my father, who is a veteran of World War II ... I'm spreading the word, and look forward to the third installment!"

Dr. Neil A. Patten, Ferris State University Professor of Communications

"A delightful read, and a recommended one for any veteran or for a family member. It's true to life, our life, as we experienced the good and bad times of our military service ... [Bazzett] got it correct!"

Vern Greunke, ASALIVES.com Webmaster, and author of *Beller's Fellars: Letters from Viet Nam, 1966-1967*

"I read *Soldier Boy* ... My main impression was that [Bazzzett is] a hell of a nice guy, raised in a family of kind and caring people, and who raised his family in the same way ... A remarkable achievement. Lord knows where this writing thing came from, but obviously he's got it. In spades."

James Crumley, author of *The Right Madness* and the cult classic ASA novel, *One to Count Cadence*